Seán Keating in Context:

Responses to Culture and Politics in Post-Civil War Ireland

Seán Keating in Context:

Responses to Culture and Politics in Post-Civil War Ireland

Compiled, edited, and introduced by

Éimear O'Connor

Carysfort Press

A Carysfort Press Book in association with Peter Lang

Seán Keating in Context:
Responses to Culture and Politics in Post-Civil War Ireland

Compiled, edited, and introduced by Éimear O'Connor

First published as a paperback in Ireland in 2009 by
Carysfort Press Ltd
58 Woodfield
Scholarstown Road
Dublin 16
Ireland

ISBN 978-1-78997-060-9

Typeset by Carysfort Press Ltd

Cover design by Margaret Hamilton

For Dad

Acknowledgements

My first acknowledgement must be to Yvonne Scott and Rachel Moss of TRIARC – Trinity Irish Art Research Centre, for their continued encouragement and support. Without my position as Post-Doctoral Research Fellow at TRIARC this publication would have been entirely impossible. I am also grateful to my friends and colleagues at TRIARC; Riann Coulter, Olivia Horsfall Turner, and Caroline Maloney. I'd also like to thank Roger Stalley, Philip McEvansoneya and Ruth Sheehy.

If I could have a second first acknowledgment, it must be to Catherine Keating and Justin Keating and their families. Because of their generosity I have had unparalleled access to material on Seán Keating from which the contents of this book originated.

I would like to thank Dan Farrelly, of Carysfort Press, for editing my work and for his support and encouragement. I'd also like to express thanks to Lilian Chambers of Carysfort Press for her eagle eye and supreme editorial skills, and to Barbara Brown for her consummate attention to detail.

There is a wonderful collection of material in NIVAL at NCAD and I'd particularly like to acknowledge Edward Murphy and Donna Romano. Special thanks are also due to the Egan family who have allowed me access to superb material which I will revisit at length. I wish to extend my sincere gratitude to the staff at the National Library of Ireland, The Centre for the Study of Irish Art at the National Gallery, and the National Archives who are extraordinarily helpful.

For personal support and encouragement I am indebted to Dad, Viola, Joseph and Ann Marie, James, Marcus, Sinéad and Frank, Jake, Roisin, Shane, Yeshua, John, Eoin and Eimear, Jane and Nicky, Lisa and Mickey, Kate and John, Aaron, Kevin, Darragh, Dan and Una, Mary Mc, Paula Murphy, Bart and Ann Felle, Clara Cullen, Ann Marie Long, Una Walker and Brian McAvera, Corina Pennie, Jo and John, Roger and Nuala, Jane E, Michael D, Niall MacF, Paddy H, Peter, Clare, Imelda, Mary, Maimie and last, but definitely not least, Vincent and Dermot.

Abbreviations

DMSA	Dublin Metropolitan School of Art
FCNI	Friends of the National Collections of Ireland
IELA	Irish Exhibition of Living Art
KPPC	Keating Papers, Private Collection, catalogued by Éimear O'Connor
MGMA	Municipal Gallery of Modern Art
NCA	National College of Art
NCAD	National College of Art and Design
NIVAL	National Irish Visual Artists Library
RDS	Royal Dublin Society
RHA	Royal Hibernian Academy

Contents

Contents   xi

Context

> The trouble with Mr John Keating, RHA, until recently the President of our Academy, is
> that he has been too often seen in the singular and not enough in the plural.[1]

Seán Keating, former President of the Royal Hibernian Academy, died on 21 December
1977. Written into Irish art history as one of the 'official' artists of the Irish Free State,[2]
he was at the same time frequently condemned, particularly after the 1950s, for his
cultural production which was seen by some critics as lacking in anything 'recognizably
Irish'[3] and he has been continually damned for his ostensibly negative attitude to modern
art. It is true that Keating consciously and consistently retained the courage of his
artistic, social, and political convictions even against the rising tide of modernist rhetoric
and expression. But the full story of his contribution to the cultural dialogue in post-Civil
War Ireland had, to date, been lost, largely owing to a narrative of twentieth-century art
history biased in favour of work made in an obviously modernist, or abstracted style over
academic work in general and the Royal Hibernian Academy in particular.[4] Thus, and
regrettably, by the time of his death Keating and his work as an artist, teacher, and
cultural commentator was largely forgotten or out of fashion. This lapse has created a set
of conditions that have allowed Keating to be continually posited as the traditionalist
against whom Irish modernism could be mediated by critics and art historians alike. But
it has to be noted that the fact that an artist worked within the guidelines espoused by
the academy does not at all imply that he or she was, or is, conservative or right
thinking.

As a result of recent research it has become abundantly clear that Keating was, like
many of his time, an extraordinarily interesting and interested man who was prepared to
roll up his sleeves and contribute in whatever way possible to the cultural creation of
postcolonial Ireland. *Keating in Context: Responses to Culture and Politics in Post-Civil
War Ireland* offers for the first time since his death, a clear indication of Keating's
political beliefs and his views on an 'Irish' school of art. At the same time the articles and
broadcasts, many of which have just recently come to light, also signal his interest in and
knowledge of world politics and, ultimately, his utter frustration and disillusionment
with national and international cultural and political developments. The fact that
Keating kept his manuscripts is significant; he gave voice to what he wanted to say in the
earlier articles and broadcasts, but ultimately, as will be seen, he found it necessary to
return to those very same issues and republish – sometimes in Irish – because little or
nothing had changed. Moreover, while his articles and broadcasts were at the time

---

[1] P.H.G., 'President Lauds Irish Painter', *Irish Independent*, 10 May, 1963, p. 5.

[2] See for example Brian Fallon, *An Age of Innocence, Irish Culture 1930-1960,* Gill and
Macmillan, pp. 237-238.

[3] Ibid.

[4] RHA.

frequently radical and often thought-provoking, in the twenty-first century they clearly and unequivocally signal his political and social value system which was premised on left-wing socialist ideology. That said, owing to the conditions created by the imposition of censorship, Keating's socialism was, of necessity, largely self-censored.

ᔕ

In the early years of the twentieth century many Irish artists; writers, poets, musicians or painters dedicated themselves to the project of imagining and thus creating a nation. A necessary constituent of that mission from a political and cultural perspective was the systematic and at times forceful tension between tradition and modernity which was created by differing opinions, arguments, discussions and dialogues between those with individual views pertaining to who the 'Irish' were and what 'Ireland' should be. Within this sphere there were many voices, and many contested views of the concept of 'Irishness' exemplified for example in the varied responses from the general public, from William Butler Yeats and from the journalists working for daily newspapers to John Millington Synge's *The Playboy of the Western World* in 1907.

Keating willingly immersed himself in the artistic discourse of the day, hopeful that his contribution and that of his colleagues would eventually help to build a New Ireland and indeed, and Irish school of art that would reflect the political reality at home and abroad. But what was Keating's concept of an Irish school of art? It has been assumed to date that it was premised on a refusal of modernist in favour of academic work. But it seems clear that although he had little time for some work that was modern, Keating's idea of an Irish school was not at all centred on the academy or even on the Dublin Metropolitan School of Art. Perhaps surprisingly, his 'Irish' school was an environment that encouraged artists through the provision of official patronage which, in turn, would allow art to emerge. While he may have been forceful as a teacher, Keating was not publicly didactic about 'how' art should be made, his only concern was that it should be 'good' art, whatever that turned out to be.

As a result of economic and political conditions it was not until the 1940s and 1950s that the cultural history of Ireland in the twentieth century was put to paper. These were the years that coincided with the formation of organizations with a more modernist persuasion such as the Irish Exhibition of Living Art, the Cultural Relations Committee and The Arts Council of Ireland. Thus and understandably, most of the histories were written by those that privileged modernism, all of which was analogous to the conditions created by The Emergency during World War Two. It was at this time too that contemporary commentators and writers came to depend on the creation of a set of binary oppositions between controversy and celebrity in the arts which was evident in the sensation caused by 'the Rouault controversy' as it is still called. Keating, along with many others, contributed to that particular debate and ultimately the painting at the centre of the hullabaloo, *Christ and the Soldier,* was accepted by the Hugh Lane Gallery where it hangs still. There were several more controversial dialogues over the following years to which Keating contributed.

Known as a teacher and painter with a high degree of skill at drawing and large-scale mural work, Keating was elected an Associate of the RHA in 1918 and a full, or Constituent member in 1923, becoming the President of the organization in 1950 subsequent to the death of the then President, James Sleator, who died in the academy building in January of that year. During his career Keating was to produce several hundred paintings, thousands of drawings, sketches and studies, numerous large-scale murals and ephemeral work. As a representative of the RHA he, along with several other civically minded artists and citizens, voluntarily contributed his time to the board both of the National Gallery of Ireland and of the Hugh Lane Gallery. In Keating's case his contribution to both establishments lasted over thirty years. From 1919 until 1937 he worked on a part-time basis at the Dublin Metropolitan School of Art. Subsequent to the 'French Report' on the school in 1927 the Dublin Metropolitan School of Art became the National College of Art, and Keating was appointed Professor of Anatomy, a position that he held until his retirement in 1958.

Keating was also a keen, if critical, cultural commentator, and from an early stage in his career he took whatever opportunities were available to contribute to discussion and debate on the subject. In 1924 he published his first article which was provocatively titled *The Slave Mind of Ireland*. Keating started then as he meant to continue and his next deed was a semi-official report on the state of the School of Art as a result of which he found himself in serious trouble. But that did not stop him. In the early 1930s Keating was offered the opportunity to make a series of broadcasts, in all of which he voiced his concern about the way in which Ireland was developing culturally in the aftermath of the War of Independence and the Civil War. To some degree his Presidency of the RHA from 1950-1962 meant a form of self-censorship which put paid to those obvious opportunities to publish and broadcast and Keating began instead to take up the argument in support of academic art in general, and the RHA in particular, in the face of what he saw as 'phoney journalism' that created divisions where in reality there were few, and against a form of modernism that supported those who wanted to get rich quick, yet undertake no form of study for the privilege.

There is no doubt that Keating was a *provocateur* and from the beginning of his career, he focussed very forcibly on the lack of suitable government support for the arts which, as he saw it, negated any and all hopeful discourse pertaining to the development of an Irish School of Art. At the same time he could not tolerate the activities of 'Elaborators'[5] who as far as he was concerned, churned the imaginary cauldron of trouble between academic or more traditional artists and those of a modernist persuasion. Their work, he believed, was akin to 'Lough Ness Monsters' and 'Flying Saucers'. Always opinionated, never afraid of contentious situations and aware of the

---

[5] Keating's term for untrained art critics.

cultural, political, economic and social significance of the arts to a newly emerging nation Seán Keating was, to use his own words:

...torn by the discrepancies and inhumanity of what I see around me even in this civilised and humane state of ours, or comparatively so, because it seems to me that ever since Christ was murdered, the real worship of ninety per cent of the human race has been mammon, and not Christ. [6]

With the formation of the Cultural Relations Committee in 1949, and the enactment of the Arts Act which enabled the establishment of the Arts Council in 1951, the development of the story of the history of twentieth century art began in earnest. But unfortunately for Keating and other members of the RHA, this coincided with government support for modern as opposed to academic art. Thus an up-to-date evaluation of Keating and his career – with recognition of those tensions necessary to the development of modern Ireland in the twentieth-century, but conceptualized and contextualized in a new, more all encompassing framework – has become essential. This has been made possible largely owing to the recognition of the work of authors such as, for example, Declan Kiberd, Luke Gibbons, Ian McBride, Ciarán Benson, and Benedict Anderson, whose theoretical approaches have been applied to the Irish situation and have thus been brought into the tool box of many twenty-first-century Irish art historians.

While it is difficult, and perhaps problematic, depending on personal perspective, to place oneself in the highly charged atmosphere that must have prevailed in Ireland in the early years of the twentieth century, it is to some degree necessary at least to attempt to assemble a view of the past by recourse to information and, if possible, imagination, so that contextualization is not merely an exercise in rhetoric but an endeavour to understand genuine people in real situations for which their actions, whether political, cultural or otherwise, had certain meanings then, even if, of necessity, they have a different import now.

The Early Years.

John Keating, as he was known to his family and friends, was born in Limerick in 1889 the eldest of eleven children, seven of whom survived into adulthood. In later years Keating said of Limerick that it:

stank. It literally did stink. There was an enormous dump at the south side of the docks behind Barrington's banks where all the refuse of the town was blown out and blew around in the wind. The corporation men set fire to the dump where they could, and it smouldered all over the town. There was a tannery near St Mary's Abbey. It stank. Sewers emptied into the river. There were no regulations about slaughter houses. Food was exposed in the open air. Three or four bacon factories added to the flavour, and

---

[6] John Skehan, 'Palette and Palate', *The Word*, April 1965, unpaginated.

Nicholas Street, Mungret Street and down by the old mall were sewers. It was so old and dilapidated, it stank with decay. I knew where I was in Limerick by the smell.[7]

But there were, evidently, good smells too:

George's Street had a fine grocery shop which called itself an Italian warehouse and had a pleasant, peculiar smell; I don't know what it was. There was a biscuit factory in Bedford Row which had a nice smell, but then there was a chicken shop across the road which added a horrible smell.[8]

While he was from a lower middle-class family and living in reasonable comfort, Keating was aware of the atmosphere and of the poverty in the city which, as he remembered it, was:

very class conscious, strongly divided into various sections of the population. A few very rich people kept us apart...there was a mass of ordinary, rather poorish citizens.[9]

Keating's natural inclination was to identify with the term 'worker' rather than an 'artist' or a 'merchant' and he therefore tended to proletarianize the account of his schooling. But education was important to his parents Annie and Joseph and the Keating siblings were all well educated. John and his brothers Joseph and Paul were sent to Leamy's School in Hartstonge Street in the city and then to St Munchin's School, which was fee paying, for the duration of their secondary education. Keating often said that he did not like school, but even if that was the case, he remained in class until the age of fifteen, although he retained a life-long critical view of the education system in Ireland. He believed that the system as it was offered nothing to encourage self-esteem or self-knowledge. Notwithstanding the trials and tribulations of student life in those years Keating seems to have been quite a good student. He had a natural facility for language and was aided in his love of French by his teacher, Dr later to become Bishop Keane, who possessed a 'sardonic humour and a violent temper which would make him go crimson with rage, but which he could control'.[10] The family home was busy, but full of books, and early in his life Keating developed a love for reading which remained with him through adulthood.

Interviewed in 1977, not long before he died, Keating said that he was:

lower middle class ... the son of a ledger clerk, born in a back street of Limerick. My mother thought of me as a dunce. She was a practical woman, a worrier. She'd get impatient with my father. He would never make a decision. He was something of a dreamer. She didn't know what to do with me. I was no good at anything. I had a good alto voice so she got me into the church choir. There was a Belgian choirmaster there. He was very good. I used to sing at all the masses and ceremonies. [11]

---

[7] Helen Buckley, 'Seán Keating, Artist Extraordinary', *The Limerick Leader,* 26 February, 1972, p. 13.
[8] Ibid.
[9] Ibid.
[10] Ibid.
[11] Tanis O'Callaghan, 'Profile of Seán Keating', in *Image,* November 1977, p. 45.

As a result of time spent in school and in the church Keating also became very good at Latin and had an excellent knowledge of biblical stories which was to prove useful in his artistic career. Keating found his schooling uninteresting and lacking in challenges and he left in 1905 and thereafter spent some idyllic months hunting, smoking and generally doing nothing much. Ultimately, Keating became bored with roaming the streets and countryside of Limerick. He had always shown talent for drawing and, although there is little direct evidence, it seems clear from articles that Keating published and broadcast in later years, that he may have wanted to go to art school from quite a young age. His mother, who worked as a dress maker, put up the money to send her eldest son to the Limerick Technical School to train to become an art teacher. He entered the school in 1907, did extraordinarily well, and by 1911 Keating was in receipt of a scholarship to the Dublin Metropolitan School of Art (DMSA) to train as an artist and art teacher under luminaries such as William Orpen (1878-1931), Oswald Reeves (1870-1967) and James Ward (1851-1924).[12]

Dublin and beyond

The students at the DMSA were highly competitive and deeply politicized and Keating found himself among several extraordinarily talented men and women such as Margaret Crilley (1881-1961) and Harry Clarke (1889-1931) amongst others, all of whom were to become well-known as the century progressed. Clarke and Keating became good friends during those years, though it does appear that their association trailed off after the latter's marriage in 1919. The school was a busy representative microcosm of Irish society at that time; in 1914 two staff members and fourteen students joined the British army, as Keating's brother Claude had done the same year, while at the same time the roll books included names associated with the Nationalist cause such as Willie Pearse who left in 1912 and Countess Markievicz who was a student at the night class prior to 1916.[13] The atmosphere at the school was, naturally enough, highly charged and proved a motivating and provocative environment for Keating, who from the outset was anxious to prove his credentials both as an artist and as a man of political conviction.

Keating's adherence to cultural nationalism only became evident in his paintings made during and after 1914. This was as a result of his love of the language and traditions of the Aran Islands which he first visited with Harry Clarke in 1913. After 1915 his allegiance to the West of Ireland signalled his alarm and unease at events that were unfolding during World War One from which he wanted to get as far away as possible. Once the political potential of the 1916 Easter uprising had been revealed to Keating the Aran Islands then came to represent the concept of 'Irishness' and place from which, in

---

[12] Keating's artistic training at the DMSA and many other themes alluded to herein are discussed in the author's forthcoming publication, *Keating Reconsidered.*

[13] See John Turpin, *A School of Art in Dublin Since the Eighteenth Century*, Gill and MacMillan, pp. 192-194. Lessons in the Irish language were available to the students and Willie Pearse had been one of the teachers prior to leaving in 1912.

line with other communities around the world who had sought refuge in their own landscape, a new school of art could be wrought. Keating was very specific in his attitude about the West of Ireland. He understood that the modernist project across Europe had taken elements from other marginalized communities and placed them out of context in order to create something new.[14] Thus his clarion call for artists to return to the West of Ireland was rationalized and well thought out and premised on the belief that a new school of art could not be born from the ashes of any aspect of the ascendancy.

The finest, most hopeful, and indeed rather idealized example of Keating's view of the islands in the years prior to 1916 was *Aran Man and his Wife* (1914). By 1915 his cultural nationalism had become fused with a strong belief in separatist nationalism, which was perhaps best exemplified in *Men of the West,* painted in 1915 but exhibited for the first time at the RHA in 1917. Whereas Keating later placed great significance on the project to modernize Ireland through the Shannon Scheme and international participation in, for example, the New York World's Fair in 1939, as time progressed he became deeply conflicted and ultimately frustrated and disillusioned at the loss of the traditional values that had been associated in his mind with the Aran Islands. This was made more evident once Keating began to use a camera and a cine-camera to record life on the islands, as a result of which he accidentally or otherwise, realistically documented the collapse of the old traditions. He never again produced such an idealistic image of the islands, and eventually the landscape and people of the West became a focus for several allegorical and realistic representations of his political disenchantment. Finally, his dissatisfaction at the political and economic conditions was made abundantly clear in paintings such as *Economic Pressure* (1948) and its pendant *Ulysses in Connemara* (1949-50) which, when compared with the idealism of *Aran Man and His Wife,* offers a sad reflection on the hope that had been invested in the Nation by the people of Ireland.

If paintings such as *Men of the West* and *Men of the South* are viewed as confident separatist Nationalist visual statements, Keating's loss of belief in violence as an instrument to gain independence becomes clear in images such as *On the Run, War of Independence* (1922) and unequivocal in *An Allegory* (1924), which was painted after the end of the Civil War.[15] It can be difficult to create successful allegorical images and, given that many of his paintings can be considered in these terms, Keating's ability to do so throughout his career warrants serious recognition. *An Allegory* was the first of a series of symbolic paintings that insist on contextual knowledge from the viewer in order to be properly understood, while at the same time they offer meaning with national and international resonances. Consequently many of Keating's better-known paintings can be understood as allegories including most if not all of his directly political work from 1915 to 1924 along with powerful images such as *Night's Candles are Burnt Out* (1929)

---

[14] Consider for instance the work of Paul Gauguin in Tahiti and that of many of the Cubists and the Fauves.

[15] Keating did not mention the War of Independence or the Civil War in any great detail during interviews except to say that he came to disagree with violence. But it is clear from personal notes that he was haunted by what he had seen.

and *Homo Sapiens-An Allegory of Democracy* (1929) and even *Race of the Gael* (1928).[16] There are lesser-known allegorical paintings too such as *Don Quixote* (1926) and *Sancho's Master* (1927) which are illustrative of the artist's interest in sourcing and visually highlighting contemporary political and social significance from the canon of iconic literature. Further examples of allegorical work include the little-known *Sacred and Profane Love* (1937) and better-known examples such as the aforementioned *Economic Pressure or a Bold Peasant being Destroyed* (1949) and *Ulysses in Connemara* (1950) each of which can be seen as a challenging critique of the state of Irish and global civilization.

Owing to the attitude of the Department of Education, which refused him leave of absence in 1924, Keating could not commit to the project of continual documentation of the historical events that were going on around him; hence there is a dearth of obviously politicized paintings after this date. Nevertheless he found ways to articulate his hope for the future, as is evident in, for example, his work on the Shannon Scheme, in which he visually reiterated his belief in the project to modernize Ireland in the 1920s. He also established artistic methods in order to communicate his continual frustration at the stultifying social, political, religious and economic conservatism together with what he believed to be destructive Americanized consumerism within post-Civil War Ireland. This is evident in paintings such as *Homo Sapiens-An Allegory of Democracy* and *Sacred and Profane Love*. To his great delight Keating discovered that he could be largely unambiguous about his principles in interviews, published articles and broadcasts, thereby signalling not only his philosophy and ideology, but also the fact that there was more than just the immediately obvious in many of his paintings for those who cared to look.

In 1919 Keating was appointed to a part-time position as assistant teacher of anatomy at the DMSA and as such he replaced William Orpen who left the school in 1914. As a former student and now teacher Keating had been acutely aware of the results, or lack thereof, of the Parliamentary Inquiry into teaching at the school to which Orpen, to his detriment, had honestly contributed.[17] Keating had experienced several years of hardship since qualifying as an artist and art teacher in 1914 even though he spent the best part of 1915 as Orpen's studio assistant in London. He returned to Dublin full of idealism and hope but by 1918 he had little work and no apparent prospects of a job. Early in 1919 Keating asked his friend Harry Clarke for work but there was none

---

[16] Keating did not believe in the pure Irish race and thus the painting offers a critique of the possibilities available to Ireland if the Government would provide educational and creative opportunities.

[17] William Orpen submitted to the enquiry that Industrial Art and Fine Art teaching should not be under the supervision of just one man as Headmaster. He was critical of the school for turning out art teachers as opposed to artists. Orpen suggested that the teaching methods at the DMSA were suitable for industrial training, but not for fine art, and that the RHA drawing school should take over that particular aspect. See Turpin, *A School of Art*, pp.217-226.

available at the glass studios at that time.[18] That same year he ran into serious trouble with the RHA who had elected him an Associate of the organization the previous year. It was not a story of which he could be proud, but the circumstances illustrated well the problems associated with payment for commissions.

In 1918 Keating was commissioned by a certain gentleman to make a portrait. Whether or not the patron was pleased with the result is not clear, but it is certain that Keating had serious difficulty in obtaining payment. Irritated by lack of imbursement Keating exhibited the portrait with the self-explanatory title *Warned Off* in the 1919 RHA exhibition. The patron was not at all amused and he made a formal complaint to the RHA council who took the matter very seriously indeed. Finally, after due consideration that included discussion on possible expulsion, the council voted instead to send Keating a formal warning and the painting was removed from the exhibition and was subsequently purchased by the patron's wife. Keating was fortunate to survive the incident and the entire episode offers an early indication of his strong-minded, if at times somewhat hasty, individuality. Although he found his experience with the RHA Council over *Warned Off* distressing and he was remorseful for causing embarrassment to the Academy, it did not prevent him from always taking an active interest and role in the continually contested cultural dialogue, even at the risk of his career, and he was elected a full or constituent member of the RHA in 1923.

Responses to Culture and Politics 1920s

Keating was tall, thin and good looking with piercing blue eyes and a mop of dark hair. He had an inquiring intellect along with an instinctive and persuasive communicative ability that drew people to listen to him whether they wanted to or not. He seems to have had an impish, mischievous sense of humour and he loved a joke and an outlandish story. These aspects of his personality are evident not only in many of his paintings and drawings, but also in his articles and broadcasts which were imbued with humorous irreverence tinged with well-informed iconoclasm. There is little doubt that Keating's position and approach demanded notice and it is hardly surprising therefore that he was asked to contribute an article to *The Voice of Ireland; A Survey of the Race and Nation from All Angles* in 1924. The book was published in the same year that Keating exhibited *An Allegory,* an iconic painting that emphatically emphasized the futility of the Civil War while at the same time illustrating the artist's lack of support from then on for violent separatist nationalism. Keating's contribution to *The Voice of Ireland*, which was his first venture into printed media, was titled 'The Slave Mind of Ireland' and it was forcefully categorical about the national state of mind as he saw it. In essence Keating used the opportunity to berate the Irish as a 'nation of self-excusers' who blamed everyone and everything including 'the English and the climate' for the 'rotten' state of things in Ireland. As far as Keating was concerned this was the 'slave mentality' of

---

[18] See Harry Clarke Papers, NLI, MSS.

Ireland the antidote for which was the requirement to 'look at ourselves, even if the sight [makes] us sick.' Throughout the article Keating alluded to issues that continually perplexed him in the DMSA but that were also applicable to society; there was 'no standard of achievement ... no test by which any man can judge himself ... ' He referred to social and cultural problems such as the lack of art, literature and the death of 'public conscience'. Ultimately he felt that:

> unless we take off our coats and dirty our hands, if need be, we Irish are doomed and damned to the bottomless pit of futility. And we shall have nobody to blame but ourselves.[19]

The article is demonstrably a literary articulation of Keating's visual intent in *An Allegory* and as such, it should be read in conjunction with study and analysis of the painting. At the same time 'The Slave Mind of Ireland' was an extraordinary and brave assessment of the nation as Keating understood it, which signalled the manner in which he intended to continue in order to endeavour to provoke social and cultural change in post-Civil War Ireland.

It was his aptitude for conversation amalgamated with his idea of what the DMSA should be that got Keating into serious trouble at the school with the then headmaster George Atkinson in 1925.[20] Keating unknowingly took up his part-time position as assistant at the DMSA against the expressed wishes of the headmaster, George Atkinson, and at a difficult time in the history of the school wherein all of the old problems that Orpen had addressed in 1906 were still in evidence. His relationship with Atkinson was probably not helped by the fact that when 'The Slave Mind of Ireland' was published Keating was mistakenly described in the book as 'Professor of Drawing and Painting from Life in the Dublin Metropolitan School of Art' an honour that he was not given until 1937, and even then against the expressed wishes of George Atkinson.

In the meantime some attempt had been made to rectify the anomalous situation in the visual arts in Ireland when the second Dail Éireann, which sat in session from 26 August 1921 to 9 January 1922, 'considered that there should be a Minister of Fine Arts'.[21] During the same year, on the invitation of Father Timothy Corcoran, S.J., Professor of Education at University College, Dublin, Thomas Bodkin wrote a 'lengthy report regarding art as part of general education.'[22] Corcoran gave Bodkin's report to the Minister of Education, J.J. O'Kelly. As a result of Bodkin's initial report, and a political will to create a system that could support Irish art in Ireland, a non-cabinet post was

---

[19] John Keating RHA. 'The Slave Mind of Ireland', in *The Voice of Ireland: A Survey of the Race and Nation from All Angles,* William G. Fitzgerald (editor), Virtue and Company, Dublin and London, 1924, pp. 83-85.

[20] Atkinson was appointed to the staff of the DMSA in 1914 and he became headmaster in 1918.

[21] Brian P. Kennedy, *Dreams and Responsibilities: The State and the Arts in Independent Ireland,* The Arts Council of Ireland, 1991, p. 5.

[22] Ibid., p. 7. Keating undertook a commissioned pastel portrait of the Very Reverend Timothy Corcoran in 1942. The portrait is part of the UCD art collection.

instituted with George Noble, Count Plunkett, at the helm as Minister.[23] The ministry existed for nineteen weeks and it is evidence of at least some official interest in the Fine Arts. Nonetheless, the Ministry of Fine Arts was abolished subsequent to the Treaty of Independence in 1923 after which there was little official interest in the visual arts. But the political lack of will did not dissuade artists and public personalities who endeavoured to contribute in one form or another to the rapidly developing and extraordinarily fascinating discourse that began to emerge now that the previously 'imagined' nation had come into being.[24] In 1922 Bodkin followed up his earlier study with another report to the new Minister of Education. In this second report Bodkin tacitly acknowledged the official desire to recreate Ireland as explicitly Irish as he called for an immediate restoration of the Ministry of Fine Art. He recommended that the new Ministry should be given officers, who would be placed within all other government departments, in order to advise on design issues pertaining to everything from stamps and uniforms, to public buildings. He also suggested that the advisors could be consulted on the criteria for art education in schools and on the care and maintenance of museums and galleries. When the recommendations were completed, the document was given to the Department of Education. Bodkin was thanked for his work and his report was unceremoniously shelved. This was a portentous act or non-act for the cultural community in Ireland; it was the moment when it first became apparent that there would be no significant changes in favour of the arts in general, and the visual arts in particular, either economically or otherwise from the new Irish Government.

At the same time conditions at the DMSA were continually difficult and although it had been suggested that a Professorship of Painting from Life should be established as early as 1906 the appointment had not been made when Keating joined the staff in 1919. Having been under the 'control of Westminster' since 1849, the DMSA found itself, in the aftermath of the Treaty of Independence, under the 'direct ministerial control of Dáil Eireann' in 1924.[25] Because the school was no longer directed from England the students did not compete for examinations and national competitions run by the British Board of Education and as a result they 'lost the stimulus of a larger field of competition.'[26] This is a tremendously significant point, which, combined with economic shortages, ultimately led to severe difficulties in the development of Irish culture and the associated discourse during the twentieth century. Nevertheless, in line with the wish to recreate and establish Ireland as Irish, students at the DMSA were prepared for national competitions such as the RDS Taylor Award, the Irish National Art Competition organized by the RDS, the Royal Society of Arts competitions, and after 1924; the Aonach Tailteann.[27]

---

[23] Ibid., p. 5.
[24] For a discussion on the 'imagined nation' see Benedict Anderson, *Imagined Communities,* Verso, London and New York, 1991.
[25] Turpin, A School of Art in Dublin, p. 233.
[26] Ibid.
[27] Programme for the DMSA, Kildare Street, Dublin, for the academic session 1932-33, Department of Education Archives, Department of Education, Dublin.

As the author of 'The Slave Mind of Ireland' and creator of powerful associated imagery, analogous to his position as assistant in the DMSA Keating was known to be 'fearless in speaking his mind, a trait which won him deep respect but also some bitter enemies'[28] and so it seems hardly surprising that he would be called upon for his opinion on the situation at the DMSA. Although he subsequently became completely disillusioned with Irish politics Keating had been pro-Treaty, a political stance which afforded him opportunities for sympathetic consideration from the government. This was not unusual for the time and while there is no demonstrable proof, it seems likely that even though George Atkinson continually recommended that he should be fired, Keating's position as assistant teacher at the DMSA seems to have been assured at least until the change of government in 1932. There came an evening in 1925 that Keating was at a gathering in the house of a friend. He was introduced to Joseph O'Neill who was Secretary to the Minister for Education, Eoin MacNeill, who, in turn, was a nationalist and a revolutionary, former chief of staff of the Irish Volunteers and co-founder of the Gaelic League.

One can only imagine the discussion and atmosphere in that house in 1925, but the result of the meeting was the artist's 'Report on the Metropolitan School of Art', requested by Joseph O'Neill, which was subsequently forwarded to Eoin MacNeill and to George Atkinson. Keating had very strong opinions about the situation at the school, which had drastically worsened since independence owing to the lack of any type of official support, whether academic, economic or material. Evidently, one of the main issues concerning Keating was that the DMSA should have academic standards akin to those of universities:

> It is clear that the school should be either reorganised as a University for those who intend to make Art their profession, or that it should be abolished. [29]

Keating identified the problem or the 'root of the decay' as 'the system itself' noting that 'nothing but a complete readjustment will make any permanent improvement'.[30] By 'system' he meant the management of the finances of the school, the lack of an entrance examination and the fact that the DMSA was 'neither an elementary nor a secondary school nor a university'. Keating noted, too, that owing to the deficiency in academic entrance standards and to the 'absurdly low fees' the school was becoming more or less a 'kindergarten' and, ultimately, a finishing school for young ladies.[31] While an apparent sexist bias has been noted in Keating's document in fact his concern was not female students *per se*, of whom there were many working successfully at the school, but a flaw in a system in which there was no entrance examination.[32] As a result, those lacking in

---

[28] Brian P. Kennedy, *Dreams and Responsibilities*, p.17.
[29] John Keating RHA, 'Report on the Metropolitan School of Art made to Mr Joseph O'Neill at his request in 1925, p. 3. National Archives, file S 3458.
[30] Ibid.
[31] Ibid.
[32] Turpin, John, A School of Art in Dublin, p. 263

facility or talent proved a hindrance to a school that was already deficient in materials and facilities. For Keating, discipline and the reorganization of art teaching were the fundamental issues at stake, and not gender equality.[33]

The dearth of art education in the primary and secondary school system, which had affected Keating in his early years, was obviously on his mind, as were the difficulties encountered when trying to combine training at night with a day job, when he suggested that:

> ...students should be full-time day workers; there should be no night classes of any kind. Students should have a good knowledge of the technique of their trade acquired in primary and secondary schools, technical schools and workshops, and they should pass an entry examination which would include a test of general education... [34]

In addressing the RDS Taylor Scholarships, Keating noted that, although the DMSA students did reasonably well, their work was not of the same artistic standard as that accomplished ten years previously under the directorship of Orpen. This was, as far as he was concerned, a direct result of 'confusion and lack of direction' from within the school. His argument with the school authorities was that there was too much emphasis on 'get rich quick illustrators and secondary teachers of art'.[35] This was an issue to which he would continually return throughout his career. Returning to Orpen's opinions given at the 1906 Parliamentary Enquiry into the DMSA and the Slade School training ethic Keating noted that:

> The formula for the making of a good School of Art is 'By Artists for Artists'. A School of Art needs a few Artists, a few students, a registrar, and money in reason. Big buildings, elaborators, expensive apparatus do not count at all. [36]

Keating pointed out that after a day's work the young men attending the classes were ambitious, but 'too exhausted ... and quite unfit for the mental and physical strain of learning to draw ... ',[37] while at the same time, the day class was in danger of collapsing owing to a 'pretence of discipline and no authority to enforce order', which meant that the DMSA was 'a bedlam of noise and idleness'.[38] Significantly, Keating suggested that the annual outlay of £4,330 could not be justified on a 'system which in the nature of it can give no results to the individual or to the State'.[39]

While Keating's report was well-intended it was not well received by George Atkinson who perceived the comments contained therein to be a personal slight on his managerial skills. Atkinson had worked hard to get the DMSA through the severe economic and

---

[33] In later years Keating often utilised the talents of his students, both male and female, in some of his large scale ephemeral work.

[34] Keating, 'Report on the Metropolitan School of Art', p. 4.

[35] Ibid., p. 3.

[36] Ibid., pp. 4-5. In later years Keating approved of the idea to create an art scholarship to allow students to travel abroad. See 'Proposal to Create a Travelling Art Scholarship', c. 1950s.

[37] Ibid., p. 2.

[38] Ibid.

[39] Ibid., pp. 2-3.

artistic difficulties caused by World War, the unrest of 1916, and the Civil War that ensued after the 1921 Treaty. He firmly believed that he had 'created a more lively spirit within the school' and that 'students were assisted towards new developments and informed of new tendencies'.[40] With lack of funding and materials and the inertia of political motivation, there is no doubt that Atkinson had a difficult job as headmaster. But the historic ill-will between the two men led to mutual distrust and misunderstanding even though they both had good intentions with regard to the school. Their relationship was also badly served by Joseph O'Neill, who, for some inexplicable reason and without permission, removed Keating's signature from the document before forwarding the report to Atkinson. For his part Keating was quick to tell the headmaster that he was the author of the text, explaining that it was not 'inspired by any malice towards him personally.'[41] But the damage was done and the two men were barely on speaking terms until both were given permanent positions within the school in 1937.

Having received both Atkinson's and Keating's reports the Department of Education decided to hold yet another enquiry into the situation at the DMSA. In due course they sought the help of group of experts from France, known as the 'French Committee'.[42] The 'French Report' was given to the Department of Education in 1927; however the report proved to be extremely problematic because it was scathing of all members of staff including Atkinson and Keating for whom, for various reasons, they recommended immediate dismissal.[43] During his meeting with the Committee, Atkinson was asked if he got on with all members of staff and he said that he got on with everyone, except for one, whom he apparently did not name. The French inspectors noted that they subsequently found out that the person to whom Atkinson was referring was John S. Keating.[44] But Keating's opinions about the serious lack of facilities and academic standards had not changed since he submitted his report to O'Neill in 1925. However, it seems evident that the French Committee mistook his demeanour as unconventional, which it probably was, and also lacking in discipline. Given Atkinson's obvious prejudice against him the accusation of indiscipline was hardly fair and their notes about him attest to the real difficulties Keating was having:

> one has the feeling that students come here (to Keating's class) in order to amuse themselves...Mr Keating tells us that the pupils are too weak and too badly prepared when they come to him but that he is obliged to take them. He has only to submit...as all

[40] Turpin John, *A School of Art in Dublin,* p. 259. Turpin cites the 1934 Headmasters report on 'The Present workings of the Metropolitan School of Art', Department of Education Files.
[41] Keating to Minister of Education, 2 May, 1932. National Archives, file S 3458.
[42] Department of Education sought advice from the Department of External Affairs. It seems to have been decided, with the unavailability of Orpen and Tonks, that an outside opinion or objective view, whether English or European, was necessary. The Department of External Affairs suggested utilizing the advice of Count O'Kelly, Irish ambassador to Paris. He in turn, recommended the input of a number of experts, all of whom were French.
[43] Turpin, A School of Art in Dublin, p. 270.
[44] Ibid., It is not clear if Keating was asked whether or not he got on with all members of staff.

his protests, even those directed to the Minister, have availed him nothing…He believes in a serious entrance examination.[45]

Dermod O'Brien PRHA and Thomas Bodkin were the Irish representatives during the tenure of the French Committee. But the report was produced without reference to them. As a result Bodkin wrote a 'minority' report in which he called for a more measured and restrained response than simply dismissing staff. He noted, as both Orpen and Keating had done, that lack of finance and facilities, discipline and academic standards were at the root of many of the issues regarding the school.[46] He also noted that artists would not willingly spend most of their lives teaching, but that it was necessary in order to survive. In order to accomplish standards of excellence in art education, Bodkin recommended the introduction of entrance examinations and student progress reports, all of which could be facilitated by a board of advisors.[47]

In the end, having taken the trouble to bring in the members of the French Committee, the Department of Education did nothing with their report. Bodkin's 'minority' document was also shelved. Whether or not Keating was aware of the level of criticism towards his expertise is not apparent.[48] In 1932, the Cumann Na nGaedhael government lost the general election and Fianna Fail, under the leadership of Eamon de Valera, became the new incumbents in Dáil Éireann. The atmosphere between Keating and Atkinson was severely strained, and the DMSA was still suffering from lack of funds and facilities. Perhaps sensing an opportunity to instigate change, Keating sent a letter to the Department of Education requesting official action for the school, and he enclosed a copy of his 1925 report to O'Neill.[49] Keating also included a cutting from *The Irish*

---

45 The Supplementary French Report. Department of Education Archives.
46 Ibid. Turpin quotes from a memorandum from Bodkin to Minister for Education, 1927, Bodkin Papers, M. 6968/107, TCD, MSS.
47 Ibid.
48 Turpin notes that had something been done on both the French Report *and* Bodkin's subsequent report that the conflict of the late 1960s and 1970s may have been avoided. He notes that the French report recommended a new management structure of administrative board and a college council to control academic affairs. He notes, that 'unlike Bodkin, two of the inspectors from France were deeply experienced in art education and its place in a State system', p. 272. This is a moot point however, and arguably, little could have changed without further financial resources and a new approach to junior and secondary education. Turpin also gives a detailed account of contemporaneous letters to newspapers regarding the school and lack of facilities during the late 1920s. He further examines the role of Atkinson as headmaster of the school, pp. 271-281.
49 When Fianna Fail won the election in 1932, Bodkin was out of favour as he had been close to the Cumann na nGaedhael government. He had previously drafted speeches for President Cosgrave for the opening of exhibitions at the National Gallery and regarding the Lane Pictures. In 1929 Bodkin tried to influence Cosgrave to set up a Ministry of Fine Art but was unsuccessful. Bodkin then wrote to the Minister for External Affairs, Industry and Commerce, Patrick McGilligan, requesting help with regard to the Fine Arts Ministry. Bodkin was director of the National Gallery at the time. He damaged his career by making ill-advised comments after a public lecture in Rathmines in December 1929. Cosgrave commissioned him to write

Times to 'illustrate the point' and promised 'more evidence if necessary' on the conditions at the school, noting too that he was not 'isolated' in his opinions, as there had been a 'steady current of dissatisfaction with the state of affairs for several years, criticisms expressed in public and private'.[50] Bodkin sent some proposals regarding a Ministry of Fine Arts directly to de Valera in February 1933. But de Valera appears to have considered Fine Art among 'the luxuries of a certain kind, which had been part of life in the mansion of Anglo-Ireland ... the preserve of the landed gentry'.[51] Once again, Bodkin's proposal was sent to the Department of Education, where it was shelved. Thus too the die was cast for the trajectory of Keating's career as an artist but also as a writer and broadcaster.

Eventually the DMSA was reorganized and academically re-structured very much along the lines that Keating had called for. He was appointed to the position of Professor of Painting and Anatomy, but not before a series of rows and discussions during which Keating had to cope with forces against him including Atkinson, and one John Ingram, Chief Inspector of the Department's Technical Branch, who, it seems, harboured an ultimately unsuccessful plan to turn the premises into a technical school.[52] Even when the various positions at the school were advertised as a result of the reorganization in 1936, Keating had to fight against an obligatory age limit which, if left in place, would also have had repercussions for Albert Power, James Golden and Austin Molloy.

Notably, although Seán Moylan was a Republican and anti-Treaty, he and Keating were friends since the early 1920s the year that the artist first painted him. When the Fianna Fáil government under de Valera took control in 1932, Moylan was elected for Cork North. He became Parliamentary Secretary in 1937 and Minister for Education between 1951 and 1954. Although Keating's political persuasion had been pro-Treaty, he became terribly disillusioned by the failure of the Cumann nGaedhael government to do anything radical to support the development of the arts in Ireland. He was optimistic that Fianna Fail would do better, but as time when on and nothing changed he became entirely disheartened with politics. However Keating remained on exceptionally friendly terms with Seán Moylan which may have, to some degree, contributed to his survival at the DMSA. Keating lost a good friend and a political ally when Moylan died unexpectedly in 1957.

---

about the Hugh Lane pictures in 1930 and although The Arts Council was instituted in 1951 subsequent to further input from Bodkin, he did not receive an appointment to the new body. See Brian P. Kennedy, *Dreams and Responsibilities*, pp. 23-27.

[50] Letter from John Keating to the Minister of Education, 2 May 1932, National Archives, file S 3458.

[51] Brian P. Kennedy, *Dreams and Responsibilities*, p. 30.

[52] Notebook containing sketches and diary entries for 1936. This entry was 'written in waiting room of PS Department in Govt buildings whilst waiting for possibility (Moynihan) of a promise that the procedure would be followed'. The interview with Mr Moynihan took place on 2 August, 1936. KPPC 536/48(1)/2.

Responses to Culture and Politics 1920s and 1930s.

Throughout the 1920s Keating was extraordinarily busy at home, at the DMSA and further afield; he finished his first major religious commission for Clongowes Wood College in 1922 and then began a series of illustrations for John Millington Synge's *The Playboy of the Western World* which was published in 1927. By the late 1920s he had become interested in what was then known as the Shannon Scheme. This was a project between the fledgling Electricity Supply Board and the German company Siemens to harness the power of the water at Ardnacrusha in County Limerick in order to create hydro-electricity.[53] The project demanded engineering prowess that had not been seen since the formation of the Irish Free State and the project garnered attention from journalists, writers and artists alike. Keating's interest and association with the Shannon Scheme was initially political and subsequently artistic; the modernity of the scheme appealed to his vision of a New Ireland and as a result he made it his business to sketch and paint the people, the machinery and the massive concrete water dam in a series of history paintings for which he has become exceedingly well-known.[54]

From the 1920s onwards various censorship regulations were introduced to Ireland, the subject of which provided the topic of sometimes heated debate among cultural commentators, writers and artists alike. It seems that the first hints of Keating's left-wing political persuasion became evident in *An Allegory* and abundantly clear in his work on the Shannon Scheme as evidenced in images such as *Night's Candles are Burnt Out* and *Der Uberman*. Keating and those of a similar persuasion had to mediate and temper their visual and literal utterances in the shadow of the censorship laws in a form of self-censorship that was necessary in order to remain below the censor's radar. Thus, it is difficult to define exactly what type of Socialist Keating was. While he was not obviously as intense as those that followed James Connolly, the world-view that he made available to the public from 1924 onwards was certainly tinged with a sound knowledge of left-wing ideology which becomes more apparent in broadcasts made during the 1930s.

Ireland's first radio station 2RN was established in 1926 under the directorship of civil servant and fluent Irish speaker Seamus Clandillon. By the early 1930s Keating was working on large-scale mural schemes for the Irish Hospital Trust, which, in turn, sponsored a programme on 2RN. In 1931, perhaps owing to Keating's relationship with 'the Sweep', the Director of 2RN asked him to give a talk on art. There had been some public complaints about the programming on the station and it may be that the Director

---

[53] The Ardnacrusha project was started in 1925 and completed in 1929. For information see Andy Bielenberg, *The Shannon Scheme and the Electrification of the Irish Free State,* The Lilliput Press, Dublin 2002.

[54] Many of these paintings are in the ESB collection. Keating was not commissioned by the ESB or the government to make the work, although his political associations likely provided the necessary introductions to the site. On completion of the series Keating held an exhibition in his studio at the DMSA to which he invited the management of the ESB. It is notable that there were other artists working at the site one of whom was George Atkinson.

wanted to create some interesting debate while at the same time engaging with a new audience. As it turned out Keating undertook a series of nine broadcasts over the next two years, and several more between 1936 and 1937. Once again, Keating started as he meant to continue with 'A Talk on Art' in which he castigated 'Elaborators', or those who lectured and wrote and expounded on art without knowing much about it.[55] He also took issue with those who expected that artists would not and should not behave like average human beings, and those who believed that an understanding and appreciation of art was only in the remit of the upper or educated classes, thereby highlighting what was to be a continual preoccupation with art snobs and cant. Revealing his Socialist persuasion, Keating told his audience that the 'ragamuffin on the street' picking out music on a mouth organ, or the woman who picked out colours for her house furnishings, or the girl who decided to 'grow a fringe' were all contributing to 'art' and that in essence, the public was being 'intimidated by critics and lecturers'.[56] His argument was that people should trust their own judgement about their artistic instinct and not allow themselves to be swayed by those who thought, because of their class and education, that they knew better. Importantly, in terms of generating confidence in the general public, Keating noted that:

> when a man paints a picture that picture is a direct personal appeal to any individual who may happen to see it. And a farmer or shop-keeper, if he is sufficiently interested, can appreciate or depreciate it just as well as the critics and alleged connoisseurs.[57]

Clearly Keating was an unconventional thinker who was not going to bow to social conventions and as such he became part of a *milieu* of like-minded people in Dublin many of whom were attracted to unusual clubs, theatres and galleries. There were many alternative exhibition venues in Ireland during the 1920s and 1930s, but one in particular proved important in Dublin. The Daniel Egan Salon opened in 38 St Stephen's Green in 1926. It grew from a framing and antique business run by the Egan family since the mid-1850s which started initially in Clare Street, moved briefly to Bachelor's Walk and finally to 26 Ormond Quay.[58] Joseph Patrick Egan joined the gilding shop of his father's business in 1915. Two years earlier he had become a student at evening classes in the DMSA and therefore it is extremely likely that he came to know Keating and others who often worked together in the building late into the night.[59] The young Egan came to know Sir Hugh Lane very well and worked with him at the Municipal Gallery in Harcourt Street. As it turned out, when the gallery opened in its permanent home at Charlemont House in the early 1930s, it was Joseph Egan who moved the paintings from one side of the city to the other, and who re-hung them in the new space.

---

[55] See 'A Talk on Art' by John Keating RHA. broadcast 27 March 1931.
[56] Ibid.
[57] Ibid., p. 5.
[58] The Egan Papers are deposited with NIVAL. I would like to thank the Egan family for their permission to access and publish from the papers.
[59] Joseph Patrick Egan had a younger brother called Patrick who also became a student at the DMSA about the same time.

Joseph took over his father's business in 1918 and ran it successfully until the damage caused to Ormond Quay as a result of the bombing of the Four Courts resulted in many shops in the area having to close. However, in 1921 Joseph opened what turned out to be a successful exhibition of 'modern work' by Irish artist W.J. Leech, thus giving him the impetus to continue the framing and antique business but now with a gallery. In February 1925 Joseph closed the Ormond Quay premises and moved to 38 St Stephen's Green on the south side of the city. In September of that year the Daniel Egan Salon opened with an exhibition of 'modern paintings' by Irish and continental artists. In offering the gallery to rent and titling it a 'salon' Joseph's idea was that the space should be used for exhibitions, meetings and other cultural activities and thus the gallery attracted a more alternative crowd.

The Radical Club, which met in the Daniel Egan Salon, came into existence in 1925 in order to provide a forum for those interested in literature, art, and other 'kindred activities.'[60] The proposed activities of the Club suggest that the organizers were interested in attempting to provide an alternative space, akin perhaps to the Futurist and Dada venues in Europe, although it was never as politically radicalized.[61] There were three groups within the Club, one involved with literature, a painters group, and a committee that organized social activities. In May 1926 the Radical Club painters group organized an exhibition that included work by artists of a more obvious modernist persuasion alongside those who were perhaps more traditional in their approach. The list of exhibitors included Harry Kernoff, Maurice MacGonigal, Cecil Ffrench Salkeld, Letitia Hamilton, Grace Henry, Leo Whelan, William McBride, Hilda Van Stockholm, Charles Lamb, Nano Reid, Patrick Tuohy, Dorothy Blackham, Jack B. Yeats, Oliver Sheppard, Estella Solomons, Patrick Trench, May Guinness, Mainie Jellett, and Keating who signalled his approval for the venture by showing; *The Hunter, Feast of St Bridget* and a study for *Men of the South*. Given his attitude in general and his socialist persuasion in particular, it seems hardly surprising that Keating became a member of the 'Radical Club' where people from every class with all types of background could meet to socialize, to exchange ideas, and in the case of artists, to show work. Furthermore, even though he was a full RHA, Keating could see the worth in an environment where there was no argument among artists about the 'Irishness' of Irish art, or the value of academic as opposed to modern art, even if the 'Elaborators' were hard at work.

The Radical Painters exhibition was opened by William Butler Yeats, who studied at the DMSA for two years before deciding on the trajectory of his literary career. During his opening speech Yeats stated that while he 'might quarrel' with the moderns, it was because 'none of his generation could really care for the extreme left of the art movement, complete Cubism, complete Futurism.'[62] However, even if he did not favour a more modernist approach, Yeats could see that some of the artists on the extreme left

---

[60] Book of newspaper cuttings, 1925-1937, Daniel Egan Papers, NIVAL.
[61] The cabaret section of the Radical Club was introduced in July 1926.
[62] Book of newspaper cuttings, 1925-1937, Daniel Egan Papers, NIVAL.

were re-introducing the Adriatic by 'bringing art back to [the] strong colour and rhythm of Asia, which was bringing to art a new world of expression'.[63]

In October 1926 the Egan Salon hosted another exhibition to which they invited artists of all persuasions, including Keating who exhibited *The Goosegirl* (1918). This exhibition was organized by Joseph Egan who used the occasion to tell the press about the plans for the gallery for the season, which included literary evenings and the production of satirical and humorous plays. President Cosgrave was invited to launch the new exhibition and during the speech he said:

> The artist must be able to show what he had created. Without this he all too easily might shut himself in a circle from which escape might prove impossible ... and to exhibit his work is a question of life or death for the artist, a *sine qua non* of his art.[64]

Cosgrave acknowledged that while art education in Ireland was severely wanting, if artists were left to their own devices they would develop their own personalized insight and thus begin to create work that was honest and genuine and yet Irish for its veracity, a concept which Keating repeatedly expounded.

The Daniel Egan Salon remained in operation throughout the 1920s and into the 1930s and there were several excellent exhibitions shown, which were well received by the press. Ultimately, however, Joseph Egan found that sales were not going too well, attendance at openings was falling off and as a result of this and other factors, including competition from the Waddington Galleries, he could not continue to operate the business. The gallery ceased trading in 1937 and Joseph Egan left Dublin for London.

While it is generally accepted that Ireland was a conservative country, particularly after the formation of the Irish Free State, at the same time there was a radicalized left-wing element in society that the government tried, at times ineffectively, to stifle. Keating and his wife May, whom he married in 1919, were left-wing thinkers. May's political beliefs and motivation were far further to the left than her husband's. Their friends and acquaintances included Hanna Sheehy-Skeffington (1877-1946), 'an advocate of socialism, republicanism and individual rights who constantly challenged authority and the state'.[65] May worked in a secretarial role for Sheehy-Skeffington, possibly before her marriage to Keating in 1919, and the two women remained friends until the latter's death in 1946. May was a member of the USSR Society, also known as The Friends of Soviet Russia, a politically radicalized group based in Dublin. Sheehy-Skeffington and the artist Harry Kernoff (1900-1977), who was on friendly terms with Keating, were also members of this group all of whom were keenly interested in political and social developments in Russia at the time. In 1930 Sheehy-Skeffington, Kernoff,

---

[63] Ibid.
[64] Ibid.
[65] Maria Luddy, *Hanna Sheehy Skeffington,* published for the Historical Association of Ireland by Dundalgon Press Ltd, Dundalk, p. 6.

Maud Gonne MacBride (1865-1953) and Charlotte Despard (1844-1939)[66] travelled as a delegation from the Friends of Soviet Russia to Leningrad on a Soviet ship the *Co-Operabzi*.[67] The tour lasted eight weeks from August to September, during which time Kernoff collected Russian propagandist posters which he exhibited in the Daniel Egan Salon in October 1930. He also gave a talk on the social conditions in Russia in the Mansion House in September of the same year.[68] Kernoff was interested in the methods of art teaching in the USSR, but, more importantly, he was struck by the Socialist value of art as propaganda and he came to believe then that 'all art' was 'propagandist art.'[69] For her part, Sheehy-Skeffington was enamoured of the Russian enthusiasm for 'work and the machine' and of the 'freedom from tyranny of fashion and clothes'.[70] Although Sheehy-Skeffington did not become a Communist she was an 'active sympathiser' and she helped to revive the Revolutionary Workers Groups from which Communism would emerge in Ireland in 1933.[71] But there was in the meantime a terrible fear of Communism among those in Government and an initiative to withhold passports from Irish workers attempting to travel to the USSR was instigated in 1931, to which the Friends of Soviet Russia responded by holding a rally in Middle Abbey Street in May of that year.[72]

As a result of the lost promises that followed the War of Independence, and the Civil War, and of the nature of the economic and cultural conditions in the country by the early 1930s, Keating had been well disabused of any idealistic illusions that he may have held prior to 1921. He was disappointed by what he understood to be an inherited colonial departmentalism and as he grew older he became even more radicalized. This aspect of his philosophical and political standpoint is abundantly clear in a frontispiece illustration made in 1931, which supports and conflates the ideology of early Russian Socialism with his own views. On this occasion Keating re-used the family vignette from *Night's Candles are Burnt Out,* a painting with which the artist had already acknowledged a positive alliance between modernity and Socialism. The group consisted of Keating, May and their son Michael, now transposed to illustrate *The National Ideal, A Practical Exposition of True Nationality appertaining to Ireland* by Joseph Hanly.[73] But instead of pointing towards the huge concrete dam at Ardnacrusha, symbolic for the

---

[66] Née French, Charlotte Despard was an English born but Irish based political activist, novelist and member of Sinn Fein. Her home while in Ireland was initially in Roscommon, and after World War One, in Dublin. In 1908 she joined Sheehy-Skeffington and Margaret Cousins to form the Irish Women's Franchise League. Despard, along with Maud Gonne, formed the Women's Prisoners' Defence League during the War of Independence.

[67] Harry Kernoff Papers, NLI MSS 24,942.

[68] Harry Kernoff Papers, NLI MSS 24,942. The exhibition ran from 20 to 25 October that year.

[69] Harry Kernoff Papers, NLI MSS 24,943.

[70] Hanna Sheehy-Skeffington Papers, NLI MSS 24,163.

[71] Luddy, *Hanna Sheehy-Skeffington,* p. 40.

[72] Harry Kernoff Papers, NLI MSS 24,942.

[73] Published by Dollard Printinghouse Ltd, Dublin, the frontispiece was titled *Dia, Tir is Teanga* (God, Land and Language).

artist of the modernity of the Shannon Scheme, the family now direct their gaze towards a bright mandorla which contains a crucifix alongside a hammer and sickle, the recognized iconography of Russian Socialism but, in this instance, tempered with religion. The image at once combines Keating's Socialist inclination with the Christian beliefs of the author who wrote in the publication about the 'significance of nationality' in order 'to show how some of the more important forces that promote nationality might be developed and utilized, in unison, for the spiritual and material national good...'.[74]

Later that same year Keating lent an oil painting titled *The Hunter* (1924) to an exhibition by artists who were 'dissatisfied with their treatment by the hanging committee of the Royal Hibernian Academy which had rejected their pictures'.[75] The exhibition was organized by former IRA member and art student at the DMSA, Ben O'Hickey, and the group became known as the Association of Irish Artists (AIA).[76] Unlike the Dublin Society of Painters exhibitions or the later Irish Exhibition of Living Art exhibitions, the AIA show, which was held in the Mansion House in Dublin, was held in direct opposition to the RHA and was in fact a *salon des refusés*. Evidently the committee asked Keating to go to the opening of the exhibition, an invitation to which he 'readily agreed'.[77] The prevailing atmosphere among critics towards art that was refused by the RHA or that was in any way different is evident in Keating's broadcast made subsequent to the opening:

> *The Press, scenting the prospect of a row in public between the Big-Wigs and the Rebels, gave the matter a little more publicity than it usually does to things relating to Art. In any other city in the world (except perhaps Belfast) there would have been some fun. Accusations, explanations, recriminations, defamations – oceans of ink would have been spilt, and possibly a little blood – from the nose. But not in Dublin ... Because I happen to be an Academician, I was given to understand that I had done something very wrong [in attending the opening]. A prominent Dublin man who is deeply interested in Art said to me "What do you mean by encouraging these fellows? You know in your position you shouldn't do it" I said "What is my position?" He replied "A member of the Academy." In that reply is condensed the whole case against academies.[78]*

In consideration of Keating's critical demise subsequent to 1950, this broadcast is crucially important because it clearly offers his opinion on the idea or concept of an Academy and how it should work. In order to develop his argument Keating took the fact that at least one member of the public thought that as a member of the RHA he should not have condoned the 'rebel' exhibition by contributing paintings to it. Given his

---

[74] Joseph Hanly, *The National Ideal, A Practical Exposition of the True Nationality appertaining to Ireland,* Dollard Printinghouse, Dublin, 1931, 'Preface', p. 1.
[75] John Keating RHA., 'Talk on Artists and Academicians', 22 May, 1931.
[76] O'Hickey had formerly headed up the Bansha, North Tipperary branch of the IRA. Keating's *Tipperary Hurler* (1928) is also based on O'Hickey and on John Joe Hayes, star hurler with the Tipperary team in the 1920s.
[77] Keating, 'Talk on Artists and Academicians', 22 May 1931.
[78] Ibid.

previous history with the RHA it must be concluded that Keating knew that he ran the risk of getting into trouble with the Council, but yet he felt strongly enough not only to contribute to the show, but to make the broadcast too. He noted in response to his critic that:

> To suggest that an Academy has no use for youth or courage or novelty or enterprise [or] for indignation against injustice –real or imaginary –is to suggest that it [the Academy] is dead.[79]

Furthermore, and importantly acknowledging the inherent and very human flaws in Academicians, Keating said:

> as long as privilege and authority are dear to humans, as long as middle-age brings caution and laziness, so long will academicians tend to conservatism, arrogance and the vices of middle age. That is why in my opinion, every institution ought to be abolished every 25 years.[80]

Although it is evident that Keating was not on the selection panel for the annual RHA exhibition that year, he made it clear that he thought that some of the paintings that had been rejected were of equal quality to those that had been accepted and therefore the 'rebel artists' had, in his opinion, a valid grievance. At the same time Keating also acknowledged the exuberance of youth and the cyclical nature of the process of art production:

> The rebel artists of today who appear in the streets without a hat, who have no property beyond youth and high spirits, who are all bones and hopes instead of all fat and regrets – will, in their turn, wear top hats or red robes...they will write letters after their names and will reject and condemn the pictures of their young contemporaries...but their rebellion is a healthy sign.[81]

In denunciation of the system employed at the RHA Keating said that:

> To have a rule – such as we have – that a member is entitled to be exhibited because he is a member, is dangerous. It puts a premium on privilege, on arrogance, on laziness, and [it] puts an edge on the criticism of the outsider.[82]

At the same time, Keating was sympathetic to the Academy which he could see was caught between a rock and a hard place and as such it had a relationship comparable with bazaars and charity:

> Promoters of bazaars go to endless trouble. They meet, discuss, arrange, give interviews, get photographed...An ocean of money is subscribed...and spent like water on the thousand and one unnecessary elaborations...and when it is all over the charity concerned is presented with about sixpence to every pound.[83]

---

[79] Ibid.
[80] Author's emphasis.
[81] Ibid.
[82] Ibid. This system has not been changed to date.
[83] Ibid.

Throughout 1931 Keating continued to broadcast about art and culture. In June of that year he offered his thoughts on 'Snobbery in Art' the perpetrators of which were essentially 'raging' with a thirst for 'the limelight' and were to a large degree responsible for encouraging a general lack of self esteem about issues pertaining to art among the general public.[84] Keating followed that up the same month with a talk on the 'Future of Irish Art' in which he returned to the theme of a national lack of interest in 'the look of things', which he understood as a lack of esteem about the value and availability of art in everyday life and 'something that we couldn't afford'. In language that seems suitable for the economic environment in the twenty-first century Keating sarcastically called on the Irish public to get into 'Americanism' and buy whatever they could (including art) in order to bring about an economic recovery:

> *Personally I think that we might as well go on a spree as not. Heretofore we were told and believed that economy and prudence were virtues. Now the Governments of all the nations give an example of mad extravagance to their citizens. The most eminent economists tell us that the remedy for economic depression is to spend freely. If you haven't got the money, buy in credit...Spend quick and get rich quicker...Tell your boss what you think of him and go on the dole...*[85]

In a statement of pure irony that signals his attitude to social welfare Keating created a 'haven for the artists' by suggesting that because compulsory third party car insurance was about to be introduced, the State could also introduce 'compulsory portraiture for motorists' which could be replaced at a price 'calculated by Income Tax Officials...'

> *Does that sound too ridiculous? Is it more ridiculous than having to pay taxes to keep people idle...* [86]

In the same broadcast Keating referred to the 'Soviet Five Year Plan', noting that notwithstanding its 'rightness or wrongness' there was no doubt that it resulted in five years of 'concentrated thinking' in an experiment to investigate methods of properly and 'systematically' industrializing a country. Whether or not one would agree with Stalin, Keating still felt that the programme was better than 'five years of destruction, mass murder, and pestilence and moral bankruptcy' in Russia. He then signals his interest in Socialism by noting that nobody knew if the Five Year Plan was going to be a success but:

> *We do know that it isn't going to be safe to try the experiment. We also know that our permission to try it will not be requested.*[87]

---

[84] See 'Snobbery in Art', 2 June, 1931.
[85] See 'Talk on the Future of Irish Art', 9 June 1931.
[86] Ibid.
[87] Ibid. Under the first Five Year Plan, introduced in 1928, the State controlled large and medium enterprises but it left smaller businesses which employed twenty people or fewer to private enterprise. Stalin's emphasis at this stage was on industrialization of the country in order to keep capitalist countries out. The first Five Year Plan ended in 1932.

Keating's deeply critical attitude towards 'Americanism' came about largely as a result of his visit to New York in 1929. He was invited there by Helen Hackett who ran the eponymous gallery that became well-known for showing the work of Irish artists from the late 1920s until the mid 1930s. Keating visited New York in December 1929 and was not at all impressed with what he saw as rampant consumerism, noise and commercialism. On his return Keating painted a little known allegory titled *Homo Sapiens-An Allegory of Democracy* in which he is obviously severely critical of the morals of the human being. He set the terrified man, who looks very much like the religious figure in *Night's Candles are Burnt Out* (1929) high above what appears to be a bird's eye view of New York. Around him are the symbols that were, and to a large extent still are, important to the human race; justice, religious and military activity. Yet, the man seems frightened and imprisoned by that which the human race had created in the name of democracy. He purposely did not sell *Homo Sapiens* but exhibited it for the first time at the RA exhibition in London in 1930 and in the same year he showed a study of the work at the Carnegie Institute in Pittsburgh. In 1932 the painting was exhibited at the Oldham Gallery in England before being sent to the Irish pavilion at the Chicago World's Fair in 1933.[88] He then showed it at the annual RHA exhibition in 1934, and at the National College of Art exhibition in 1941. In 1953 Keating sent the painting to an exhibition in the National Library of Wales, Aberystwyth, which was organized by the Cultural Relations Committee. He showed it again at the retrospective of his work held at the Hugh Lane Municipal Gallery in 1963 and yet again at the RHA in 1966. In fact, Keating felt so strongly about the effect of man on the world and on each other that in 1931 he published the image as a Christmas card which he sent to all his friends and clients.

In August 1931 Keating used his broadcast to respond to letters that he had received from parents who wondered whether or not their children were 'artists'. His advice was sympathetic, fatherly and even handed. He acknowledged that all parents think that their children are wonderful, and whether or not a child was an artist, to send him or her to art school anyway, if they expressed a desire to go, because it would do no harm. Ultimately, he felt, the child would have a good sense of whether or not he or she would make it. He pointed out too that the life of an artist was hard as they had to 'meet the insatiable Demon within' and be prepared to 'take the consequences of being an artist' which were not at all pleasant.[89] His second broadcast in August addressed his concerns about what was being produced for the cinema. Keating enjoyed films and was a member of a club in Dublin, however he was deeply critical of what he described as 'dope' which was available on general release to the public in the early 1930s. Clearly Keating felt that capitalism was at fault for the ignorant and unwholesome content and

---

[88] Keating also showed *Holy Joe in the Mountains* (1929) at the Chicago World's Fair.
[89] See 'Art as a Career', 4 August 1931. At this stage Keating's sons were aged four and one respectively.

the 'false view of life' that cinema offered. The content of the films seemed to suggest that money and the acquisition of wealth was the essence of life. Thus he noted:

> As long as private enterprise is allowed to conflict with the general welfare, so long will millionaire producers sell vulgarity, sensationalism and clap-trap – because it is cheap...[90]

At the same time Keating could see that without the pressures of capitalism the cinema could provide mental freedom to everybody and thus it contained the inherent possibility to become 'the most powerful instrument of general enlightenment' that had emerged to date.[91] Yet again Keating's attitude to the all persuasive influence of America on Irish advertising cinema can be seen in his little known allegory *Sacred and Profane Love* (1937). The foreground of the painting illustrates normal everyday life: a father or perhaps a grandfather holding onto a pram while the mother, modelled on Keating's wife May, cleans her son's nose while people of every generation, some fashionable, others not so, are walking the path as if it were a stage set. The scene in the foreground is, as far as Keating was concerned, the result of 'sacred' love while the billboard in the background advertising some new cinema production is 'profane'. Interestingly, the painting was first shown in the Carnegie Institute in Pittsburgh and then Royal Academy in London in 1937 before being moved to the Royal Scottish Academy in 1938. Keating held on to the painting and showed it for the first time in Ireland in an exhibition of his work at the Kenny Gallery in Galway in 1973. With regard to rampant consumerism and commercialism, Keating's thoughts seem prophetic:

> To endeavour to promote a social conscience in the name of God and at the same time to permit – under the guise of modernism and advancement – the activities of a naked commercialism (which has fallen into disrepute among the very people who created it) is a process of auto-frustration. Unbridled self-interest and reckless exploitation of the moral and physical needs of the human race has brought about the state of things in which collapse is inevitable...I suggest that it might be better for us – even from the financial point of view – to take the tax off Beethoven and put it on Ballyhoo.[92]

In November 1931 the subject of Keating's broadcast was the public misconception about art and artists. Essentially Keating's point was that artists were expected, to some degree, to behave like performing monkeys and to answer ridiculous questions posed by people who really had little or no interest. The entire charade conspired, as far as Keating was concerned, to add 'another brick to the facade of Bunk in Art'.[93] Taking up the case on behalf of artists Keating highlighted the dreary and miserable aspects of their life; little or no money, the need of patronage without which a good reputation was entirely impossible and yet it was all a vicious circle which served to make the young artist ill and thus, a bad conversationalist for the 'bunk in art' contingent. During the

---

[90] See 'Art and Cinema', 28 August, 1931.
[91] Ibid.
[92] See 'Be not Solicitous'.
[93] See 'Another Talk on Art' 28 November 1931.

same broadcast and using photographers as an example, Keating gently but firmly castigated those who patently were not artists but who saw anyway a commercial opportunity available to them at the School of Art. These photographers, not realizing the difficulties involved in learning the required skills, joined the classes at the school in order to provide 'genuine hand-painted oil portraits' to their clients. But they were disappointed to discover that there were no quick answers to learning 'how to paint a nose' and thus they became disillusioned and suspicious of artists. At the same time Keating's comments on the matter also serve to illustrate his continual frustration and dissatisfaction at having to teach in circumstances that allowed people into class without a basic entrance examination that would investigate the presence or otherwise of a basic artistic talent. The 'elaborators' do not escape Keating's attention and his final comment during this broadcast was to encourage people to eat eggs if they liked eggs, and to look at pictures, sculpture and architecture if they liked art.

Keating reproduced 'Another Talk on Art' as an article titled 'The Voice of One' in December 1938.[94] While there are minor changes to the published article, it is clear that he still felt very strongly that several issues to which he referred initially had not been addressed to his satisfaction. In fact the subject of 'Elaborators' and 'bunk in art' and 'bunkum in excelsis' was the mainstay of most if not all of his articles and broadcasts. However, the topic of entrance examinations to which he tacitly referred in 1931 and again in 1938 had not been properly dealt with when the Dublin Metropolitan School of Art became the National College of Art in 1937. It took a little time for the new regime to settle down and entrance examinations were not introduced until 1942.

In April 1932 Keating delivered a broadcast titled 'Art in Ireland'.[95] The essence of his message in this instance was that although the Irish were in possession of 'artistic sensibilities', there was no Irish school of painting in evidence. Given that at this time he was teaching at the DMSA and was a member of the RHA and well-known in Ireland and America for his work, Keating's attitude may seem surprising. Indeed, when his paintings were shown in America between 1929 and 1939 Keating was invariably described by art critics as leading the vanguard of an 'Irish School of Art.' But the reality, as Keating understood it, was entirely different, and during this broadcast the artist touched on themes that he had spoken about and visually represented previously in paintings such as *An Allegory*. He felt very strongly that Ireland was still borrowing from English convention and that the 'system of art education inaugurated by Prince Albert' was still in operation but that it was 'part of the Victorian smoke-screen of Democracy and Humanitarian Liberalism behind which went on the real business of Empire-mad industrialism and privilege'. Thus he felt that, owing to lack of opportunity, there was no Irish artist on a par with Courbet, Monet or Zuloaga who had each made work that was indicative of their sense of nationhood. Consequently in his opinion, we

---

94 See 'The Voice of One', *The Leader,* 17 December 1938.
95 See 'Art in Ireland' 23 April 1932.

could 'never build an Irish "school" of art out of the debris of the Ascendancy'.[96] Keating acknowledged that there were two 'good' galleries in the city, but they were hampered in the ability to purchase works of excellence owing to a severe lack of funding and they showed little evidence of an 'Irish school'. But it is really the final paragraph of this broadcast that best exemplifies Keating's attitude to art, artists and art training in Ireland at that time. It is clear that membership of the RHA and a job at the DMSA was not fundamental to his thinking:

> we have in Ireland at the moment a number of young Irishmen of talent and individual character actually painting Irish things in Ireland. Here is all the material for an Irish School, if the individuals were sufficiently self-conscious and cohesive to be aware of it, and if they were given the necessary encouragement. This must be in the form of a provision for continuous work on public buildings, offices, Churches, theatres and the recording studio.[97]

This was a logical and forward thinking proposal but it was not until 1997 that the Irish government introduced the 'Percent for Art Scheme' which allows 1% of total build costs towards commissioning and implementation of an associated art project.

The following October Keating returned to the subject of an Irish School of Art and the inherent faults in the system set up under Prince Albert.[98] At the same time he remained critical of the School of Art, which was not, as far as he was concerned, a 'cradle for the development of a national culture'.[99] Indeed, Keating's attitude to the method of teaching at the School is significant given his negative treatment at the hands of some Irish art historians:[100]

> as long as the machine is revolving, as long as the students are passing examinations which lead nowhere (except to poorly paid jobs as teachers), so long is the end considered to be attained... You haven't got anything to say? Well, copy the Renaissance and improve your taste – or copy the Gothic, or the Moorish or the Chinese.[101]

Perhaps the most important element of the broadcast was Keating's discussion about nationalism in art as evidenced in other countries such as China and the South Sea Islands. His point was that the artists of these countries developed their own culture based on their surroundings and not by reference to examples from other places. Implicit in Keating's argument is the fundamental flaw that he saw in seeking a new art for Ireland in forms or 'isms' that had been developed in, for example, France. The essence of his argument was that Irish artists should return to their own 'place', as those

[96] See also 'The State of Painting', date of broadcast/talk unknown but c. Late 1940s. This document may have formed the basis of a lecture on modern art delivered by Keating to students of University College Dublin in November 1948.
[97] Ibid.
[98] See 'Talk on Art', 30 October 1932.
[99] Ibid.
[100] See for example Turpin, 'Keating and MacGonigal in the School of Painting' in John Turpin, *A School of Art in Dublin since the Eighteenth Century'*, Gill and Macmillan, 1995, pp.330-347.
[101] Ibid.

of other countries had done, in order to develop a national school of art. For Keating that place was the West of Ireland in general and the Aran Islands in particular. There were more pragmatic reasons for his ideas. Keating felt that Ireland had no choice but to return to her own native culture because Europe and the machine age had given 'the Great War, the Treaty of Versailles, thirteen years of neurasthenia, war debts and influenza – and now the Great Slump'.[102]At this stage his vision for Ireland was:

> *self-supporting, self-confident and self-respecting…rid of idlers and wage-slaves…with an economic equilibrium that could be trusted to stay put…a time when the awful doctrine of every man for himself and the devil take the hindmost – that damnable first article of the creed of all imperialists and money-grubbers – will stand revealed as an insult to man's intelligence.*[103]

Whether or not that vision came to fruition is a matter of opinion, but it would seem, by reference to Keating's later paintings, that he was to become even more disillusioned about the manner in which Ireland was governed and the failure of humankind around the world to learn from previous mistakes. The artist, Keating felt, had the capacity to show the truth to the world, and thus had the ability to create an 'anti-toxin for humbug' because the capitalist was not interested in him until he was dead. Thus Keating's vision for an Irish school of art was not premised or dependent on an architecturally designed building complete with every *mod con*. It was instead, an environment that provided opportunity and appreciated the output from those who proved that they had something to say.[104]

In 1932 the aforementioned AIA held another *salon des refusés*, this time at the Daniel Egan Salon. Yet again, and notwithstanding the critical attitude to this involvement with the organization the previous year, Keating gave his implicit and explicit support by lending *Race of the Gael* (1928) to the exhibition. As the painting included a portrait of Ben O'Hickey the loan seems to have had an intentional *double entendre*.[105] Keating's meaning in the painting, as is quite often the case, is not immediately obvious. The title might suggest that he subscribed to the concept of the pure Irish race, but in fact, as he wrote to Helen Hackett of the eponymous gallery, he did not believe in such an idea at all. He placed Ben O'Hickey, a dark haired former member of the IRA, dressed in this instance as a farm hand or labourer, and Brigadier Ben Carty, who was blond or grey, and perhaps more sartorially elegant than his younger colleague, in a landscape that is largely imaginary. In the style of late Renaissance

---

[102] Neurasthenia is a form of chronic fatigue.

[103] See Keating 'Talk on Art', 30 October 1932.

[104] See also Keating 'A Modern School of Painting', date of article or broadcast unknown but post 1933.

[105] Ben O'Hickey, who was Keating's student at the NCA, exhibited *A Southern Village* and *The Late Rory O'Connor*. The other model in *Race of the Gael* is Brigadier Ben Carty. The exhibition included work from Shane Kilgariff, John Dixon, J. Fitzpatrick, Phyllis Godfrey, F. Fahy, Mary McCord, Teresa Mulpetre, W. Montgomery, Kevin O'Grady, S. Fitzgerald Smith and J. Forsyth Taylor. Book of Newspaper cuttings, Daniel Egan Papers, NIVAL.

courtly Mannerism, their gaze does not engage the viewer as both look to some distant point. This is a by now well-known artistic device that denotes the sitters as knowledgeable, sophisticated and capable. While both had associations with political factions in the pre and post Civil-War era, they serve in this instance to mediate the artist's message; that Irish men of all types, from every background, were intelligent and educated and could therefore run the country successfully, perhaps better than the politicians who claimed to be in control. It is notable that while Ben O'Hickey holds a rifle, it is laid to rest against his left shoulder, signalling a refusal of violence in favour of political dialogue. It is also significant that Keating made sure to send this painting to the RA in 1929, where it was hardly noticed owing to the attention given to his 'problem' painting *Night's Candles are Burnt Out* (1929), and then to the Carnegie Institute in Pittsburgh and the Helen Hackett Gallery in New York that same year. Thus, Keating's refusal of violence, which was first signalled in *An Allegory* in 1924, was now reinforced in an image that publicly privileged peace and intelligence above all else.

The press described the AIA exhibition as 'the rebel gallery', full of pictures rejected by the RHA and painted by artists who were 'rebelling against autocracy.'[106] While there is no evidence one way or the other, it seems plausible that the size of the small house in which the RHA was based in Ely Place may have been prohibitive in terms of the number and scale of work that could be shown at any one time. Doubtless too, the RHA members were keen to hang their own work given that it was proving extraordinarily difficult to sell art because of the general economic conditions. Moreover, Joseph Egan noted at the time that in fact while the group was a 'protest against the RHA' he thought that the 'standard of work was very poor.' At the same time Egan noted that the exhibition was 'getting plenty of publicity'[107] possibly at least partially owing to Keating's involvement. Mrs Reddin, who opened the exhibition, described it as a 'step in the right direction and deserving in encouragement', and the newspapers took a more lenient view of Keating's involvement, noting of his contribution *Race of the Gael,* that it was one of the largest canvases in a show that included over one hundred works.[108] The AIA was notable for its strongly confrontational approach towards the RHA in the early 1930s and Keating's willingness to become so publically involved deserves recognition. However, as Keating had predicted in his radio broadcast on Art and Academicians the initial energy did not last and the group did not exhibit again as the AIA after 1932. [109] For his part, Keating's main artistic concern was to finish his major commission from the Haverty Trust to paint an image to commemorate the history of Saint Patrick which was shown, along with paintings on the same theme by Leo Whelan and Margaret Clarke, as part of the celebrations to mark the Eucharistic Congress held in Dublin that year.[110]

[106] Book of newspaper cuttings, Daniel Egan Papers, NIVAL, NCAD.
[107] Joseph Egan, Daniel Egan Papers, NIVAL, NCAD.
[108] Book of Newspaper Cuttings, Daniel Egan Papers, NIVAL, NCAD.
[109] May 1931.
[110] Titled *St Patrick Lights the Paschal Fire at Slane*, the painting was given by the Haverty Trust to the Irish College in Rome in 1937.

Keating was kept busy over the next number of years, not least with the ongoing issues between himself and George Atkinson at the DMSA. He worked hard in the studio at home and at the school and he showed work in galleries in Dublin, all over England, in Scotland and in New York. While many of the paintings that he undertook were portrait commissions, a large amount of the work shown at exhibition were paintings and drawings of the Aran Island people. In spite of the censorship laws, during the 1930s several short-lived, vaguely radical newspapers emerged. One of these was called *The Irish People*. It appeared in February 1936 and had its last publication in April of that year. The stated aims of *The Irish People* are of significance, not least because Keating published a scathing article in the first edition of the paper. It was hoped that the broadsheet would provide a forum for 'expressing all the forces working for the unity and independence of Ireland' which was as 'sharply felt within the mildly anti-imperialist trade union movement in Belfast as among the irreconcilables of Kerry'.[111] It also offered a forum for 'expression to the various progressive cultural and social movements' and the editors encouraged 'rebuffed writers, the labour movement, the youth movement, Gaelic League workers and national teachers' to use the paper to air their grievances. Contributors to the first edition of the paper included Mrs Sheehy Skeffington, Erskine H. Childers, Peadar O'Donnell and 'Cu Uladh'.[112] Later contributors included Harry Kernoff whose article was titled 'Root Causes of the Lack of Artistic Appreciation in Ireland' and Maurice MacGonigal whose essay was called 'The Culture of a Nation is not born in Defeat'.[113] Belfast born and based Captain Denis Ireland contributed several articles on Marx, Marxism and Lenin and he offered his views on Communism in the final edition of the paper.[114] Keating was asked to contribute a response to the question 'Is there any rage in you against our cultural shortcomings?'. The result was 'Art Does not get a Chance in Ireland' which is a distillation of all of Keating's previous ideas about the development of Irish culture. As far as he was concerned the entire cultural edifice had to be pulled down and re-constructed before anything close to culture could emerge because there was no artistic freedom, no support for art and artists except mere words, and even less interest from official quarters. His words well reflect his sentiment and at the same time they appear to contain significance for the twenty first century:

> *As long as we permit lying advertisements worded in revolting terms to cheat sick and frightened people out of money for nostrums...as long as we permit anyone who thinks himself a builder to run up an ugly structure in any place that suits him for any purpose...as long as private interest can postpone or defeat schemes for improvement or draw rents from slums...as long as we build hospitals in noisy and depressing slums and let private jealousies defeat necessary and obvious amalgamations and constantly*

---

[111] *The Irish People (Muintearr na h-Eireann)*, first edition, 29 February, 1936, p. 4.
[112] 'The Hound of Ulster' was Peadar Toner MacFhionnlaoich (1857-1942). He was President of the Gaelic League between 1933 and 1942.
[113] 14 March and 28 March 1936 respectively.
[114] The final edition of the paper was 11 April, 1936.

protect privilege and authority against reason and common sense...as long as the whole mental background of the people is formed on the concept of a remorseless struggle for existence presided over by an angry god...or a soulless machine – the State – there is no room for beauty or culture.[115]

In November of that year Keating made a broadcast titled 'If I were Director of Broadcasting', which initially appears to be a tongue-in-cheek comment at the influence of some over others.[116] The content of the article, in which Keating styles himself a dictator, is utterly preposterous and, in an effort to use humour to encourage people to think about authority and what it should mean, it is obviously iconoclastic. He had little time for the dogmatism of hierarchical organizations that sought control over the populace and this included political, social and religious institutions. At the same time Keating was critical of a common people that appeared mindless and willing to be influenced by inflexible authorities. The subtext of this attitude was an acknowledgement that, owing to the prevalence of dogmatism from which Ireland was supposed to have ridded herself, there could not be anything fashioned as 'national' if a hierarchy or hierarchies were still in control of the mind of the people at large.

It would seem too that Keating may well have had the Spanish Civil War (1936-1939) in mind while writing 'If I were Director of Broadcasting.' May Keating had been educated in Spain and only returned to Dublin in 1916 on the death by accident of her then *fiancé*. It is hardly surprising, given the Keatings' self-evident politics, that they along with many others in Ireland would become involved with the Republican side in the Spanish Civil War. The Irish Catholic Church supported Francesco Franco in his bid to rule Spain and as a result the Bishops gave their *imprimatur* to a series of pro-Franco collections which were taken up during mass on the Feast of Christ the King in October 1936, just a couple of weeks prior to Keating's broadcast on Directors and Dictators.[117] The newly formed Christian Front was engaged in similar anti-Republican and pro-Franco activities outside church gates and in meetings all over the country. The task of exposing the use of religion to cloud the real issues pertaining to the political struggle in Spain fell to people associated with the left such as Peadar O'Donnell (1893-1986) and Father Michael O'Flanagan (1876-1942).[118] As if to prove his credentials as a left-wing liberal Keating showed a full-length portrait of Father O'Flanagan in the RHA in 1936. Central to the political issue was that General Franco wanted to control Spain while the Spanish people had voted four to one in favour of a Republican government which had

---

[115] 'Art does not get a chance in Ireland', in *The Irish People* (Muintearr na h-Eireann), first edition, 29 February, 1936, p. 4.

[116] See 'If I were Director of Broadcasting', 14 November 1936.

[117] The collection took place on 25 October 1936.

[118] Peadar O'Donnell took the anti-Treaty side during the Civil War. He is known as the author of several publications including *Salud! An Irishman in Spain* (1937). Father O'Flanagan or Flanagan as he was variously known was Vice-President of Sinn Fein in 1919 and President of the organization from 1933-35. For further information on the Irish Republican fight in the Spanish Civil War see Michael O'Riordan, *Connolly Column*, New Books, Dublin, 1979.

in turn the support of the 'Catholic masses and the Basque Nationalists, Communists, Socialist and Republican parties.'[119] The authorities were frightened by Communism and the fact that the Spanish Republic had the support of Marxists and Socialists was arguably the reason that the Catholic Church favoured Franco. But it would seem that many did not know or at least did not acknowledge that Franco was backed by two strong Fascist powers, Germany and Italy, who were apparently prepared to 'plunge the world into war to set up a Fascist dictatorship in Spain.'[120] Fascism was on the increase across Europe and it was considered by many in Europe as the enemy of liberty. General Eoin O'Duffy became the leader of the 'Blueshirts' in Ireland in 1932 which was, in effect, an arm of the Fascist movement. It was a politically far-right organization with a fastidious fondness for Mussolini. As a result of all manner of manoeuvrings the Spanish Republic and those associated with it became the subject of mass hysteria and as a consequence people began to believe that attacks on priests, nuns and churches in Dublin were imminent. It is by now well known that many Irish men joined the Republican side of the Spanish Civil War in 'International Brigades' including Tyrone born poet Charlie Donnelly (1914-1937) who died at the Battle of Jarama in February 1937.[121] At the time Donnelly was under the command of his old friend Frank Ryan (1902-1944) who headed up a battalion known as the 'Connolly Column'. May Keating, along with Hanna Sheehy-Skeffington, Nora Connolly O'Brien (daughter of James Connolly after whom Ryan's Brigade was named) and the writer Dorothy Macardle were members of a radical group known as the Spanish Aid Committee who in turn helped to organize 'an all-Ireland Ambulance Corps for the Spanish/Irish Republican forces.'[122] The project won the support of prominent Trade Union leaders many of whom made 'generous but anonymous subscriptions to the Irish Aid Committee for the Spanish Republic.'[123] Keating cannot have been impervious to the activities of his wife and friends and his portrait of Father O'Flanagan offers a clear indication of his Socialist credentials and with all of this in mind his article 'If I were Director of Broadcasting' does seem to take on another meaning altogether.

During a broadcast aimed at children in 1937 Keating took the opportunity to gently advise children not to be persuaded from their own thoughts and opinions by hierarchical people or institutions. His views on the subject can be interpreted in the light of the debate around national culture and more generally in relation to world politics. It would appear that Keating felt that if children were encouraged to recognize

---

[119] O'Riordan, *Connolly Column*, p. 32.
[120] Ibid.
[121] Ibid, p. 43. O'Riordan notes that the majority of Irish people who fought on the Republican side in Spain were poets, writers and playwrights. See also Joseph O'Connor, *Even the Olives are Bleeding,* New Island Books, Dublin 1991 for an analysis of the life and work of Charlie Donnelly.
[122] O'Riordan, *Connolly Column*, p. 36.
[123] Ibid. O'Riordan notes that one Trade Union representative refused to remain anonymous. He was John Swift, retired General Secretary of the Irish Bakers' Union.

their own opinions about art, for instance, they would grow up with firm convictions and the ability to refute broad-scale dogma. With this in mind Keating told the children that it was important and essential to trust one's own judgement about life in general and art in particular.[124] His comments also shed light on his attitude when interviewed about certain aspects of modernism particularly from the 1940s onwards. He always had a view, which was usually presented with more than a tinge of humour and indeed iconoclasm. At the same time he tempered his remarks by noting that whatever had been said was his opinion and ultimately he expected that others would have their own thoughts on the matter at hand. Hence his continual attitude to 'elaborators' and culture-mongers who he felt were feeding into a national lack of self-esteem in matters pertaining to culture. On the other hand Keating was always aware of political developments in the world and thus he was continually frightened by violence and surprised that at a certain social level nothing had been learned from previous wars and conflict. Remarking about his job as an artist Keating encouraged children to look at the pictures around them, to go to galleries, which were no longer merely for 'the rich' and to look at prints in books. By doing so he felt that children would be exposed to everything and if it meant 'nothing' that was alright and not to pretend otherwise:

> There is almost sure to be some form of skill or expert work that will interest each of you. Stick to that – and don't despise others who happen to have different tastes.[125]

As the world edged towards World War Two the government of Ireland adopted an internationally neutral position and concomitantly created the conditions that have now become known as 'the Emergency'. The result was a culturally exciting atmosphere especially in Dublin as conscientious objectors, pacifists and others took up residence without fear of conscription. It was in 1939 that pacifist Herbrand Ingouville-Williams (d.1945), Kenneth Hall (1913-1946), Basil Rakoczi (1908-1979) and his young son Tony arrived initially to the West of Ireland before settling in Dublin by the end of that year.[126] While it is often written that Ireland was at that time 'culturally conservative', it really must be made clear that that conservatism was created by the fusion of the principles of church and state and many people, including Keating, were continually agitating against both institutions.[127] It is also argued that artistic movements which had formerly been seen as threatening were successfully presented by a 'younger generation' in Dublin at this time.[128] It is true that Mainie Jellett's work was assessed in biological terms by George Russell (OY) in the early 1920s, but he had come to accept her work by the later part of that decade. Moreover Jellett, born in 1897, can hardly be seen in terms of a younger generation and so too Norah McGuinness who was born a mere four years later in 1901. However, the two women, along with several others, can be seen in terms of the

---

[124] See 'Talk to Children', 28 October 1937.
[125] Ibid.
[126] See S.B. Kennedy, *The White Stag Group,* The Irish Museum of Modern Art, 2005.
[127] Ibid., p. 20.
[128] Ibid.

development of artistic concepts born of the European modernist movement. While Ireland was apparently 'closed' to the war, Rakoczi and Hall as 'The White Stag' brought their own brand of European modernism to Dublin where there were many artists, including Jellett and McGuinness, that were open to their ideas.

There is no doubt that the cultural environment changed rapidly during the early 1940s, particularly in Dublin. That should not suggest however that there was an ongoing and personalized conflict between Irish artists who favoured European modernism and those that privileged a more 'academic' approach. There were several exhibition venues all around the country where artists of all persuasions exhibited their work in the hope of selling. It is true that Mainie Jellett was the author of extremely critical reviews of the RHA in the early 1940s, but while her remarks were robust, she did not personalize them and members of the academy, including Keating, would have concurred with her concerns. While Keating and Jellett are frequently positioned against each other by art historians, in fact while their visual differences are acutely apparent, there is no evidence to suggest that they disliked each other and there is plenty to suggest that they had similar social concerns.

Responses to Culture and Politics 1940s.

It was in the context of 'The Emergency' that Keating published his provocatively titled article 'A Spanking for Intellectuals' in March 1940.[129] Yet again Keating referred to national and international cultural and political conditions by returning to the issue of the 'critic' and his or her desire to 'improve' others while refusing to comprehend their own lack of self-awareness and their 'inability to realize the absurdity of trying to force living things into dead logical systems' thus leading to the 'shocking display of envy, malice and all uncharitableness' evident in the 'conversation of Intellectuals.'[130] Keating blamed the universal educational system for the 'ignorance and inefficiency' among 'Intellectuals' which would be 'unthinkable among ordinary workaday people'. Moreover, although education had been the privilege of the elite and the 'clerical', he was critical of the system made available to the ordinary people as a result of the Industrial Revolution because ultimately it was 'only for the purpose of making them more efficient slaves and not to enlarge their minds or teach them to think.'

> Meanwhile the Intellectuals go on talking about art, religion, politics, [the] economy. Nobody listens to them and they don't listen to each other. And the common man – like the maddened beast in a forest fire – stands bewildered amid the glare and crash of falling bombs and shattered hopes ...
>
> The workers will have to use their heads as well as their hands – and the Intellectuals their hands as well as their heads – if the human race is to survive. Think or die. Work or rot.

---

[129] See Keating, 'A Spanking for Intellectuals', March 1940. The article was published in *The Irish Digest,* March 1940, pp. 18-21.
[130] Ibid.

Even if the cultural conditions in Ireland during the early 1940s were exciting, there was still no state support for art and artists in the country. At the same time there was a commonly held view that there was no 'Irish' art since the Viking Age owing to the historic state of affairs with England. Thus the critics who wanted an 'Irish School of Painting' found room to make comparison between 'traditional' and more experimental work by reference to the RHA and to artists such as Jellett respectively. It is true that during this time there was more intense criticism of the RHA but it has to be said that Keating agreed with it. Moreover, it seems that there is some misunderstanding about Keating's idea of a 'national' school of art. It is true that he called on artists to look to the West of Ireland, but this was because he saw that otherwise 'Irish' art would be premised on ideas generated in other cultures and taken out of context to create 'modern' art. At the same time the West of Ireland ultimately became the focus of Keating's frustration and discontent at the lost promises of the Irish State, which can be seen in work such as *Goodbye Father* (1936-8), *Economic Pressure or a Bold Peasant being Destroyed* (1949) and *Ulysses in Connemara* (1950). Keating was aware that there was no 'Irish' school, but his concept of what that might be was not premised on a building, but rather on freedom of expression and the provision of patronage, all of which is evident in many broadcasts and published articles from the 1930s and 40s.[131] It is manifest too, that Keating hated pretence and flattery in the art world, and on the death of the sculptor Andrew O'Connor, he railed against the establishment for its non-acceptance of the sculptor's work, though they turned up to 'heap praise' at his funeral.[132] Evidently he found 'post-mortem flattery' even worse:

> The Irish native is a past master of the liturgy of ceremonial hum-bug and this talent is traceable through our whole social system ... it seems to me that there is always a note of subdued relief in the panegyric...The panegyrist is a lucky fellow. For ten minutes or longer he stands in the reflected glory of something bigger than himself, something which he, [and] possibly he alone, has never really understood. He satisfied both his conscience and his audience by delivering a high minded and generous critique without danger of being contradicted in public by the subject of his criticism.[133]

Owing to several issues that occurred in the early 1940s Keating has retrospectively been assessed as 'right-thinking' and, as a result of his academic training, somehow boring.[134] The saga of the 'Rouault Controversy' in 1942 and the foundation of the Irish Exhibition of Living Art, both of which have been assessed in detail on several occasions by art historians, have contributed to the prevailing misconceptions and

---

[131] See Keating, 'I'd say that it would be better not to hang any picture than to hang a bad one', *The Irish Digest,* September 1940. The article was published in Irish and is reproduced here in both Irish and English.

[132] See 'J'Accuse' in Irish with English translation. The article first appeared as Seán Ceitínn, 'J'Accuse', *Comhair,* Meitheamh 1942, pp. 5-6. The date of this article is significant with regard to the RHA and Rouault Controversies. The association with the Dreyfus affair in France is somewhat provocative.

[133] See Keating 'Post Mortem', date of article or broadcast unknown but circa mid-1940s.

[134] See for example Dorothy Walker, *Modern Art in Ireland,* The Lilliput Press, Dublin, 1997.

misunderstanding of Keating. As S.B Kennedy has noted, the discussion about the 'Rouault Controversy' occurred in *The Irish Times* and Keating was but one of the contributors to it.[135] He was on the Board of the Municipal Gallery at the time and he did not like the painting and voted against it. However, he was also on the Board of the Municipal Gallery in 1956 that accepted the painting and Henry Moore's *Reclining Nude* which had been rejected in 1954.[136] Another issue of concern in terms of an up-to-date evaluation of Keating was the rejection of a painting by the RHA in 1942. Louis le Brocquy's *The Spanish Shawl* was rejected by the selection panel of the RHA in 1942. It is not apparent if Keating was on the selection panel for the RHA that year, nor is it apparent whether he approved or otherwise of the painting. It is clear however that Keating and le Brocquy enjoyed a friendly relationship in the late 1930s and early 1940s, although the younger artist was critical of the older over the refusal of the Rouault painting.[137]

The reason for the rejection of *The Spanish Shawl* has not come to light; it may be that the RHA found it to be too modern and indeed there are some problematic technical issues with the construction of the composition, or it may simply have been due to a lack of space. At that time the RHA was based in an old residential house, which was subsequently knocked down and rebuilt; it was not an ideal location for exhibitions in the first instance. The result of all the criticism and the rejections and the discussions and developing knowledge about modern art was the foundation of the Irish Exhibition of Living Art by Mainie Jellett, Louis le Brocquy and others in 1943.[138] Several well-known artists showed work at the inaugural exhibition including Dermod O'Brien PRHA and Keating who gave the ESB permission to show *Tip Wagon at Poulaphouca* (1942).

---

[135] S.B. Kennedy, *Irish Art and Modernism, 1880-1950*, The Institute of Irish Studies, The Queen's University of Belfast, 1991, pp. 87-88.

[136] Keating remained on the Art Advisory Board of the Municipal Gallery until at least 1972 when the then Director ceased to publish the names of those on the committee.

[137] Letter 5 December, 1941, from le Brocquy's address at 15 Upper Fitzwilliam Street, Dublin. KPPC 1/1/1/. See also NIVAL, le Brocquy files in which there is an envelope that contains the information and which is addressed to Louis le Brocquy, c/o The School of Art, Kildare Street. The colour chart was titled 'Artists' Colour Chart of Dangerous Mixtures' and it illustrates aspects of the deterioration of colour in certain colour combinations, where were caused by chemical reaction. It is noted on the Chart for example that 'cobalt violets must not be touched by a steel palette knife' and that 'Composite tints, or colours sold under proprietary names, should be referred to the Chart under the names of their constituents, which may be readily ascertained from the colourman's catalogue'. It is further noted in the small print on the bottom of the Chart that 'It is not advisable to use pigments of poor quality or pigments which are not listed by their manufacturers as "permanent" or "durable"...' Le Brocquy's research into the chemical aspects of paint is not surprising. He started his student career as a chemistry student in Kevin Street Technical College. See Ronan Farren, 'Homage to a Great Painter', in *The Evening Herald*, 19 November, 1981, p. 10.

[138] The IELA papers are with NIVAL at NCAD. It is clear from the minutes of the organization that Mrs Sybil le Brocquy did not set up the IELA. She was invited to join the IELA committee at a later date in order that she would take care of public relations.

Moreover the relationship between the two organizations remained entirely amicable and good-humoured.[139]

Throughout the 1920s, 30s and 40s Jellett was at the forefront of the Irish Cultural Renaissance. Her aesthetic was different to that of Keating, but essentially they both wished to create an 'Irish' identity for Irish art, the former premised on the West of Ireland and the latter on a more abstract mode of expression with roots that originated in Parisian modernism of the early twentieth century but with an eye to ancient Irish history:

> *If an Irish artist of the eighth or ninth century were to meet a present-day Cubist or non-representational painter they would understand each other.*[140]

Jellett made a major contribution to the development of and discourse on Irish art through exhibitions of her work, teaching, broadcasts and articles and it was extremely unfortunate for Ireland that she died at such a young age. Ultimately Jellett's position as imperative to the development of the history of Irish art in the twentieth-century was reinforced by the publication of *The Artist's Vision* by Eileen MacCarvill in 1958. Jellett's approach was undoubtedly directly supportive of modern art that could be representative of contemporary society and as such her tendency was, understandably, to encourage people to look at unfamiliar art without condemnation.

But even if their aesthetic approach was entirely different both Keating and Jellett had similar ideas about viewing art:

> *We must learn to trust our own reactions, and not to expect the artist to hand out a tabulated list of facts and formulae of what to see in his pictures. I think that even with the most realistic of story-telling pictures you will not find two people who will react in the same way to one picture...*[141]

The two artists also held similar views about the availability of art to the general public, although their opinions manifested in different ways; Jellett produced a lot of work that was similar in style to that of her friends and collaborators Evie Hone (1894-1955) and Albert Gleizes (1881-1953) with whom she helped to develop the technique of 'Translation and Rotation'.[142] The abundance of similar work meant that it could be marketed cheaply so that the general public could afford to purchase it. In that way, her artistic meaning could be disseminated from the working class to the bourgeois. On the other hand Keating, owing to his class, was more dependent on showing work at the RHA in order to make a living. He did reproduce several paintings and drawings as Christmas cards, post cards and posters throughout his career, but the ephemeral nature

---

[139] The RHA minutes over various years show that the IELA wrote for permission to use the RHA's crowd control chains, a request to which they always agreed.

[140] Jellett, 'A Word on Irish Art', in Eileen MacCarvill, The Artist's Vision, with an introduction by Albert Gleizes, Dundalgan Press, Dundalk, 1958, p. 105.

[141] Mainie Jellett, 'Looking at Pictures', in MacCarvill, The Artist's Vision, p. 71.

[142] See 'Forward' and Albert Gleizes, 'Homage à Mainie Jellett', (translation from French) in MacCarvill, The Artist's Vision, pp. 9-24 and 35-44 respectively.

of the work has meant that it is now forgotten. Fundamentally however, Keating's message about critics and cultural matters was promulgated through articles and broadcasts in which he was extremely forceful. But while Jellett's lectures and articles were more focussed on the production and viewing of art, Keating's were far more critical of the lack of official support for the arts, which, had it been available, would have provided the environment to create 'Irish' art. Moreover, he continually disapproved of the deficiency of good art criticism.

It is hardly surprising therefore that both Jellett and Keating were asked to contribute to *The Irish Art Handbook* which was published in 1943. Jellett's article, titled 'An Approach to Painting', indicated the importance of her training in Paris with Andre Lhote (1885-1962) and Gleizes and of her eventual discovery and absorption of Chinese art. She believed that:

> the art of a nation is one of the ultimate facts by which its spiritual health is judged and appraised by posterity, and in many cases, when all else has disappeared the clue to a whole civilisation may be traced through fragments of pottery, sculpture, or other artistic manifestations which may remain.[143]

For Jellett, the 'modern movement' in art was inspired by truthful ideals that were a 'means of purification and a revitalization of the art of the late nineteenth and twentieth centuries ... that had shaken the materialism of the so-called academic tradition and shown those who were alive enough to see, where the true traditions lie'. Yet, illustrating the constant and necessary tension between tradition and modernity, she was unequivocal about modern movement which demonstrated 'with clarity and success' that to carry on a 'livening tradition is to understand and *venerate* the great works of the past and to realize the unchanging artistic laws behind them ... which must be reinterpreted by each period in turn so as to express its need and character ... and so to represent the art of the period'.[144]

Keating's brief contribution to *The Irish Art Handbook*, titled 'Reflections', demonstrated that, owing to lack of government funding and to various internal issues, art institutions were still, twenty years after the foundation of the Irish Free State, 'refrigerators' and not the 'incubators' that they could and should have been if the cultural, political, and economic conditions had been suitable.[145] It is significant too, particularly in consideration of the cultural climate of the time and subsequent art-historical analyses that place him as anti-modern, that Keating wrote:

> The only honest contribution that we in Ireland can make on behalf of art and civilization is to make the best possible use of the comparative peace we have got to allow freedom and facilities to creative workers, and to leave art to look after itself.[146]

---

[143] Mainie Jellett, 'An Approach to Painting', *The Irish Art Handbook,* Dublin, 1943, pp. 17-20.
[144] Jellett, 'An Approach to Painting', p. 18.
[145] See Keating, 'Reflections', 1943. Keating used this phrase again in a lecture to the Architecture Society of Ireland, see 'The Future of Irish Architecture', undated but c.1950s.
[146] Ibid.

Adhering to his belief that critics were responsible for the perceived trouble between the 'moderns' such as Jellett and the 'academics' like himself, Keating once again reiterated that while good criticism was essential, it was simply not 'enough' to read books and then assume oneself to be knowledgeable. He believed that for the most part, critics were not 'soaked in their subject' and therefore they were causing misunderstanding among the public by issuing 'laudatory phrases' about better-known artists and 'mild' to 'not-so-mild' reproof for those who were not yet established. As the quote above suggests, Keating simply wanted 'freedom and facilities' so that creative workers could get on with what they did best.

If freedom and facilities were not available through conventional means, like-minded people found creative outlets for their work anyway. The Egan Salon, which had provided a forum for those of a more rebellious persuasion, had closed in the late 1930s, but there are many other galleries, clubs, groups and publications for like-minded people in the country. One of these was The Runa Press which was established in Monkstown, County Dublin by English born Rupert Strong (1911-1984) and Eithne O'Connell (1923-1999) in the early 1940s.[147] Strong came to Ireland to train in Freudian psychoanalysis with Jonathan Hanaghan . In turn he became a founder member of the Irish Psychoanalytical Association. He published several books on psychoanalysis and poetry.[148] In 1943 The Runa Press published a paperback pamphlet titled *Tidings* which featured work by, among others, Strong, O'Connell, and Jonathan Hanaghan, and two poems by White Stag member Basil Rakozci.[149] Significantly the cover featured a drawing by Keating which was titled *The Postman*. The drawing was a witty commentary on the content of the pamphlet and thus it was a smart message for several reasons, not least that it directly associated Keating with some of the alternative writers and poets in Ireland at that time.[150]

Dermod O'Brien (1865-1945), who had been President of the RHA since 1910, died unexpectedly in October 1945. Always an academic painter, O'Brien was nevertheless valued by everybody involved in the development of Irish culture in the post-revolutionary era for his moderate and accommodating approach to aesthetic developments. O'Brien supported the Dublin Painters when they set up in the 1920s and he also gave encouragement to the IELA in the 1940s. He and Keating, both from Limerick, wanted to create a municipal gallery in that city along the lines of the Hugh Lane in Dublin. To this end they were both actively involved in encouraging artists to contribute to a collection of work which had no official home until the gallery finally

---

[147] Strong and O'Connell married in 1943.
[148] Hanaghan was the founder of psychoanalysis in Ireland in the 1930s and published several books including *Freud and Jesus*, Runa Press, 1960.
[149] *Tidings,* December 1943.
[150] Keating was on friendly terms with Rupert and Eithne Strong, and also with Patrick Kavanagh, there is no evidence however of a direct friendship with Basil Rakozci. The next publication in the series from The Runa Press was titled *Apocalypse* and it featured a drawing by Stephen Gilbert and poetry by Herbert Read and Jonathan Hanaghan among others.

opened in Pery Square in the city in 1947. Both artists were awarded the Freedom of the City of Limerick for their involvement in its cultural development in general, and for their contribution to the foundation of the Limerick City Gallery in particular, O'Brien in 1936 and Keating in 1947. The loss of O'Brien at such a difficult time in the history of the RHA and at a significant moment in the development of the discourse on Irish art was, to put it mildly, deeply regrettable. James Sleator (1885-1950) was elected President of the RHA on O'Brien's death.[151] He was a highly regarded artist who worked on two occasions as William Orpen's studio assistant. He had been a founder member of the Dublin Society of Painters in the 1920s and he was also on the first executive committee of the IELA, so he obviously subscribed to O'Brien's principles.

Sleator was apparently modest and unassuming and his tenure as President was taken up with issues pertaining to the house that the RHA purchased as its permanent home in 1939. The Academy had been renting various premises around Dublin since the destruction by fire of their building in Abbey Street in 1916. The loss of the building caused severe fragmentation in the manner of the day to day operation of the Academy, the disparate nature of which has ramifications even still. During the 1920s the Council of the RHA authorized the use of a studio belonging to Professor D. Gogarty MD at the rear of Ely Place in Dublin from which they ran the 'Life School',[152] while the painting school operated from 6 St Stephen's Green in Dublin.[153] In 1939 the Academy purchased Professor Gogarty's home, a rambling old building called Ely House, in 1939.[154] The house was unsuitable for use as offices and exhibition space, but the Council were anxious to have a home in the fashionable south side of Dublin city. Again at an inopportune moment in the history of the development of Irish art, the architecture of Ely House and its associated lack of exhibition space at least partially accounted for the fact that unpopular choices were made and some paintings, including le Brocquy's *The Spanish Shawl,* were refused for the annual shows. In April 1946 a 'building committee' was formed from among the membership of the RHA in order to oversee the

---

[151] Jack B. Yeats and Lucius O'Callaghan were also candidates for election. Minutes of the General Assembly, 18 October, 1945. James Sleator received 10 votes, Yeats received 5 and O'Callaghan received 1. RHA Archives.

[152] All RHA meetings were held in the Royal Irish Academy of Music building at 36 Westland Row at this time. Prior to 1920 the RHA meetings were held at the offices of Mr Albert E. Murray in Dawson Street, and, latterly, at premises in South Frederick Street in Dublin. At a meeting held in 36 Westland Row on the 29th November 1920 George Atkinson, seconded by Caulfield Orpen, proposed that the site on Abbey Street be sold for £10,000, as it was proving a liability.

[153] Between 1916 and the 1920s the painting school operated from an address at Lincoln Place in Dublin.

[154] The RHA Council purchased Ely House from Oliver St John Gogarty who emigrated to America in 1939. The purchase of Ely House also included the garden of George Moore's former house on Ely Green.

refurbishment of the premises at Ely Place.[155] This committee was further supported by the 'Fund Committee' which included Sleator, Keating, the Lady Glenavy, Ernest Hayes, and Frances Hicks with the purpose of raising funds initially to refurbish and then to rebuild the RHA on the site at Ely Place. However, suitable funding was not forthcoming and the project to demolish Ely House and rebuild on the site did not proceed until the 1960s.[156]

In the meantime, by the end of the 1940s the idea of an Arts Council to promote and foster the arts in Ireland had been mooted by senior civil servant Paddy Little. While the government was deliberating over the issue, the editor of *Hibernia* magazine, Basil Clancy, wrote to the Taoiseach, Eamon de Valera, to suggest the formation of a committee that would encourage the development of Irish culture at home and abroad.[157] Although de Valera was not particularly concerned with the arts at home, he was keen that Ireland should have a bright and new cultural identity abroad, and in 1946 a 'memorandum was presented to the Government proposing a small committee of ... twelve persons of well-recognized cultural qualifications whose function would be to examine and make recommendations to the Minister for External Affairs ... in connection with cultural activities abroad'.[158] But it seems that de Valera was not interested in the development of culture in itself, but rather as a means to a political end. The underlying argument for the formation of the proposed committee was that 'cultural propaganda was not suspect as obviously political propaganda tends to be'.[159] Interestingly, given the national and international denunciation of de Valera for sending condolences to Germany on the death of Adolf Hitler in 1945, it was also noted that the proposal to set up a cultural committee was not 'subject to the conventional limitations which diplomatic representatives are bound to observe' and that if foreigners became interested in a country, it followed that they then generally became 'sympathetic'.[160] Moreover, a major advantage of the development of international cultural propaganda was 'that its primary impact is on the intelligentsia – the very people who, in most

---

[155] Minutes of the General Council, 18 April 1946. The members of the 'Building Committee' were Leo Whelan, Maurice MacGonigal, Letitia Hamilton, Lucius O'Callaghan, Ernest Hayes and Frank McKelvey. RHA Archives.

[156] Building developer Mathew Gallagher provided funding for the construction of the new premises on the site of Ely House. The building was not completed until 1987.

[157] Clancy wrote to deValera in 1947. A general election took place in 1948 and Clann na Poblachta and Fine Gael formed the first inter-party government with Fine Gael's John A. Costello as Taoiseach.

[158] Brian P. Kennedy, *Dreams and Responsibilities, The State and the Arts in Independent Ireland,* The Arts Council, Dublin, 1991, p. 61, from S.P.O., S 13773A, 9 April 1947. The Minister of External Affairs in 1947 was Eamon deValera and in 1948, Sean McBride founder of Clann na Poblachta assumed the role under the new inter-party government.

[159] Ibid.

[160] Ibid., from a memorandum titled 'Cultural Publicity Abroad: Proposed Establishment of Advisory Committee', dated 2 June 1947, S.P.O., S 13773A.

countries, are in the best position to influence Press, radio and public opinion'.[161] As exemplified in the commissioning and subsequent treatment of Michael Scott's pavilion and the associated art work in 1939, de Valera was interested in the use of art as propaganda to advertise Ireland as a new post-colonial nation, but always premised on recourse to ancient myth, legend, and the story of colonial domination. Hardly surprisingly, therefore, the Government rejected Paddy Little's proposal for an Arts Council in 1947, but somewhat bizarrely they voted to establish an Advisory Committee on Cultural Relations in order to 'promote Irish culture abroad'.[162] Meanwhile, the outstanding issue of the development of an Irish Arts Council actually to encourage the development of culture in Ireland before export abroad was of little importance to de Valera and the idea was postponed until John A. Costello's new inter-party government took over in 1948.

Responses to Culture and Politics 1950s – A Complex Decade

The formation of the Cultural Relations Committee in 1949 and Arts Council in 1951 seemed to signal official support for cultural developments in general, and the visual arts in particular. But unfortunately, as will become clear, the manner in which the first official exhibition of Irish art in America in 1950 was handled by the Cultural Relations Committee and the Academy, served further to alienate the RHA from critics who supported a more abstract form of modernism. Nonetheless, it was during these years that some artists, who are now associated with a more modernist aesthetic, were elected Honorary, Associate, or Constituent members of the RHA. By 1950 both Grace Henry and Mary Swanzy had been elected as honorary members, while Louis le Brocquy and Cecil Ffrench Salkeld were on the list of Associate membership. In 1950, Patrick Hennessy (1915-1980), whose work was premised on sound academic training but with a modernist, almost surreal edge, had been elected an RHA.[163] Though Keating was not President when Hennessy was elected, evidently, he did like his work.[164] By 1955, le Brocquy had been elected a Constituent member of the RHA, while Salkeld remained on the list of Associates.[165]

The Cultural Relations Committee was appointed by Minister Seán McBride in 1949 with two personalities from the world of Irish art and architecture, Michael Scott and Eileen MacCarvill, selected to serve on the board.[166] Both were well respected, and

---

[161] Ibid.

[162] Ibid. The Advisory Committee was given an annual income of £10,000 rather than the initial £5,000 proposed by Basil Clancy.

[163] Catalogue for RHA exhibition, 1950. Hennessy was elected RHA in 1949. KPPC 2095/17/16.

[164] Keating frequently refers to Hennessy in diary entries for the time.

[165] Catalogue for RHA exhibition, 1955. KPPC 1096/6/16.

[166] The other members of the initial committee were The Hon. Justice George Gavan Duffy (Chairman), Senator Michael Hayes (Vice-chairman), Professor Seamus Delargy, M.A., Richard Hayes, L.R.C.P.I., D.Litt., Senator Patrick McCartan, M.D., John MacDonagh, Roger

intellectually and critically associated with modernism. In consideration of the fact that the Committee was to oversee the development of Irish culture abroad, it is of great significance that not one member of the RHA, an organization of professional artists well qualified in the area of visual arts, was appointed to the committee. In retrospect, this was a serious error on the part of the Minister, who with a little more foresight could have encouraged the RHA out of its perceived stasis by virtue of inclusion. Instead, members of the IELA representing the more 'modern' aspect of Irish visual art were appointed, thereby rendering the immediate remit of the committee abundantly clear and reiterating and thereby officially institutionalizing the opposing views on academic and modernist art that had previously only been apparent among critics and to which Keating had constantly referred over the previous years.

The initial suggestion for an exhibition of Irish art in America was proposed by artist Cecil Ffrench Salkeld ARHA (1904-1969) in late 1949.[167] As a result of a conversation with Dr George Potter of the *Providence Journal,* Salkeld sent a minutely detailed four page proposal to the Cultural Relations Committee.[168] Significantly, he invited the Committee to consider officially supporting an exhibition of Irish art 'of all schools' and of 'no school' to tour the United States of America. He attached a comprehensive list of suggested artists from the RHA, the IELA, and the Oireachtas Exhibition group.[169] Salkeld noted that:

> there are excellent painters in each of these groups. But there are also many good painters that are in none of them. And an exhibition, to achieve International level, must not be selected from any limited point of view: no prejudice as to technique employed, as

McHugh, M.A., Ph.D., Senator E.A. McGuire, Professor T.W. Moody, F.T.C.D., Liam O'Laoghaire and The O'Rahilly, Barrister at law. CRC, NIVAL.

[167] Cecil Ffrench Salkeld, 'Memorandum undated for the consideration of the Cultural Relations Committee, pertaining to late 1949'. CRC, NIVAL. For an overview of Cecil Ffrench Salkeld's life see Cyril McKeon, 'Cecil Ffrench Salkeld 1904-1969' in *Martello Arts Review,* Winter 1992, Duke Press, Dublin, 1992, pp. 1-5, and a poem in the same publication, Gearailt MacEoin 'The North Room' a tribute to Cecil Ffrench Salkeld', pp. 54-55. Determined to illustrate his professional standing and connection in Irish public life, Salkeld offered the names of referees at the bottom of his letter of introduction to the Committee. The list included D. O'Donovan, Secretary of the Department of Social Services, Frank Hugh O'Donnell of the IELA, H.L. Morrow, Productions Director with RTÉ, James Sleator, PRHA, Evie Hone of the IELA, publisher Seamus O'Sullivan, Maurice Walshe and Frank O'Connor.

[168] Dr George Potter had been prominently associated with the recent establishment in the Providence Public Library of the Alfred M. Williams Memorial designed to promote an interest in the study of Irish Culture. Appendix to 'Memorandum for the consideration of the Cultural Relations Committee', Ibid. Thus, the proposed exhibition was to travel initially to the Irish Centre in Providence, Rhode Island.

[169] The list of one hundred and twenty names included many Constituent and Associate members of the RHA, including Keating, Kernoff and Salkeld, and well known names from the IELA, le Brocquy who was by then an Associate of the RHA, McGuinness and Hanlon, as well as lesser known and completely unknown names from the world of Irish art. CRC, NIVAL.

to 'school' adhered to, or as to 'Message' – Gaelic or otherwise, should be permitted to influence the composition-one might almost call it the 'creation' – of an exhibition.[170]

Salkeld proposed himself as the single selector for the exhibition, noting that this would provide the necessary 'unity' and cohesiveness of the exhibition which should not be 'just good enough' or 'not too bad', given that 'too many such exhibitions have lowered Ireland's artistic reputation in the past'.[171] He proposed that in order to obtain the required standard, Irish artists were to be 'circulated' about the proposed exhibition, and from the entrants approximately one hundred paintings and some sculpture would be chosen and shown in Charlemont House or the NCA for one week prior to their exhibition in various venues across the United States of America. The show was to be titled 'An Exhibition of Modern Irish Painting and Sculpture' and duly advertised as a 'non-profit seeking, non-commercial undertaking'.[172]

James Sleator, as President of the RHA, involved himself in negotiations with the organizing committee for the American exhibition and, given that the remit was 'all schools' and 'of no school', he insisted that they chose work by professional as well as lesser-known artists. The Cultural Relations Committee also decided to support Salkeld's idea.[173] Unfortunately Sleator died unexpectedly in mid-January 1950 thus leaving the RHA without a President until March of that year.[174] But the activities of the Cultural Relations Committee and the group that were organizing the exhibition were being closely observed. There ensued a commotion over the requirement that all of the paintings were to be framed in a similar manner in order to allow for a degree of cohesiveness in the exhibition. There were also issues about the selection process and concerning the proposed venues in America. Thus a letter appeared in *The Irish Press* under the pseudonym of 'Mac Alla', the contents of which caused some consternation among the members of the CRC.[175] The author of the letter wanted to know 'who would sit in judgement on the submitted work'. The writer, who was obviously an artist or somebody that was knowledgeable about the whole process, noted that 'we were led to

---

[170] Salkeld, 'Memorandum for the consideration of the Cultural Relations Committee'.

[171] Evidently Salkeld attached a memorandum on one such 'badly organised' exhibition, but this is not available in the file.

[172] Salkeld', Memorandum for the consideration of the Cultural Relations Committee'. Salkeld's proposal included a comprehensive list of items including packing, shipping and insurance, all of which he had organised in advance of applying to the CRC. He sent the letter with appended list of artists' names, to Ms Sheila Murphy of the Department of External Affairs, Iveagh House, Dublin.

[173] The CRC consisted of ten members who all worked on various sub-committees for film, theatre, Fine Arts and music. The members of the Fine Art sub-committee were Senator McGuire, Mr Figgis, Mr Ralph Cusack and Michael Scott, both members of the IELA. Cusack had previously been associated with the White Stag exhibitions held in Dublin during the war years.

[174] Sleator had been at a meeting with Keating and others the previous day. He died in the Academy building.

[175] Mac Alla, 'Cat Jumps Out of Cultural Committee Bag', *The Irish Press*, 20 January, 1950, p. 4. 'Mac Alla' is a derivative of a Gaelic word meaning echo.

believe that we would have an opportunity of viewing this exhibition in Dublin before it started on its American tour. We were led up the wrong path. Somebody or something has decided it will go to America without being seen by the public here'.[176] Moreover, the artists had been informed that to enter work for selection would cost nothing, yet all paintings accepted were to be reframed at the artists' expense 'in order to harmonize with the rest of the framing in the exhibition'. While most of the artists unwillingly agreed to this, 'Mac Alla' noted that only Keating RHA was refusing outright to reframe his work, because 'the procedure was without precedent and it was the artist's right to frame his or her work in a manner suitable to subject and theme'. Moreover, 'Mac Alla' wrote that most of the artists approached on the matter were, quite literally, afraid to have their name appear in print as it could be 'artistic suicide'. However, Maurice MacGonigal was of the opinion that all the trouble could have been avoided if artists had been invited to exhibit instead of contributing to a selection process. 'Mac Alla' pointed out that the original itinerary for the exhibition was to include 'several different cities in North America' but that it had come to his attention that it would now be shown in two venues in America, the Rhode Island School of Design Museum, Providence, and an unidentified location in Boston, and at the National Gallery in Canada. In a wry attack on untutored 'modernists' and useless judges, 'Mac Alla' referred to one Thomas Henry Barnardo, an untrained 'newcomer' to art who had been painting for 'a few months' and whose *Wicklow Path* had been chosen for the exhibition. The young man 'admitted to a few lessons from George Campbell' but that his artistic career really started 'last summer when he was sick for a while and to pass the time, he tried painting'. Therefore, if the standard of the proposed exhibition was as high as the CRC had anticipated, young Thomas Henry Barnardo plainly 'had the makings of a genius'.[177]

The letter was the subject of serious debate at a meeting of the CRC sub-committee on Fine Art the following month, although nobody was aware of the identity of the author.[178] The cracks in the intended CRC exhibition had been publicly unveiled by none other than Keating himself, who wittily invented the pseudonym of Mac Alla in order to develop a forum through which to vent his frustration at the CRC in general, and the process in particular.[179] Keating took pleasure in his provocative alter-ego and he did not reveal himself to anybody at the time.

By February 1950 a list of eighty nine works for definite inclusion in the exhibition had been established, but Jack B. Yeats had thus far refused to be involved. At this point, the Minister for External Affairs intended personally to 'approach' the artist in order to

---

[176] Ibid.

[177] Ibid.

[178] Notes from the Sub-Committee on Fine Arts, CRC, 9 February 1950 in which 'Mac Alla' is described as a columnist for the Irish Press. CRC, NIVAL.

[179] KPPC, Diary, January 1950, in which Keating identifies himself as the author of the letter in the Irish Press.

persuade him to submit work.[180] The sub-committee initially invited Thomas McGreevy to write an introduction to the catalogue for the exhibition, which was to open in the Rhode Island School of Design Museum in March 1950.[181] It was also arranged that McGreevy would accompany the exhibition around the United States. While McGreevy had placed extensive notes 'at the disposal of the Committee', he preferred 'that his name should not be used'.[182] The fact that McGreevy intended to put his name forward for election to the post of Director of the National Gallery of Ireland may have convinced him to remain anonymous. The sub-committee 'did not regard McGreevy's material as suitable' and proposed to have the 'views of the [full] Committee on the matter'.[183] The sub-committee was 'authorized to ask Elizabeth Curran to undertake the task' of writing the introduction to the catalogue. It is notable at this stage, that five of the twelve members of the CRC were also closely associated with the IELA.[184]

In the meantime it was necessary for the RHA to elect a new President and so an extraordinary general meeting was held in March 1950. Keating's name had become associated with the position at an early stage although he did not think that he would be elected. On that occasion F.G. Hicks took the Chair and present were the Lady Glenavy, Letitia Hamilton, Margaret Clarke, Brigid Ganly, Jack B. Yeats, George Collie, Maurice MacGonigal, Lucius O'Callaghan, Leo Whelan, Ernest Hayes, Laurence Campbell, Patrick Hennessy, Simon Coleman, Harry Kernoff, Seán O'Sullivan, William Conor, Micheál deBurca, and Keating. Keating was elected to the position with twelve votes

---

[180] Minutes of the Twenty Third Meeting of the Advisory Committee on Cultural Relations, Iveagh House, 16 February, 1950. CRC, NIVAL.

[181] The show was to travel to Boston Symphony Hall and Ottawa.

[182] Minutes of the Twenty Third Meeting of the CRC. McGreevy's catalogue notes range through the history of Irish art from 'Cormac's chapel...Knockmoy Abbey, Garrett Murphy, Thomas Cooley, James Barry, the devastation of the penal laws and the Irish revival of the nineteenth century'. He then mentions the exhibition held in Dublin by John Yeats and Nathaniel Hone the Younger in 1901, Hugh Lane, and gives a long and rambling account of William Orpen's career. He then mentions that 'Irish art followed two paths along with academic art', the singular route of Jack Yeats and the direction forged by Mainie Jellett and Evie Hone. The final paragraph of his introduction is a tribute to Michael Healy and Harry Clarke for their glass and Frances Kelly, Father Hanlon, Norah McGuinness, Thurloe Connolly, Nano Reid, Patrick Scott and Louis le Brocquy as Ireland's 'contemporary painters' whose work 'speaks for itself'.

[183] Ibid. At this stage, the full committee of the CRC included Eileen MacCarvill and Mrs Sybil le Brocquy who had been co-opted in order to bring the group to the required number of twelve people.

[184] Elizabeth Curran was the daughter of art critic, C.P. Curran. The CRC sub-committee on Fine Arts worked under five headings, music, film, visual arts, literature and publishing. The visual arts committee consisted of Senator McGuire (chairman), Mr Scott, Mr Figgis, Mr Cusack and Mrs Le Brocquy. The music committee members were Mrs MacCarvill, Mr McDonagh, Mr Figgis, Mr Cusack and Mr Ryan. The film committee was Mrs MacCarvill, Dr MacCartan, Mr Scott and Mrs Le Brocquy. The literature committee members were Dr Moody, Dr Delargy, Dr Hayes, Mrs MacCarvill and Mrs Le Brocquy and the publishing committee members were Mrs MacCarvill and Dr Hayes.

while his nearest rival, Leo Whelan, received seven. At the same meeting Maurice MacGonigal was elected Keeper of the Academy which allowed him the privilege of living in special quarters within the RHA house.[185] Given Keating's rather less formal relationship with the Academy, particularly during the 1930s, he may in fact have seemed an unlikely candidate for the position. But it was well known then, although more recently entirely forgotten, that Keating was left-thinking, inclined towards rebelliousness, opinionated, outspoken and involved in many art institutions in Dublin, all of which singled him out as an ideal candidate for the position at a time when the RHA was being pushed to one side by modernists and art critics associated with the Cultural Relations Committee. Keating's first conflict as newly elected President of the RHA was with the Cultural Relations Committee and the organizers of the exhibition of Irish art that was to travel to America later that year.

It was Elizabeth Curran's introduction in the catalogue for the exhibition that caused serious consternation in RHA and which raised Keating's wrath. With regard to the RHA Curran wrote in her introduction that:

> an Academy (founded in 1823) without any tradition at all, but which at least made provision for an annual exhibition where outmoded pictures, the backwash of 19th century painting, were shown without true discrimination ... The Royal Hibernian Academy, like most academies of art, except by reaction, has played little effective part in the movement of art in recent years. It is true it includes painters of distinction; Mr Yeats for example ... but collectively, it is of little importance. It is an academy in no true sense of the word but rather a society of artists with some official recognition. It lacks direction and standards. Its painting school has been discontinued. Its bent is towards insipid naturalism but this is redeemed not merely by Mr Yeats's annual entries, but by the canvases of Mr Leech and younger academicians like Mr Seán Keating, Maurice MacGonigal etc.[186]

Keating had no time for personal accolades when everything he stood for was being attacked by people he assumed to be ill educated art critics. The Academy wrote to the Minister and the Cultural Relations Committee protesting against 'the manner and matter of the preface to the US Exhibition,' which was 'in very bad taste.'[187] The letter acknowledged that the Academy was, at times, deserving of criticism, but that ultimately this should not have been a concern in the introduction for the catalogue of an international exhibition purporting to show all aspects of Irish art. For the Academy it was all made worse by the fact that the introduction to the catalogue was written under the aegis of the Irish Government. It does appear that Curran was somewhat unfair in

---

[185] RHA Archives, minutes of Extraordinary General Assembly of the RHA, Wednesday, 15 March 1950. As President of the RHA Keating also became an Honorary Royal Academician and an Honorary Royal Scottish Academician.

[186] KPPC 1174/16. Catalogue for the exhibition.

[187] See 'Letter from John Keating PRHA to the Cultural Relations Committee 1950 – on behalf of the Council of the RHA.'

her analysis of the RHA at that time, and she did not consider the financial constraints that consistently inhibited the development of art and critical practice in Ireland. Evidently too, Curran's deference to Keating in her article was merely a ploy, as even the artist himself would have acknowledged that, owing to his busy schedule and constant fatigue, he was not making work to the best of his ability in the late 1940s and into the 1950s. Indeed, the paintings that he sent to the exhibition included an old example of his work, *Men of the West* (1915) and a landscape titled *Sunset in Fog* (1949-1950). It was true that the RHA painting school had been discontinued during the war, but the decision to close was made by the RHA Council owing mainly to lack of facilities and of governmental support. The very fact that the RHA existed at all suggests that it played a major role in the 'effective movement of art', even if only as a foil by which other forms of more modern art practice could be measured.

After an extraordinarily difficult year, one that signalled the beginning of Keating's critical downfall, he published an article in *The Bell*, which was then under the directorship of Seán O'Faoláin. Yet again, Keating referred to lack of patronage, and an institutionalized lack of interest in the arts. Keating's Socialist ideals are self evident in 'Painting in Ireland Today', in which he wrote with deep conviction about the plight of artists, lack of patronage, and lack of governmental interest in art. The article was published just before the formation of the Arts Council. Keating wrote:

> The artificial antitheses between Art and Modern Art is largely a by-product of phoney journalism. It equates with Loch Ness Monsters, Yellow Perils and Flying Saucers. Art was always modern in the sense that sincere artists were always experimenting, and insincere ones were always imitating them in the hope of attaining the end without understanding the means. In Art, as in other things, movements are inspired by saints and missionaries, and stifled by theologians and functionaries.[188]

The 1950s was a decade of profound change in Ireland, when the generation born after the fight for freedom in the early years of the century had reached maturity. They had no memory of the tumultuous years between 1916 and 1923, but were kept aware of the vital struggle for freedom from colonial rule through family histories and through the manner in which their parents and grandparents chose to vote in general elections. However, the shortages and difficulties caused by World War Two were in living memory. People wanted employment, improved education, larger houses, and a better life. The arts became popular, not for their ability to mirror political developments as had previously been the case, but for their social capacity. While organizations involved in art teaching and public exhibitions suffered from lack of development owing to financial constraints, there were lively debates about the Arts Council and other issues in the pages of daily newspapers. These debates were often fanned by the best-known protagonist of the time, Seán O'Faoláin, founder and editor of *The Bell* and impartial

---

[188] See Keating, 'Painting in Ireland Today'.

director of the Arts Council of Ireland between 1956 and 1959.[189] Ultimately, as will become apparent, the tense relationship between Keating as PRHA and O'Faoláin as Director of the Arts Council contributed significantly to the artist's critical decline during the 1950s.

There were other art-related matters throughout the 1950s that are still linked with Keating because he was President of the RHA. One of these was the rejection of Louis le Brocquy's *The Family* initially by the Friends of the National Collections and secondly by the Arts Advisory Committee to the Municipal Gallery in 1952. Victor Waddington wrote in the first instance to the committee of Friends of the National Collections with a request that it might consider contributing to the purchase of le Brocquy's painting which in turn would be offered to the Municipal Gallery through the Arts Advisory Committee.[190] Waddington suggested that the FNCI should 'remove their restrictive clause [which would] enable them to buy works of painters of this, as well as other countries', which in turn would ensure that the FNCI would 'become a more potent force and would gain a much more sympathetic and real support than they have had so far'.[191] Evidently concerned by his suggestion, the FNCI 'unanimously agreed' that it would not support the purchase of *The Family*, and furthermore, the Secretary was directed to write to Waddington in order to 'make it clear to him that members of the Council [were] not bound by any restrictive clause, but are free to frame or alter policy as occasion demands'.[192]

It is frequently suggested that it was the Arts Advisory Committee to the Municipal Gallery that rejected the painting to begin with, but it is important in terms of chronology to note that their decision came after that of the FCNI.[193] Although it is

---

[189] O'Faoláin was Director of The Arts Council from December 1956 to July 1959. For a discussion on the early years of the Arts Council, see Brian P. Kennedy, 'Better sure shot than scattergun: Eamon deValera, Seán O'Faoláin and arts policy', in Gabriel Doherty and Dermot Keogh, *De Valera's Irelands*, Mercier Press, Dublin, 2003, pp. 115-131.

[190] Council Meeting of the FNCI held on the 25January 1952, the Earl of Rosse took the Chair and the sitting committee was Mr Frazier, Miss McGuinness (Norah), Miss Yeats (Anne), Mr de Vere White, Miss Curran (Elizabeth), Mr Briscoe (Ben), Mr Maher, Mr McGreevy (Thomas – Director NGI), Mr Kelly (acting Curator of the Municipal Gallery of Modern Art), Mr Westropp and Mr Figgis. Minutes of Council Meeting, 25 January, 1952, FNCI, NIVAL.

[191] Ibid. Waddington's letter was read into the minutes.

[192] Ibid.

[193] See Dr Síghle Bhreathnach-Lynch, 'Louis le Brocquy's *A Family*: An unwholesome and satanic distortion of natural beauty', *Circa* online. Dr Bhreathnach-Lynch notes that it was 'the committee responsible for acquisitions at Dublin's Municipal Gallery of Modern Art' that 'rejected' the work, p.1. Dr Bhreathnach-Lynch acknowledges in footnote 11, that it was the FNCI that initially rejected the work, and that then it was offered to the Arts Advisory Committee of the Municipal Gallery of Modern Art, who also rejected it. Medb Ruane notes that the painting was 'rejected out of hand' by the Hugh Lane Municipal Gallery when it was offered as a gift, but without acknowledging that the FNCI had initially rejected the painting prior to the Arts Advisory Committee, see Medb Ruane, 'The Family', in *The Irish Arts Review*, Summer 2002, p. 23 while Brian Fallon asserts that the FNCI bought the painting and

evident that Keating did not like the work, he did not make any argumentative public comments about the refusal of the painting. He voted against it as did five other members of the eleven strong committee. Ultimately the controversy was to contribute quite significantly to the construction of Keating as a bore with little or no time for modern art. Yet the annual RHA exhibitions included work by artists who were not members of the Academy, but who entered their paintings or sculptures in the hope of being selected to hang alongside that of the members of the Academy. Keating was on the selection panel for the duration of his presidency and some of the artists whose work was chosen during this time were known for their interest in experimental forms of modernism.[194] In 1950 *Landscape with a Bakers Van* by Belfast artist Colin Middleton (1910-1983), who was described as a Surrealist painter,[195] was among those selected for exhibition.[196] Middleton also showed with the IELA and with Victor Waddington. Also selected that year was *Fisherman's Wives*, by another Belfast artist, Dan O'Neill (1920-1974), who, unlike Middleton, was largely self-taught, and who also exhibited on a frequent basis with the IELA and Victor Waddington.[197] O'Neill was represented again in 1955 when he showed a work titled *Peace*.[198] In 1958, *Rocky Island Shore* and *Interior with Figure* by Gerard Dillon (1916-1971), another self-taught artist from Belfast, was selected for exhibition.[199] Dillon was on the committee of the IELA, and also exhibited with Victor Waddington and the Dawson Gallery. Significantly the RHA chose to publish black and white images of four paintings from the 1958 exhibition in the catalogue, one of which was the aforementioned *Interior with Figure*.[200] Work by Pauline Bewick, David Clarke, Fr Jack Hanlon and sculptor Yann Renard-Goulet were selected for exhibition in 1960. The black and white images in the catalogue for that year include *The Travellers* by Norah McGuinness, HRHA, in which the influence of le Brocquy is unmistakable.[201] Also illustrated was *Nathaniel* by Henry Healy, ARHA, which demonstrated the obvious influence of Picasso. Thus while work shown at the annual

---

'presented it to the Municipal Gallery', see Brian Fallon, 'Painter of the Psychic Skeleton', in *The Irish Times,* 24 October, 1996. Apparently Keating told Fallon that the painting was 'unacceptable and unworthy' while Mrs Clarke stated that it was 'obscene'.

[194] The records of meetings of the RHA do not record individual responses to paintings submitted for selection.

[195] See for example, Eileen Black and Anne Stewart, *Treasures from the North, Irish Paintings from the Ulster Museum,* The National Gallery of Ireland, p. 60 which notes that Middleton first began to 'experiment with Surrealism in 1937'.

[196] Middleton continued to exhibit with the RHA until 1955, at which point there was a break until 1967. He was elected an ARHA in 1969 and an RHA in 1970.

[197] KPPC 1095/17/16.

[198] KPPC 1096/6/16.

[199] Catalogue for RHA exhibition, 1958. Dillon first exhibited with the RHA in 1943. KPPC 1096/8/ 16

[200] Ibid., p. 25. The other images were *20th September, 1803,* Maurice MacGonigal, RHA, *Old House, Dublin,* Harry Kernoff, RHA and *New Ropes, Loughshinney,* Patrick Leonard, ARHA.

[201] Catalogue for RHA exhibition, 1960, figure 4. KPPC 1097/1/ 16.

RHA exhibitions was for the most part by members of the Academy, there is no doubt that attempts were made to at least begin to encompass more experimental art forms.

Throughout this time, and notwithstanding internal art-political issues, Keating kept a wary eye on world affairs. He had been utterly appalled when the atomic bomb was released over Hiroshima and Nagasaki in 1945 and he found political developments around the world extremely worrying and he was not at all enamoured when in August 1953 the USSR announced that it was about to test a hydrogen bomb in an effort to lead the international arms race against America.[202] That same year an anti-war publication titled *Ireland: Neutrality and Peace,* appeared in association with the Dublin Trade Union Council. There were several articles from those involved in culture and politics, or both, including Harry Kernoff and Peadar O'Donnell. Keating's contribution brings to mind the first article that he ever published in 1924 and if he was subject to self-censorship then, his 1953 article does not suffer from ambiguity:

> Up to the present man has been fortified in his struggle with the material universe by his belief in a reasonable expectation of life, liberty and the pursuit of happiness. When the Americans atom-bombed Hiroshima, destroying the just with the unjust and sterilizing the survivors, they made a more brutally effective statement of the mechanistic theory of existence than any materialist has ever proposed. But it blew away forever the clouds of sentimental humbug and hypocritical 'patriotism' from the face of war. Now sincere Christians and convinced materialists can, and must, agree to declare against war. Not to do so is to become an accessory to mass murder.[203]

Throughout the 1950s Keating's record as a cultural commentator and protagonist on behalf of artists became obfuscated in the face of continuing controversy. In 1955 he became involved in a row with art critic James White which took place in the daily newspapers. At the centre of the spat was a drawing by Keating titled *The Matriarch* which had been given by the Haverty Trust to the Municipal Gallery that year. Keating was a member of the Arts Advisory Committee to the gallery and he was also a Haverty Trustee at the time. In accordance with the terms of the Haverty Bequest, a formal application had to be made by the gallery or institution in order to receive work purchased by the bequest fund, and the Director of the Municipal Gallery had applied for two drawings or paintings as a result of which the drawing had been offered. Criticism of the Haverty Trust decision was immediate in the form of a letter from an 'Art Critic' in the *Irish Press.* The unidentified author highlighted the fact that of the thirty-seven paintings purchased by the Haverty Trust, sixteen were by artists associated with the RHA, while twenty-one were chosen from exhibitions held by other groups.[204] Annoyed

---

[202] The announcement and test detonation happened in quick succession in August 1953. In January of that year President of America, Harry Truman, announced that the United States had developed a hydrogen bomb.

[203] Keating in *Ireland: Neutrality and Peace,* Dublin Trades Union Council, 1953, pp. 13-14.

[204] Art Critic, 'How Haverty Trust Pictures are Selected', *Irish Press,* 23 June, 1955, p. 11. A meeting of the Haverty Trust Committee took place at the Municipal Gallery, 21 June, 1955, in order to allocate the previous five years purchases to applicants.

that *The Matriarch* had been given to the Municipal Gallery, the author of the letter suggested that the academic paintings purchased by the Trust should be allocated to institutions or galleries outside the capital, while the modern paintings should be given to Dublin.[205] The author was also annoyed because paintings by younger 'leading painters such as le Brocquy, Connolly, Middleton, Scott, Campbell, Dillon, Nano Reid, Norah McGuinness, Anne Yeats, Father Jack Hanlon, Patrick Collins, Patrick Swift, George Wallace, Caroline Scally and others' had not been allocated to the Municipal Gallery.[206]

A few days later James White's irate comments about the Haverty Trust and the distribution of pictures was published in the *Irish Press*. He wrote that 'the Art Advisory Committee of the Dublin Municipal Gallery deputed two of its members, one of whom was Mr John Keating, PRHA, to apply for such pictures as would be considered for the Dublin gallery'.[207] The thrust of White's argument was that Keating was compromised by his allegiance to both the Municipal Gallery and the Arts Advisory Committee. White also identified himself as the author of the original letter of criticism of the Trust, noting that if he thought that the Arts Advisory Committee 'would even consider the work of our best 30 contemporary artists', he would not have found it necessary to vent his concern in the first instance.[208] White was particularly concerned that Evie Hone was not adequately represented in Ireland, although her work was appreciated abroad. Finally, implying that Keating would no longer have any influence, he remarked that a new Arts Advisory Committee was about to be formed, which he hoped would begin to encourage the Municipal Gallery out of its conservatism.

Keating's response to the question of his integrity and White's 'tendentious and misleading account of how the allocations were made' was immediate.[209] He pointed out that he was in fact one of five, and not two, who made the decisions regarding where the work purchased by the Trust should go. Keating was present at the particular meeting to represent the Haverty Trust and not the Arts Advisory Committee to the Municipal Gallery. He was 'not deputed to apply for such pictures as would be considered suitable for the Dublin Gallery' nor did he 'apply' for his own picture.[210] Applications for artwork from the Trust were the responsibility of the Directors of the institutions concerned. Moreover, according to Keating, *The Matriarch* had not been specifically requested by any gallery or institution in Ireland. Therefore because the drawing had not been requested Keating suggested to the Haverty Committee that he would be happy if it remained in Dublin and the other members of the group readily agreed. Keating also noted that another painting, which was the work of a 'modern', was also given to the

[205] Ibid.
[206] Ibid.
[207] James White, 'Haverty Trust', in 'Letters to the Editor', *Irish Press*, 2 July, 1955, p. 6.
[208] Ibid.
[209] John Keating, 'Haverty Trust Pictures', 'Letters to the Editor', *Irish Press,* 12 July, 1955, p. 6.
[210] Ibid.

Municipal Gallery at the same time, a point that White had not acknowledged in his article or letter. Therefore, as far as Keating was concerned, the accusation of 'academic prejudice' was not sustainable. Moreover the conditions of the Haverty Trust were continually problematic because of the legal conditions of the bequest which specified that the RHA had to be represented on the purchasing committee. But, according to Keating, when the Trustees considered the purchase of work by members of the committee who were painters, they refrained from giving a casting vote in favour of their own work.[211] Keating proffered that 'it was obviously unlikely that the kind of people who can make an honourable gesture when it is a case of selling their pictures would be dishonourable when it is a question of merely placing them'.[212] At the same time, he strenuously rejected White's implicit suggestion that the other members of the committee would have allowed him to act unfairly with regard to his own work.

Within a couple of days White publicly acknowledged that he had received incorrect information of the identity of those on the allocation committee.[213] He also indicated that he had been misinformed, and that a picture by George Campbell, ARHA. had also been given to the Municipal Gallery.[214] However, the thrust of White's comments reveal the real dilemma of the situation. Keating, in his role as artist, President of the RHA, Trustee of the Haverty Bequest and member of the Arts Advisory Committee, was in a position of authority which had been, in White's opinion, compromised by the acceptance of *The Matriarch*. The 'whole point' of his article and subsequent letter was 'to draw the attention of the authorities to what happens when artists are allowed to judge the work of other artists', which allowed Keating 'to further the English Academic outlook ... and to make our Municipal Gallery seem as if it were placed in a small English town'.[215] While Keating did not make any further public comment, the director of the Municipal Gallery in Limerick, Robert Herbert, wrote to the paper to make apparent his great exception to White's suggestion that Dublin should receive all the 'modern' paintings, without paying heed to the fact that cities outside Dublin were equally cosmopolitan. At the same time, Herbert's letter appears to support the choices made by the Haverty Trust.[216]

The attitude of the general public to the whole affair is not apparent, as there appears to have been only one letter of response in the newspapers, in which it was pointed out that during a previous Radio Eireann programme, Keating had been attacked at the

---

[211] Ibid.
[212] Ibid.
[213] James White, 'Haverty Trust Pictures', 'Letters to the Editor', *Irish Press,* 19 July, 1955, p. 6.
[214] Ibid.
[215] Ibid.
[216] Robert Herbert 'Haverty Pictures', in 'Letters to the Editor', *Irish Press*, 28 June, 1955, p. 6.

microphone because he 'didn't like something somebody called Moore did'.[217] The author suggested that the general public did not know enough about what the 'painters of the Expressionist school meant to convey', and suggested that another radio interview should be organized with Keating representing the 'classical school' because he was a 'calm and clear speaker' and 'an artist who actually paints the new style'. Her letter finished with a proverb, 'one picture is better than 10,000 words', and therefore, 'a drawing that takes 10,000 words to explain is not a picture'.[218]

The whole affair served to illustrate and highlight the problematic legal constraints associated with the Haverty Trust Bequest and indeed, within various art institutions. The legal terms of the Haverty Bequest were unequivocal about the fact that the RHA was to be represented on both the purchasing and allocation committees. This provision was to safeguard two elements of the bequest; the purchase of paintings of Irish history by Irish artists or those living in Ireland, and the maintenance of artistic standards. In the same way, the legal structure of the Arts Advisory Committee to the Municipal Gallery was equally problematic. It was dependent on members of the council of the RHA, from the Board of Trustees of the National Gallery of Ireland to the civil appointees who were elected to the position at the behest of the city manager on behalf of Dublin Corporation. As a result, such artists, who contributed, as Keating did, to these organizations, were left in an invidious position and open to public criticism.

In 1959 Keating as President of the RHA found himself embroiled in yet another controversy, this time with Seán O'Faoláin who was then Director of the Arts Council. In that year the Council announced a new purchasing scheme with CIE to encourage the development of Irish art.[219] Under the scheme, the Arts Council selected paintings for CIE to hang in their hotels around the country, and both organizations were to contribute to the cost of the chosen works. The arrangement came about as a result of a similar scheme (1954) between the Arts Council of Ireland and local authorities under which work of merit could be purchased for donation to libraries. As long as the work was made by artists on an approved Arts Council list, it paid 50% of the purchase cost. Evidently, however, the uptake on the scheme by local authorities was not as good as the Arts Council had hoped. When the announcement about the new CIE scheme was published in the press, Keating responded on behalf of the RHA in a letter that highlighted the anomalies created by the manner in which the Arts Council was run, noting that he was not aware of the election process or the necessary qualifications of the members.

Keating pointed out that if the Arts Council did not approve of what had been selected by the local authorities, it simply refused to cover half the cost of the work. Moreover, if the local authorities did not want work by any of the artists on the Arts Council's

---

[217] Ailbhe O' Monachain, 'Re Art Discussion', 'Letters to the Editor', *Irish Press*, 28 June, 1955, p. 6.
[218] Ibid.
[219] 'Boost for Irish Artists', the *The Irish Times*, 22 May, 1959, p. 5.

approved list, nothing could be purchased at all, and all monies had to be returned to the Council offices.[220] This situation ultimately left the Arts Council as the arbiters of taste in the visual arts, a situation to which Keating and the RHA took great exception, particularly as it was abundantly clear that O'Faoláin supported more abstract forms of art. Keating felt that given that local authorities knew their population and were also aware of the limitations of their buildings in terms of the provision of space and lighting, that they should be 'allowed to know what they like and that they should be helped to buy what they want instead of what the Arts Council thinks they ought to want'.[221]

That year members of the Arts Council visited the RHA and evidently liked some of the work on show. However, when a list of approved artists was made available there was not one member of the RHA named. This meant that local authorities could not purchase the work of RHA members shown at the annual exhibitions or indeed, at other venues throughout the country. Despite the obvious difficulties, Keating approved of the scheme in principle, which he described as 'excellent co-operation between public authorities and the Arts Council' which was to be encouraged.[222] Sensing an official nudge against the art of the academy, and yet in the hope of helping the scheme to survive, Keating suggested that members of all public authorities should be encouraged to visit major exhibitions of Irish art, implicitly the RHA, the Oireachtais, and the IELA, and they should select up to six works, any one of which they would be happy to purchase in association with the Arts Council. Keating wrote:

> If the Arts Council thinks that one of its functions is to educate the public taste, it might advise the local authorities as to which of their six selections the council considers to be the truest works of art. I imagine that the provincials would willingly consider advice - when it is accompanied by half of the catalogue price. Such an approach to would-be purchasers of works of art might have better results than the present system of pre-selection, with its implication that provincial taste must necessarily need a metropolitan imprimatur.[223]

O'Faoláin's reply was to outline how the process worked. Notable in O'Faoláin's response was that:

> three times a year 75 local authorities are sent catalogues of exhibitions organised respectively by the RHA., the IELA and the Oireachtais. With the catalogues go select lists of those works of art which the Arts Council approve as suitable for purchase by local authorities under the scheme.[224]

---

[220] John Keating, PRHA, 'A Question of Taste', 'Letters to the Editor', *The Irish Times*, 23 May, 1959, p. 7.
[221] Ibid.
[222] Ibid.
[223] Ibid.
[224] Sean O'Faoláin, 'A Question of Taste to the Editor of the Irish Times', *The Irish Times*, 5 June, 1959, p. 7.

O'Faoláin suggested that Keating did not understand that as the Arts Council was accountable to the Irish government, it could not devolve decisions to other people, not least to the RHA, whose secretary evidently had the audacity to suggest that they might 'know better than the Arts Council what works of art are good enough for local authorities to buy'.[225] As far as O'Faoláin was concerned the Arts Council was 'appointed to act as a public guide in matters of taste'.[226] This attitude was to prove crucial to the developmental trajectory of Irish art and criticism from the 1950s onwards.

In a reminder to the readership of an earlier controversy, and as a means to explain why the Arts Council had chosen to ignore the RHA for the scheme that year, O'Faoláin suggested that if the President of the RHA maintained, for example, that 'Rouault was a bad painter, or that Jack B. Yeats knew little or nothing about technique, he might be right. On the other hand, the Arts Council might be right in disliking ... any paintings on display at the current exhibition of the RHA.'[227] Rather oddly, for a man who was well used to public riposte against academic artists in general, and Keating in particular, O'Faoláin reprimanded the RHA for airing their views on the matter in such an open manner, noting that he thought it was 'unwise' and that he was not sure that by appealing to 'all and sundry, the Academy was not surrendering its rank and title altogether'.[228] This was an extraordinary statement from O'Faoláin as Director of the Arts Council which served to prove his complete bias against the RHA. He also missed the premise of Keating's initial letter which had been that if the Arts Council was to help to develop Irish art then it should allow local authorities to choose for themselves and not create a list of approved artists which reflected a bias one way or the other.

The Lady Glenavy, who had never seen an entire RHA exhibition condemned in such a manner, demanded a list of the 'secret police' that made up the Arts Council and who therefore had the power to decide 'the fate of Irish artists'.[229] Artist Fergus O'Ryan noted that the attitude of the Arts Council was a 'poor reflection on the common sense of the 75 [local] councils' who were pressurized by a form of official censorship by which they could not afford to purchase works of art with O'Faoláin's imprimatur.[230] O'Ryan felt that if the local authorities were encouraged to develop their own sense of the visual arts perhaps in later years they would clamour for 'Mondrian, Klee, Nicholson, or even

---

[225] Ibid.
[226] Ibid.
[227] Ibid.
[228] Ibid.
[229] Beatrice Glenavy, RHA., 'A Question of Taste', 'Letters to the Editor', *The Irish Times*, 20 June, 1959, p. 7. The editor appended a list of names of the members of the Arts Council to the end of Glenavy's letter. They were Seán O'Faoláin (Director), Sir Alfred Chester Beatty, Dr Thomas McGreevy, Mr John Maher, Soirle MacAnna, the Very Rev. Donal O'Sullivan S.J., the Earl of Rosse, Dr R. J.Hayes, Dr G.A. Hayes-McCoy, Sir Basil Goulding, Miss Muriel Gahan, Mr Michael Scott and Mr Mervyn Wall (Secretary).
[230] Fergus O'Ryan, 'A Question of Taste', 'Letters to the Editor', *The Irish Times*, 8 June, 1959, p. 7.

Pollack [*sic*]'.[231] Aware that the Arts Council liked some of the work at the RHA, O'Ryan also asked why it had not seen fit to include at least those names on the approved list for local authorities and 'by doing so help some struggling artist ... a more worthy task than educating the members of 75 local councils'.[232] Keating singled out O'Faoláin's remarks on the length of time required to develop the 'notoriously fallible'[233] concept of taste, wryly noting that this was the very reason that local councils should be allowed to make their own judgements. Keating felt that the Arts Council should encourage public servants to attend exhibitions in search of pictures which would in turn advance their individual judgement 'instead of limiting their choice to a list which may represent the personal taste of one or two self assured persons'.[234] Responding to the biased value judgements of the Arts Council Keating commented that:

> *Assessing the merits of a work of art according to the name – however fashionable – on the label, or according to the dictates of some current cult – however bogus – may be a legitimate activity for dealers and professional culture-mongers. But a body which has been appointed 'to act as a public guide in matters of taste' should endeavour to exercise its functions on a different level – when it is spending public money.*[235]

Endeavouring to keep previous controversies about art in the public domain, O'Faoláin's retort was directed at Keating personally and not at the RHA. Two years previously a local authority librarian had chosen one of Keating's paintings for purchase under the 1954 scheme. When the Arts Council was informed about the intended purchase it could not go ahead under the scheme because Keating was not on the approved list for that year. Although O'Faoláin tempered his comment by suggesting that Keating was not motivated by personal gain in his criticism of the scheme, this was faint praise that attempted quietly, but publicly, to signal the artist's lack of integrity. Damning Keating further, O'Faoláin wrote in support of the Arts Council schemes that:

> it must more than once have been a comfort to the harassed representatives of local authorities, faced by their own local authorities on art, saying 'D'ye call that a picture?' (before a Rouault? Or before a Jack B. Yeats?), to be in a position to say that the Arts Council, officially appointed by the Government and operated under the aegis of the Department of the Taoiseach, had *fully approved* of the painting (purchased under the scheme), not just acquiesced in its purchase to flatter somebody else's taste.[236]

---

[231] Ibid.
[232] Ibid.
[233] Sean O'Faoláin, 'A Question of Taste to the Editor of the *Irish Times*', *The Irish Times*, 5 June, 1959, p. 7.
[234] John Keating PRHA, 'A Question of Taste', 'Letters to the Editor', *The Irish Times*, 10 June, 1959, p. 7.
[235] Ibid.
[236] Sean O'Faoláin, 'A Question of Taste', 'Letters to the Editor', *The Irish Times*, 19 June, 1959, p. 7.

Keating attempted to clear his name without delay, noting that if O'Faoláin was suggesting that he was motivated by personal considerations by publicly criticizing the judgements of the Arts Council then the implication was 'deceptive'.[237] He pointed out that the painting in question, although not on the 'approved list', was 'immediately purchased by a private buyer', and therefore Keating had no issue with the Arts Council over that matter.[238] But Keating, in his role as President of the RHA, had been approached by various artists who were all dissatisfied with a scheme that was based on 'approval lists'. It was essential that he should have the opportunity to address their concerns to the Director of the Arts Council. Reiterating the points originally made Keating once again criticized the 'dictatorial methods' of the Arts Council and in reference to O'Faoláin he suggested that:

> polite acquiescence in a sincere choice might be a good alternative to such 'positive approbation' as was shown by the selection of 61 exhibits from the Living Art Exhibition, 1958, and the block rejection of the Royal Hibernian Academy Exhibition, 1959. Such sweeping action may be described as a question of taste, but it is not unreasonable to suspect prejudice.[239]

There was just one further letter about the matter, which was sent 'on behalf of the people of Ireland' in order to:

> thank the gentlemen of the Arts Council for ensuring that we shall never lose our baptismal innocence by the introduction of television – like the inhabitants of England, Scotland, Wales and the Isle of Man, and other wild places … we, in art loving Mullinahone are particularly indebted to Dr Seán O'Faoláin for having preserved us from the RHA.[240]

O'Faoláin had been dismissive of Keating and the RHA for 'airing their views' about the Arts Council in public. Paradoxically O'Faoláin used his position as Director of the organization to publicly support the then Taoiseach, Eamon de Valera, against the introduction of television to the Irish Free State. It was not until Seán Lemass succeeded de Valera in 1959 that approval was given for television in Ireland.[241]

Early in 1962, Keating announced his decision to retire from the Presidency of the RHA the following October.[242] Both Dermod O'Brien and James Sleator died while in

---

[237] John Keating, PRHA, 'A Question of Taste', 'Letters to the Editor', *The Irish Times*, 20 June, 1959, p. 7.
[238] Ibid.
[239] Ibid.
[240] James Maher, Kickham Street, Mullinahone, County Tipperary, 'Letters to the Editor', *The Irish Times*, 29 June, 1959, p. 7.
[241] Paradoxically, the first ever broadcast from Telefís Éireann on New Year's Eve, 1961 featured an address by President de Valera on the benefits and disadvantages of the medium. O'Faoláin resigned as Director of the Arts Council of Ireland in July 1959, in order to take up the position of Resident Fellow and Lecturer at Princeton University, New Jersey. See Brian P. Kennedy, *Dreams and Responsibilities, The State and the Arts in Independent Ireland,* The Arts Council, 1991, p. 128.
[242] Keating resigned during a meeting of the General Assembly on the 18th October 1962.

office and Keating wanted to enjoy what was left of his years without the pressure of so many official duties. At the same time he also withdrew from the Board of Trustees of the National Gallery and from the Arts Advisory Committee to the Municipal Gallery.[243] He was seventy-three and had just completed a large-scale commission for the ILO in Geneva. Keating continued to take an active interest in the affairs of the RHA and he attended meetings of the Council intermittently until 1969.[244] When Keating announced his decision to retire, a group of his friends from within the RHA formed a sub-committee to organize a retrospective of his work.[245] It was the first time in the history of the RHA that an exhibition on the intended scale had been organized for a past President who was still living. Keenly aware of the importance of making the retrospective an occasion for Keating and for the RHA, the sub-committee sought and received permission to hold the exhibition in the Municipal Gallery of Modern Art. James White, by now Curator at the gallery, became the Honorary Secretary of the organizing committee.[246] The exhibition was opened by the President of Ireland Eamon de Valera.[247]

The foreword to the catalogue was extremely favourable towards the artist and was written by James White.[248] White acknowledged Keating as a 'sort of bulwark of tradition in Ireland since 1916...'and he further noted Keating's

> uniqueness as a painter is largely due to his uncompromising vision. If he has seemed to set himself apart from many of his contemporaries in terms of style, he has in fact never

---

[243] See James White 'Introduction', in *John Keating, Paintings – Drawings 1963*, Municipal Gallery of Modern Art, Parnell Square, Dublin, p. 10 in which White notes that Keating had 'recently resigned as President of the Royal Hibernian Academy, as he has the many other posts he held in the domain of art, in order to give himself more time, more peace of mind to pursue his dreams and crystallize them in further works of art'.

[244] Minutes of the Emergency Assembly, 23 May 1969, RHA Archives.

[245] The members of the sub-committee were Maurice MacGonigal, John Kelly, Fergus O'Ryan, and possibly, Harry Kernoff.

[246] Evidently the decision to give Keating a retrospective was discussed initially between James White and the incoming PRHA, Maurice MacGonigal, during which the curator suggested that the RHA should set up a sub committee to organise the event. The management committee of the Municipal Gallery authorised the use of the space for the show and White secured a verbal agreement for the necessary funding from the Arts Council. The catalogue for the exhibition features an acknowledgement to the Arts Council, An Comhairle Ealaíon, for 'the grant received, without which the exhibition could not have been realised'. Gal/13/38, MGMA. James White became curator of the Municipal Gallery on the retirement of Eithne Waldron in 1962.

[247] White to Mr O'Flahartaigh, Secretary to the President at Aras an Uachtarain, 19 March, 1963, seeking to know if the President would open the exhibition. The President offered to receive Maurice MacGonigal and James White at the Aras 29 March, at which stage he agreed to open the exhibition. Gal/13/38, MGMA.

[248] *The Matriarch* was included in the 1963 Retrospective.

ceased to be a modern and to address himself to modern thinkers by virtue of his single-minded attitude to life.[249]

White commented that Keating had always been determined to show the courage of his convictions and to paint images that asserted his primary values, while at the same time, refusing to bow to 'the less-than-honest opportunists who were quick to exploit the new situation'.[250] The paintings of Aran were distinguished for their 'calm, dignified gravity of gesture and countenance'[251] which, according to White, was closely allied to Synge's visualization of the West of Ireland. Keating's vision of modern Ireland was mentioned as evident in *Night's Candles are Burnt Out* (1927), and the drawings received particular attention for their 'quality of abstraction always present in art' because 'the artist, by rejecting and selecting data is all the time establishing his points of criticism or approval which go to make up not just a representation, but a statement'.[252] The exhibition received warm reviews and apart from some publicity that accrued owing to his work on the Geneva mural Keating lived out the remainder of his years in relative solitude. He was, however, re-introduced to the public again in the early 1970s when he made his television debut. His mischievous sense of humour was still apparent during an interview held with Colm O'Briain at the ROSC exhibition in 1971.[253] Keating had nothing to lose and plenty to say about several of the art-works on show. The outing garnered several younger patrons who were eager to have their portraits painted by a man who was by now, whether positively or negatively, firmly placed in the public conscience as *the* artist that best exemplified the 'Irishness' of Irish art. By this stage the extent of Keating's contribution to the concept of a school of 'Irish art' had been forgotten and as the years passed the meaning attached to 'academic art' became extraordinarily and unfairly biased against the RHA.

Towards the end of his life Keating gave one of his last interviews in which he offered a glimpse of his life and career.[254] He had voluntarily contributed the equivalent of years of his time to the boards of the National Gallery of Ireland and the Municipal Gallery and indeed, to the foundation of the Limerick City Gallery. He had produced several hundred portraits and paintings including many large-scale murals which regrettably, do not survive. He had also produced thousands of drawings and sketches, set designs for theatre and book illustrations. Most importantly in terms of a contextual understanding of the man, Keating wrote and broadcast many articles which questioned the culture and politics of post-Civil War Ireland. It is clear that even at this late stage Keating still held William Orpen in very high regard.[255] However Orpen has been

[249] James White, 'Introduction' in *John Keating, Paintings and Drawings 1963*, catalogue of the exhibition, p. 7.
[250] Ibid.
[251] Ibid., p. 8.
[252] Ibid., p. 9.
[253] Keating was also given a 'birthday tribute' on the Late Late Show in 1973.
[254] See 'Seán Keating – a Life', *RTÉ Guide*, 10 December 1971.
[255] See 'William Orpen: A Tribute'.

variously credited and discredited for his influence on Irish art in the early years of the twentieth century, and as a result Keating's reputation has suffered in terms of critical evaluation owing to his emotional rather than intellectual reliance on his mentor's artistic influence.[256] It is also clear that in old age Keating remained as stoic and wise about life as he had been throughout his career:

> *We can't stop, we've got to go on, we're in a stream…you can swim with the river or you can swim against it – swim against the river and you'll drown, swim with it and you may survive. But it isn't you that'll decide where things are going – it's the river. We're in the river.*[257]

In Conclusion

By the time that Keating died he had been forgotten by Irish art critics and to a large extent, by art historians, although he remains popular with the public at large. Always strongly opinionated, he had lived and worked through some of the most tumultuous episodes in the history of twentieth century Ireland, and indeed, Europe. In the early years of his career, Keating placed his hope initially in a Cultural Revolution and then in the New Ireland, to which he fervently wished to contribute his own nationalist vision – exemplified for example in images such as *Aran Man and his Wife* (1914) and *Men of the West* (1916). It is abundantly clear that, subsequent to the violence of the Civil War, Keating's hope and faith in the Revolution turned quickly to disillusion and frustration. It is possible to pin-point the moment when Keating first began to find alternative methods to vent his frustration and disenchantment at the Government of the New Ireland. In 1924 he had been refused permission to take leave of absence in order to paint the history that he saw emerging around him and it was from this point on, with the publication of *The Slave Mind of Ireland*, that he began to present his readers and viewers with articles and images that were replete with the veracity of modern life; loss, fear, alienation and even disgust – evident for example in most of his articles and broadcasts and in images such as *An Allegory* (1924), *On the Run* (1924), *Homo Sapiens, An Allegory of Democracy* (1930) and notwithstanding the change of government in 1932, in later work such as *Ulysses in Connemara* (1947-50) and *Goodbye Father* (1950). At the same time, Keating remained optimistic about the down-to-earth working man who, if afforded the opportunity, could and would do their best for their country, evident in paintings such as *The Tipperary Hurler* (1927), *Race of the Gael* (1927) and *Night's Candles are Burnt Out* (1928). Nevertheless, it is interesting to note that his positive view does not seem to continue beyond the 1930s, except in

---

[256] See for example, Bruce Arnold, *Orpen, Mirror to an Age,* Jonathan Cape, London, 1981, p.163; see also Ann Crookshank and the Knight of Glin, *Ireland's Painters 1600-1940,* published for the Paul Mellon Centre for Studies in British Art by Yale University Press, New Haven and London, 2002, p. 281.
[257] Keating, 'Seán Keating – a Life'.

privately commissioned portraits, although it did re-emerge in his two large-scale mural works which were made for exhibition abroad.[258]

Even though he was continually disillusioned by the politics of culture in Ireland in particular Keating maintained a strong belief in the role of the artist in society which is evident in his articles and broadcasts. But at the same time he was consistently frustrated and troubled by Irish art critics, or 'scribblers', who he felt were responsible for encouraging a discourse on art which he thought was ultimately misleading:

> *Our critics are saturated in mediocrity. The evaluating of which provides them with a little cultural butter for their daily bread, for they are partners of necessity since 'culture' does not provide a living in Ireland. In such a society talent, imagination, taste, techniques do not interest the critics. All the sycophants of the dealers, the free sherry at opening days of mushroom galleries, where the audience are elderly, idle women, silly ignorant girls, retired civil servants et al and people with nothing to do and less to spend. Painting is a mono maniac pursuit in private. Until the time arrives when artists are preserved in botanical or zoological gardens as interesting diversions for the mob and intellectuals, it will continue to be so.*[259]

To some degree the RHA has always been seen as conservative largely because of its mission to uphold academic standards. Although his concern for culture in Ireland was recognized at the time, Keating's election as President of the RHA in 1950, which coincided with the formation of the Cultural Relations Committee and The Arts Council, served to obscure his previous record. Without the knowledge and context of his previous career and of his iconoclastic observations and his artistic subterfuge Keating unwittingly became known to a new generation of artists, art historians, and critics as an opinionated, old-school 'has been'. In hindsight some of the decisions that were made by the RHA were misguided and perhaps short-sighted. However, this does not suggest that members of the academy in general, or Keating in particular, were conservative or right-wing. Rather, the polemic situation in evidence at the time now serves to highlight a tension between tradition and modernity, which was ultimately necessary for progress to happen in the first instance. It is now clear that Keating was in fact, acutely aware of this fact. In this context, in earlier years, Keating showed a confident disregard for the authority of the RHA, and throughout his Presidency of the organization, he felt strongly that there was no academy or at least no future for the organization. There were several reasons for this attitude, including lack of membership and the biased approach of the Cultural Relations Committee and the Arts Council that privileged a certain form of European inspired modernism.

Often driven by discontent, Keating seemed at times to have been either unaware or perhaps nonchalant about the effect of some of his activities on his potential livelihood. Yet he remained unafraid and always willing to engage with whomever, whenever necessary. This was an attitude that won him many friends, and several professional enemies. Although Keating seems to have been surprised by the public reaction to his

---

[258] New York 1939 and the International Labour Offices, Geneva 1962.
[259] KPPC 814/56(1)/3.

private comments about *Christ and the Soldier* ultimately, owing to his worldview, he saw the argument as parochial in the context of the Second World War. Moreover, it has to be acknowledged that art institutions and organizations were, and often still are, dependent on voluntary time, often from people who were, through no fault of their own, ill-equipped to undertake all aspects of the job at hand. Purchasing committees such as the Haverty Trust were legally required to have representation from the RHA. The Arts Advisory Committee to the Municipal were either Government appointees, some with little art experience, or members of the RHA. In the political and cultural climate that developed during the 1940s and 50s these requirements left volunteers, including Keating, in an unenviable position and unsurprisingly, open to accusations of favouritism or elitism. The Rouault Controversy, as it became known, is a case in point. That the painting was refused by the Arts Advisory Committee was perhaps ill-judged in retrospect, but that it became a controversy at all is significant and suggests a contemporary but now continual dependence on disagreement and on celebrity in order to create the story of Irish art history. In essence, the discourse of controversy and celebrity, already in evidence since Orpen's era as the star of the DMSA, became, during the 1940s, the tacitly agreed substitute for sound critical approaches. It should not matter in the twenty-first century what Kathleen Clarke, Keating, or Myles na gCopaleen thought, or that the painting was shown in the seminary at Maynooth as if in defiance of those who disliked it, although it did matter then. The argument about the painting was modern in the context of a developing post-colonial identity, and while controversial at the time, it should now be accepted as just that – part of the process of national definition.

Keating was always aware of the power of the media as a propagandist tool, evidenced in his 1930s broadcasts, and the invention of his alter ego MacAlla in the 1950s, which was used, much to his private amusement, to publicly whip the Cultural Relations Committee. Even when elderly, and not long before his death, Keating was capable of holding court through the most provocative form of public media; television. He took the opportunity during his interview with Colm O'Briain at the ROSC exhibition in 1971 to again reiterate his values about modern art. Perhaps taking positive advantage of his septuagenarian status, Keating did not hold back and his comments seemed to be deliberately theatrical and contentious. At the same time however, Keating made it clear that he was simply expressing a personal opinion which premised his belief in academic standards in drawing methods as opposed to what he understood to be get-rich-quick celebrity driven art. The outing garnered him a new wave of devoted public fans, several of whom wrote to him expressing their delight at his performance. Added to this, Keating's birthday tribute on RTÉ's Late Late Show in 1973 resulted in several portrait commissions which served to revitalize his career among the general public, if not with critics.

Keating was described at the time of his death as 'a man of great honesty and distinctiveness', he was not, according to Colm O'Briain, 'a world art figure, but that was because the entire period in which he worked was unknown internationally, and it was just becoming known now.'[260] It was acknowledged then, although forgotten later, that the artist had been 'an outspoken advocate of a better position for the artist in Irish society', whose experience over the years had proven that 'the Minister for Education was a negligible person, because [art] was always the last thing on the agenda', while 'art critics came between the artist and the public ... the critic of art is not a menace, but a nuisance'.[261] Added to this, after a lifetime of service to his easel, to his students, and to various institutions, Keating firmly believed, even in the face of his critical reception from the 1950s onwards that 'the apostolic succession of art is not broken'. There were, he thought, 'no gaps or flying leaps into the dark of futurity [sic]. Art keeps pace with life, neither too far behind nor too far in front'.[262]

Keating was not a modernist with a capital M. He never sought to remove the object, or to translate and rotate volume, or even to fragment form in the manner of the Cubists and abstract painters. He was, however, a modern man living, working, writing and broadcasting during one of the most tumultuous times of modern Irish history. Keating chose to paint the reality of modern life in all the fragmented and alienated glory that Joyce and Beckett literalized in text. Yet Keating's art was never purely academic because of its ability to mirror the social and political questions of the day. But whether he is to be judged modern or academic, or somewhere in between, or at times, a mixture of all three, it is now time that he is judged in the plural and not in the singular for his major contribution to culture and politics in post-Civil War Ireland.

There is arguably a dependence on controversy and celebrity in aspects of Irish art history which has led ultimately to a 'hello-isation' [sic] of Irish art in the late twentieth and early twenty-first century. Modern life, and indeed art, cannot exist without mediating with a past. It is this dichotomy between the past and the present that creates the new. Undoubtedly Keating was a controversial figure in the twentieth century and there were many others. Yet nearly one hundred years later, as Keating and others had foreseen, Cathleen Ni Houlihan is financially and politically shaken, a victim to the ravages of private enterprise. The world has come, once again, full circle and thus it is time to fashion that 'new dress' for Cathleen. There should be several pieces to the pattern, not least a new method by which to assess the development of Irish visual culture in the post-Civil War period. This method should encompass everyone, controversial or otherwise, modern or traditional and without damning or privileging one in favour of the other. It is perhaps therefore, a metaphor for the present and future.

Keating's articles and broadcasts examine in detail the decline of his post-revolutionary enthusiasm and thus, they offer a personalized critique of post-Civil War Ireland which is also to be seen in many of his paintings, drawings and book illustrations. They also signal the extent of his albeit self-censored but acutely evident

---

[260] Willie Kealy, 'Work and Personality Evoke Many Tributes – Keating – a portrait of the artist', *Irish Press*, 22 December, 1977, p. 4.
[261] Ibid.
[262] Ibid.

socialism. His articles, lectures and broadcasts are reproduced for the first time in *Keating in Context: Responses to Culture and Politics in Post-Civil War Ireland* in the hope that the book will contribute to the development of a more innovative discourse about the artist and to a fresh methodology for the assessment of visual art in Ireland in the twentieth century.

> If he has seemed to set himself apart from many of his contemporaries in terms of style, he has in fact never ceased to be a modern and to address himself to modern thinkers by virtue of his single-minded attitude to life.[263]

Éimear O'Connor

---

[263] James White, 'Introduction' in *John Keating, Paintings and Drawings 1963,* catalogue of the exhibition, p. 7.

Articles Lectures and Broadcasts

Keating's articles, lectures, and broadcasts have been reproduced with minimal intervention by the author. At times there are significant repetitions, but because the aim here is to achieve accurate documentation, these repetitions have been retained in Keating's text.

The Slave Mind of Ireland

by John Keating, RHA [Published in *The Voice of Ireland: A Survey of the Race and Nation from All Angles,* ed. William G. Fitz-Gerald, Virtue and Company Ltd, Dublin and London, 1924, pp. 83-85.][264]

The average decent Irishman is a disappointed perfectionist, who is either always going to do things right next week, or who has definitely, although subconsciously, decided that it is 'a rotten world anyhow'. Before we begin to discuss the question of the 'slave-mentality' of Ireland, we must provide ourselves with a working definition of 'slave'. I should say that a slave is a man who lives in permanent subjection to men or circumstances, or institutions which he despises.

To know that you are better off than your boss, and to do a bad job to spite him, instead of a good job to shame him; to take his wages instead of taking his business; to fight with your boots instead of with your brains: that is to be a slave.

We Irish are a nation of self-excusers. We are all such nice fellows that you *must* love us; besides, 'it'll be all as one in a hundred years'. The fool who first said that should have a monument of potatoes. We blame the English, we blame the climate. Everybody admits the English, and the climate – even the English! We find an excuse for slackness in the general rottenness of things; but that ought to be our reason to think and work and plan, to be hard on ourselves, to look at ourselves, even if the sight makes us sick.

We have invented a mythical gentle-man – courteous, brave and witty, musical, chaste and gallant, chivalrous to his foe and faithful to his friend; scholarly, but not pedantic; convivial, but temperate; religious, though not fanatical, and so on through the whole catalogue of inhuman perfections.

Are we really like that? Let us see:

- Courteous? – Our public officials!
- Musical? – The exclusive popularity of English music-hall aphrodisiacs!
- Scholarly? – The intermediate system of education!
- Religious? – Our parish administration!
- Loyal? – Parnell, Redmond, Larkin (to say nothing of present-day examples)!
Poetical? – The marriage system in our country parts!
- Chivalrous and imaginative? – Habitual cruelty to animals!

In Ireland there is no standard of achievement; no test by which any man can judge himself as to his fitness to teach or lead anybody, and so we have always had droves of fanatical ignoramuses, whose one line of business was politics.

---

[264] Keating is incorrectly titled as 'Professor of Drawing and Painting from the Life in the Dublin Metropolitan School of Art. He was not given this position until 1937.

Either through laziness or lack of opportunity, we never perfect – even so far as perfection is possible – our knowledge of any art or science. And since there is no popular critical standard to be attained, and since ability is not the criterion of reward, we are all filling jobs, or are anxious to fill jobs, for which we have no aptitude or desire, beyond the natural wish to pocket a cheque so many times a year.

There is one class – by far the most energetic and enterprising part of the whole population – who bend the whole force of such minds as they possess to the study of the possibilities of this, that, and the other circumstance and person in relation to some job. They learn to foresee how the cat will jump, and they recognize a psychological moment as if by instinct. Their contempt for the man who thinks he ought to get a job *because he could do it* is immense. And yet they give more imagination and labour to the art of evasion of realities than the expert does to his art of 'knowing how.'

We in Ireland do *not* breed the expert, and so the other kind flourish – the kind that do not know good from bad, that are inclined to prefer the bad because they feel more at home with it. I mean the man who never has his house in order, nor his mind; the man who says 'it'll do grand'; the man to whom mental or physical discipline is altogether intolerable. Finally, the average Irishman thinks that fat improves the fire, and he loves to queer the pitch.

To know that nobody cares ' two hoots in hell' whether you are a Catholic or a Protestant if you can do your job is to know that being a Catholic or a Protestant won't save you if you cannot do that job. Just as to know that you can marry any girl (that will have you), even if your great-grandfather *did* marry the daughter of an alleged informer, is to be a better man for yourself and for your country. If you are good for yourself, you cannot help being good for your country.

But in the town or city in Ireland, there are too many cats always half out of the bag for anyone to be too hard on anyone else. There is no money and no credit. It is all clean shirts and no supper, or all supper and no shirts. Nobody, except an Englishman, would want the supper *and* the shirts. To want something and to go without because 'you couldn't until you were asked' is to be an Irishman. To want something and to earn the price – or take it from someone who has it (preferably the latter) – is to be an Englishman.

We have no literature, nor art, nor language. Our morality consists in not being profligate. We are badly fed. We are ravaged by lunacy and consumption. Our towns are hideous. Our public conscience is dead. We are so 'nice' in our mind that we don't bother to be nice in our manners. We hate the vulgar ostentation of doing well; *thinking* well is altogether more subtle. If you love us, you must love us in spite of ourselves; otherwise, how can we know that you really love us? If you hate us, then our sense of justice burns with a holy rage, and we will practice every devilry on you as a duty. You can never put us in the wrong, because we are either so stifled with hatred that your vice is our virtue, or else we have so juggled with our conscience (in order to live at all) that we do not know right from wrong.

Evasion is an art with us. It must have been of us that Talleyrand was thinking when he said that speech was given us for the purpose of 'concealing our thoughts'.[265] We have learnt to evade everything except our mistrust and contempt of ourselves, which, strange as it may seem, lives and thrives side by side with our national vanity.

We know we can do everything, but we cannot decide to begin anything. We have two sides to our brain, but not in separate compartments, like Broadbent.[266] We can feel religious, and be pious and skeptical at the same time; and we can feel like princes, and cadge and canvass for a two penny job. We love Ireland, and hate Irishmen. We loathe oppression, habitually mistreat our animals. We are not even vulgar in our own way, but must copy the Englishman at his lamentable worst. We ignore our national assets, and proclaim our bankruptcy on the housetops. And we won't be laughed at on any account – at any rate, not in public!

What assets have we? We are clean-bodied. We would be healthy if our idiotic system of education (or lack of it) would teach our women to cook. We are quick to see essentials. We are not elaborators by nature, but rather simplifiers. We are not natural hypocrites. We are not physically degenerate – not *yet*.

We have for ages been telling ourselves that we were saints and scholars; but no saint ever thought himself anything but the worst of sinners! It was thinking himself a sinner that made him a saint. We take pride in being poor and ill-fed and ill-clad, because when honour is in jail it is a disgrace to be at large. But we must get rid of that paltry confusion of ideas that associates comfort, order and culture with luxury, Imperialism and decadence.

Anybody can be 'temperamental' on an empty stomach, and the Irish, as a race, have not had a square meal since Essex ravaged Munster.[267] We have mistaken our low vitality for philosophic indifference; and since the more we starved the nobler we grew, we did not resent the hunger of soul and body as much as we might be expected to do. This encouraged our ancient foes to indulge their passionate scientific curiosity to find out just how much we could and would endure.

We Irish must also learn to lose our sense of humour – about ourselves, at least. Until pain and confusion and *grotesquery* shall cease to be funny among us, we shall not get very far. We used to have either to laugh or to weep. Now we may sing or be silent, or shout and whistle. And being free to do all these things, we shall not want to, but shall probably work instead for a new and bloodless revolution of our polity and people.

It is the denial of the right to be happy at work – the not knowing that we *can* be happiest of all at work – that leads to the confusion of thought which connects mere wages and salary with happiness, and that, in a hapless country of broken-hearted, poverty-stricken, caste-gagged professional men. That same confusion is at the root of

[265] Charles-Maurice de Tallyrand (1754-1838), French diplomat and politician.
[266] William Broadbent (1835-1907), leading British authority on neurology.
[267] Sir Robert Devereux, second Earl of Essex was appointed Lord Lieutenant to Ireland by Queen Elizabeth 1 in 1599

our national slackness – our lack of enterprise, our indifference to the duties of citizenship, our timorous contempt and dislike for anyone who presumes to tell us anything.

It is this indifference to the vulgar hustle of mere success that has brought us to live amongst our neighbours like an old, crazy, aristocrat, droning and dreaming of vague honours and ancestors – to contrast between his pretensions and his potentialities ridiculous to everyone except himself.

Finally, unless we take off our coats and dirty our hands, if need be, we Irish are doomed and damned to the bottomless pit of futility. And we shall have nobody to blame but ourselves.

Report on the Dublin Metropolitan School of Art

by Seán Keating 1925 [at the request of Mr Joseph O'Neill, Secretary to the Minister for Education].[268]

The Dublin Metropolitan School of Art has been for at least six years past in a state of inertia. There are several reasons for its rapid decay, but the root of the trouble is in the system itself and nothing but a complete readjustment will make permanent improvement. This readjustment need not involve any more expenditure. The money granted is adequate, but hopelessly misapplied.[269]

During the period before the war the students of the school used to send works every year to compete in the National Competition in London. They always got good results. One year they got the highest possible awards in every class of work in competition with all the other Schools of Art in the British Empire. The raw material is as good now as then.

It may be argued that the system was the same then as now, but that period of success was due in the first place, to the personality and vitality of one man – William Orpen, who came as visiting teacher four times a year, and brought new life and enthusiasm to the school. In the second place there was severe discipline and a complete staff of elementary teachers, a system of cells, as it were, to hold the idlers.

The system was then, as now, rotten from top to bottom, but there was order and silence. This severe discipline and order was the result of the findings of the Royal Commission to enquire into the satisfactory state of the School.

From the time of the outbreak of the War in 1914 and the ceasing of the visits of Orpen there has been a steady decline.

In 1918, following on a deputation of serious students to the Department to complain of the state of things, there was a half-hearted attempt to brace up, which in turn faded out. Things went from bad to worse; the School was taken over by the British as a Recruiting Station, serious students deserted it, and it became a sort of club for middle class girls which is what it really amounts to at present. The young ladies have dressing rooms, a telephone, a woman attendant, their admirers ring them up, call and make appointments, there is a dance class in the winter, visitors call at any hour, students absent themselves when they please, go in and out of every room at every hour of the day; briefly, there is not even a pretence of discipline and no authority to enforce order. The School is a bedlam of noise and idleness.

The young ladies spend their time harmlessly in making little lace designs, drawings for fashion papers, dresses for fancy dress balls, etc., and give an air of pleasant pettiness

---

[268] National Archives, S 3458.
[269] This comment caused great offence to the then Headmaster George Atkinson.

to the whole place. Except for a few serious students who work by themselves in holes and corners, this is what the School of Art amounts to.

It is true that the Taylor Scholarship is always won by a student of the School of Art, but one has only to compare the Scholarship works of recent years with those of ten years ago to realize how low the standard has fallen.

The night classes are attended by young men who have been working all day, in shops and offices, and who at 6 o'clock have dashed home, swallowed a hasty tea and rushed back to the School by 7 o'clock. In a city as large as Dublin this in an outrage on health and efficiency and they ought not for their own sake to be permitted to do so. To be a dyspeptic at 25 is not a good foundation for a career. These young men have ambition, energy, and the will to learn, and often talent, but they are naturally exhausted after a day's work, and quite unfit for the mental and physical strain of learning to draw, which, let it be emphasized, is not an amusement.

Neither of these two classes of students justifies the expenditure of £4,330 per annum or more on the School of Art (see Estimates) on a system which in the nature of it can give no results to the individual or the State.

The confusion and lack of direction begins from the moment the student enters the School. It is neither an elementary nor a secondary school nor a university. The aim, so far as there is a conscious aim, seems to be the manufacture of get rich quick illustrators, and secondary teachers of 'Art' for whom there is little demand.

There is no entrance exam. Children may join, and do, thus importing an element of Kindergarten. There is a paper syllabus never possible and never attempted. The fees are absurdly low, a mere invitation to idlers and the curious and to fathers and mothers who wish to keep their children off the streets at night, or out of mischief; there is no attempt at supervision to preserve even the appearance of discipline or order.

It is clear that the School should be either reorganized as a University for those who intend to make Art their profession, or that it should be abolished.

It should consist of students who either can depend on exceptional ability to maintain themselves by scholarships over a number of years or whose relatives can maintain them during their studentship.

When parents wish to give a boy a profession – say as engineer –or veterinary surgeon –they are willing to keep him and pay for his studies until he is qualified. Why should they not do the same for Art?

The artistic young ladies have several private schools (usually conducted by older artistic young ladies) to choose from where they can do their little lace designs and fashion drawings at their own expense instead of at the public's. The night students are provided for already in the Technical Schools.

To permit students to enter a Life Class without a course of elementary instruction (exactly such as is provided by the drawing classes in the Technical Schools) is imbecile. The teacher who has got to any degree of knowledge of painting or drawing, sculpture or composition, simply cannot think or speak of Art in terms which a beginner can understand. He presupposes knowledge of technical words and allusions and a fund of experience which the student of this kind has not got. Teachers and student simply stultify each other. It would be cruel and silly to send an illiterate to a University; yet this is what happens when a raw student joins the School, asks for a class, and is permitted to enter it forthwith.

The Official Government School or University of Art, if it exists at all, should deal with the teaching of Painting and Sculpture, as a University does with, for example, Medicine and Surgery. The staff ought to be professors of the art which they teach, and not constructors of syllabi.

There should be advanced courses in Composition and Design open to Stained Glass Workers, Metal Workers, Cabinet-makers, House-painters and Textile Designers generally.

Students should be full-time day workers; there should be no night classes of any kind. Students should have a good knowledge of the technique of their trade acquired in primary and secondary schools, technical schools and workshops, and they should pass an entry examination which would include a test of general education. 50% of the sum expended on Art teaching should go to Scholarships.

The artist makes himself, but he can only make himself quicker with the help of other artists, who must, however, be convinced of his sincerity before they will help him. The artist is pre-eminently a specialist, and will not waste his time or his gifts on anything that savours of highbrowism or 'polish' or mere instruction in Aesthetics.

The formula for the making of a good School of Art is –'By artists for Artists'. A School of Art needs a few Artists, a few students, a registrar, and money in reason. Big buildings, elaborators, expensive apparatus do not count at all.

Signed by hand
John Keating.

A Talk on Art

by John Keating, RHA. [Broadcast 27 March 1931]

When the Director of Broadcasting asked me to give a talk on Art I was very much surprised and a bit reluctant.[270] I tried to hint to him that he was on the wrong track – but he insisted. 'What's all this talk about Art anyway?' I said, 'I do it – and that's all I know about it. There are several others you can get to talk about it, who don't do it, but who know all about it.' 'Ah but' said he 'that's the very reason. What we want is the straight dope.' This in matters of Art was something so entirely new that I was silenced. 'Besides' said he 'We'll pay you.' That settled it. The mist was clearing off the bog. I was on solid ground. Like any other tradesman I accepted a job for which I was to be paid – and here I am.

I can't help thinking of several people who would do this kind of thing with much more aplomb than I can – people who actually like giving lectures and reading papers – who do it gratis, or as ART FOR ART'S SAKE – whatever that may mean. Some of them know all about modern art, others all about French Impressionist Art, others all about all the Arts, and some know nothing about any of them. However, I have listened to their bunk long enough. Let them listen to mine now.

I suppose it will be thought that I am a bit prejudiced against people who lecture and write and expound theories about Art. The Elaborators – I am prejudiced against them. They are chiefly responsible for the atmosphere of illusion and mistrust that exists between artists and the general public. They have invented for artists a character that it is neither easy nor desirable to live up to.

When people have dealings with a doctor or a plumber or a lawyer or a shop-keeper, they each expect ordinary reasonable common-sense. They approach each other naturally – talking as one human being to another. But when they come into contact with an artist, they just draw themselves up and wait for the performance to begin ... Some expect him to be sub-normal. Others expect him to be super-normal. Others expect him to act like a cross between a clown and a pedigree pup. Then when he talks and behaves like any ordinary Christian, they are disappointed.

For instance, a lady gives a high-brow tea-party, and, being high-brow, she knows that to provide her guests with a real genuine artist is almost more important than to provide them with genuine sandwiches or cigarettes. Then the artist comes, and, not knowing what is expected of him (or even if he does), he just talks about the weather or motor-bikes or the tariff on butter, and the lady feels that she has been let down. She decides that as an artist he is a wash-out. Now I, as an artist, think that is a bit unfair. For the same lady does not consider that her grocer is a wash-out because he just hands

---

[270] The Director of Broadcasting in between 1926 and 1936 was Seamus Clandillon. He was replaced by civil servant and native Irish speaker Dr T.J. Kiernan.

her tea and sugar over the counter, says 'good morning', and turns to his next customer. Nor is the butcher a wash-out just because he doesn't come to give an interpretation of the leg of mutton he is sending her.

I might, if it were possible, have interruptions here. People saying: 'Oh but, legs of mutton and pounds of butter are in a different category from pictures – they are necessities of life. Art is not.' That statement sounds all right, but it is misleading.

It is true that people would never die of starvation for being deprived of pictures, but an innate artistic faculty is so essentially a human characteristic that anyone who lacked it could hardly be called human. Personally I have never known anyone who had not either active or latent artistic ability of some kind, and I hope I never will. I think it would be like meeting somebody with horns instead of eyes, or claws instead of hands – a human monstrosity.

The difficulty here arises from a misunderstanding of the word Art, thanks to centuries of misinterpreting by our friends the Elaborators. When the ordinary man or woman hears the word Art mentioned he or she immediately thinks of Raphael's Madonna or Michael Angelo and the Sistine Chapel, and when the ordinary man is ignorant of the correct attitude towards these (according to the Elaborators) he thinks it necessary to protect himself in advance with a disarming show of sweet simplicity and candour. The minute you meet him – at least the minute he meets the artist – he says: 'Of course I know nothing whatsoever about Art.'

But Art is not confined to the Raphaels and Michael Angelos. It is everywhere – in everybody. But it is very difficult to define. There are two words – one of them is 'sentimentality' and the other is 'Art' – of which I have never been able to get a definition that was quite satisfying. They are both equally ubiquitous. They get into everything. I have read Tolstoy's book 'What is Art?' but I decided when I had finished the book that Tolstoy didn't know what it is – any more than I do. It has been described as 'Life seen through temperament'. I think I would call it merely the faculty for selection.

It is Art in us that makes us discard some things and choose others when our choice is uninfluenced by any ulterior motive – in short when we choose a thing because we like it aesthetically – and for no other reason. For instance a boy, who has just got away from his mother's apron strings, goes for the first time to buy his own ties and socks. And instead of the usual socks of sensible 'heather mixture' that he was accustomed to, he chooses a pair with black and white squares or purple stripes, and an orange tie instead of the usual blue one. He is exercising his artistic faculty. Perhaps you will say that he is only celebrating his new-found freedom by getting something different at all costs. But there were so many socks and ties that were different that he had to eliminate until he finally chose what pleased him most. That is Art.

A girl looks in her looking-glass and decides that a bare forehead does not suit her, so – in spite of the fashion – she decides to grow a fringe. That is Art.

Then there is the little ragamuffin who doesn't care tuppence about either his clothes or his hair, but who sits for hours on the steps of a tenement house trying to pick out tunes on a mouth organ. That is Art. And it has been a characteristic of humans in all ages since our early ancestors living in caves used to decorate the handles of their flint-axes by cutting on them little circles and crosses and curly-wurlys – ornamentations that in no way increased the efficiency of the weapons, but which gave an outlet to the owners unconscious yearning for creative art.

Then, to come back to our own times, there is a woman who wants new curtains for her windows. She thinks that bright red and green cretonne would look lovely, but then, in her street white lace curtains are 'the thing' – all the best people have them. And so, this woman's natural human impulse to exercise her choice – her artistic instinct – is suppressed. She is intimidated by the convention which says that while bright, sharp colours are vulgar – or 'gaudy' – white lace is lady-like.

This is a fair sample of what happens all along the line in matters of Art. The public has allowed itself to be intimidated by the critics and lecturers. These – the Elaborators – tell us in technical jargon what we must admire and what we must denounce, and why. They analyse and interpret pictures and music and books for use. I was going to say that anything that one man does, another man can understand without the intervention of a third party to explain it or to write a book about it. But I suppose that is too sweeping. When pioneers in medicine, for instance, made revolutionary discoveries, an account of their work had to be transmitted and preserved. And I suppose that is true of other branches of science. But they are intellectual activities. Art is not. It is a simple, rather childish thing that needs no interpretation. When a man paints a picture, that picture is a direct personal appeal to any individual who may happen to see it. And a farmer or shop-keeper, if he is sufficiently interested, can appreciate or deprecate it just as well as the critics and alleged connoisseurs. They know whether it is 'plangent' or 'tactile' or 'canorous'. They can tell you whether it is 'lacking in volume' or whether it has 'rhythmic unity', or whether its 'architectonics' are good, or whether its 'recessional dimensions are lacking in subtlety'. But this has nothing whatever to do with Art.

If it amuses the Elaborators to talk like that, let them. But don't take them too seriously. They are only trying to confine creation within a set of rules invented by themselves. There can be no hope that the ordinary man's attitude towards Art will become more sympathetic until in matters of Art as in other things he has the courage of his convictions – or of his non-convictions as the case may be, and until he refuses to be browbeaten by the Elaborators.

It does not follow from this that one's taste cannot be improved and developed. It can be, but not from outside, nor from accepting blindly what the critics say. People must acknowledge – at least to themselves – what they sincerely like and what they don't like, and then try to develop along their natural lines.

For instance, if you admire Cinema posters, you need not force yourself to forsake them in favour of steel engravings. A thing is not necessarily good because it is old. But make a speciality of Cinema posters. Try to see as many different kinds as you can. You will begin to compare and contrast until you have created a definite personal standard. Your critical ability will develop until you are not satisfied with just *any* Cinema poster, and you will go out of your way to see what you consider a good one – and you will know why you consider it good. The same applies if you admire reproductions of the Old Masters – that is if you do really admire them.

But this whole subject of Art is in itself such a vast one, and is so obscured by the atmosphere of pseudo-culture that has evolved round it, that it is impossible to do more that touch upon it within the limits of a short talk. In the time at my disposal I could hope to do no more than to insert the nose of a crow-bar under the elaborate edifice of tom-foolery which has usually repelled the ordinary man. As an illustration of his attitude towards Art – and all that implies – I would like to tell of something that happened to me about 20 years ago:

As I was walking along a road in Co. Limerick, a man passing in a creel-cart offered me a lift, and I got up. After the usual general remarks he asked me what was my trade. I told him I was learning to be a painter. 'And a very good trade too' says he. 'I'm a butcher myself, but the butcherin' trade isn't what it used to be.' Being young and full of vanity I explained with great majesty that I was not a painter in that sense – but an art-student. He was not impressed. 'Is it paintin' pictures you mean?' 'Yes' I said, 'Art'. 'Ah, well' he said, 'b'lieve me now, an' leave your Art-painting. Sure what good is Art-paintin'?'

I often wonder...

Talk on Artists and Academicians

by John Keating, RHA. [Broadcast 22 May 1931]

About two months ago one of our daily papers issued a poster announcing in big print a war between Irish artists and the Royal Hibernian Academy. A number of Dublin painters, dissatisfied with their treatment by the Hanging Committee of the Royal Hibernian Academy – which had rejected their pictures – announced their intention of holding an exhibition of their own in the Mansion House.

The Press, scenting the prospect of a row in public between the Big-wigs and the Rebels, gave the matter a little more publicity than it usually does to things relating to Art. In any other city in the world (except perhaps Belfast) there would have been some fun. Accusations, explanations, recriminations, defamations – oceans of ink would have been spilt, and possibly even a little blood – from the nose. But not in Dublin. The choleric, opinionated, warm hearted, impulsive Irishman is a myth. At least he does not live in Dublin.

The committee of the new organization asked me to lend them some pictures – which I readily did. Then they invited me to go to the opening of their exhibition – and I went. And so the newspapers did me the honour of saying that I was 'patronizing' the affair. And because I happen to be an Academician, I was given to understand that I had done something very wrong. A prominent Dublin man who is deeply interested in Art said to me: 'What do you mean by encouraging these fellows? You know in your position you shouldn't do it'. I said: 'What is my position?' He replied: 'A member of the Academy.' In that reply is condensed the whole case against Academies.

To suggest that an Academy has no use for youth or courage or novelty or enterprise, for indignation against injustice – real or imaginary – is to suggest that it is dead. But as long as privilege and authority are dear to humans, as long as middle-age brings caution and laziness, so long will academicians tend to conservatism, arrogance and the vices of middle age. That is why in my opinion every institution ought to be abolished every 25 years. It is awful to contemplate how institutions which came into being as incubators end as refrigerators.

The rebel artists of today who appear in the streets without a hat, who have no property beyond youth and high spirits, who are all bones and hopes instead of all fat and regrets, will in their turn wear top hats or red robes or whatever the occasion demands. They will write letters after their names, and will reject and condemn the pictures of their young contemporaries. And so on ad infinitum. But their rebellion is a healthy sign. God help the country where young men are cautious. Somebody once said that a man who is not a revolutionary at 20 is a scoundrel at 50.

But to return: had the seceders a grievance? I think that in many cases they had. A just and exact appreciation of what is good in painting is impossible to arrive at, because Art has never been defined and never will be. It is the incalculable in it that gives it its only reason for existence. But in practice certain qualities are demanded – competent workmanship, absence of vulgarity, intelligibility – to put the matter at its lowest. In my opinion, some of the rejected work was, (judged on this basis) equal at least in merit to work accepted. In one case I was surprised to hear that a picture had been rejected.

It would be a good thing for members of academies as individuals, and for their academies as respectable institutions, if members were obliged to submit their works to a jury of their fellows. To have a rule – such as we have – that a member is entitled to exhibit <u>because</u> he is a member, is dangerous. It puts a premium on privilege, on arrogance, on laziness, and puts an edge on the criticism of the outsider. Too often it can be justly said: – 'Well if it hadn't been by so-and-so they wouldn't have hung it.'

Of course the truth is that nobody in Ireland – or anywhere else for that matter (except those directly concerned) is interested in Art. We all want food and clothes and amusement and comfort. But how many of us want pictures or music? A few do. The majority do not. And why should any human want to be praised and petted for doing nothing else but what he likes. The law of existence for the average man is that he does something monotonous and uninteresting for pay. It takes all his time and most of his energy.

I may say here that I think that all State aids and subsidies for Art are bad in so far as they are dispensed by institutions. The high-brows, the wanglers and the up lifters nag and worry the governments of all countries for subsidies for this that and the other. They accumulate properties and prestige, interfere between the public and the producer, and the public has the pleasure of paying for something that it doesn't understand and doesn't want, plus the honour of being sneered at for liking whatever it is it happens to like.

Of course the artist who knows his trade doesn't care. He is a skilled workman, and if people don't want pictures he can do drawings, illustrate books, design posters, decorate the insides of buildings, paint shop signs and so on. He can make a living, and does. But then there is the 'artistic fellow' who has drifted into it, who has a little money, who likes to hang round with painters and writers, who 'eats well, sleeps well, drinks well, but who when he sees a bit of work goes all of a tremble'. Occasionally he has a job somewhere in the background – the kind of job that doesn't require his daily presence at his desk or bench. He is generally the son of an autocrat father or a too fond mother, and when he left college he chose the job he hated least. He it is who plagues governments for money for Art, and pontificates and interferes – who antagonizes the artists and makes the public laugh.

Then there are the shady characters who pose as artists because they want to lead a loose life – the kind of life in which artists are popularly (and falsely) supposed to wallow. A good artist generally works about sixteen hours a day, and spends two hours more thinking out what he will do tomorrow.

But what has the existence of these playboys got to do with academies and secessions, one might ask. Well this. If you were to take a piece of the artistic life of any country at any time, academies – orthodox and otherwise – and everything else included, you would find a preponderance of playboys as enumerated above. Because such people are more frequent in Nature, and hence the personnel of institutions for promoting Art, Music, Drama, Culture etc., has the same proportion – or a little more – of elaborators and blatherers that is found in Nature. That is why institutions are generally stupid – relying on prestige instead of ability, on precedent instead of intelligence, on power rather than justice. That is why they are so fond of exercising the second-rate virtue, that is why they rely on being 'gentlemanly', and that is why they collapse.

When Whistler and his followers seceded from the Royal Society of British Artists, he said: 'We took all the artists and left all the British.'[271] What he said in effect was this: that if, as a member of an academy, you depended on being 'British' – or gentlemanly, or cultured, or middle-aged, or established or anything else, rather than on being a worker – the time would come when the good men outside were not so anxious to get in as the good men inside were to get out.

There is another aspect which concerns the rebels – and that is that they must justify their rebellion. In a year's time there will be another Academy exhibition. Will the seceders have in the meantime accomplished anything sufficient to command public encouragement, or to cause the Academy to have qualms? The answer lies with the seceders themselves. If you hit a man, knock him down. He who fights and runs away – gets a kick in that part of his anatomy which faces the enemy. And serve him right. Let the rebels work, so that when the time comes they will have the glory and the newspapers and all the rest of it. And if they keep it up the time will come when they in their turn can begin to pester the government for a subsidy, or a building or a charter.

When the French Salon, which corresponds to the Academy, rejected Courbet's pictures he hired a big wooden building, set it up in front of the Salon, hung all his pictures inside and charged double entrance fee. He had a howling success. But having tasted blood he went too far. When after 1873 the Republicans turned out the Empire, Courbet went round with his admirers and demolished certain monuments that he considered bad. The Academicians indicted him for the destruction of the property of the French people. He was imprisoned, fined, and banished.[272] So let the rebels look out. The members of Academies are old birds. They know the ropes and can afford to wait. In the American language, it's what they can do, nothing else but.

But if young Mr So-and-so of the new Association of Dublin Artists is nursing a secret ambition to 'get even' with the Academy, here is one way of doing it: First his work must be exceptionally good, and he must begin telling everybody how good it is. Then the newspapers get to hear of it, and start telling the public how good it is. The public likes to have the newspapers telling it what it already knows – that shows that it was right ... Finally the noise gets round to the Academy and they elect him an associate – because

---

[271] James Abbot MacNeill Whistler (1834-1903) , *Symphony in White, No. 1: The White Girl* was refused by the Royal Academy that year but shown to acclaim at the Salon des Refusés in Paris in 1863.
[272] Gustave Courbet (1819-1877) French Realist painter. See for example Linda Nochlin, *Courbet,* Thames and Hudson, London, 2007.

they are always on the lookout for talent, of course. Then they write him a nice letter saying that on such-and-such a date he has been elected, and will he please reply, because the King, or Lord Lieutenant, or Governor General or whoever it is, has to approve, and presumably he can't approve until he knows whether young Mr So-and-so accepts or not etc., etc. Then if he wants to impress them he lets them wait three weeks or a month, and the Secretary writes again, and he accepts.

Then, unless he has some sense – which is very uncommon – he begins to think he is somebody, and that he can now go asleep for the rest of his life. If he wants to be very grand indeed he declines the Academy's invitation to become an associate, and goes on being a genius for a few years. Then some members of the public who don't care tuppence about Art or Academies, but who like to see justice done (when it doesn't cost them anything) begin to ask why So-and-so is not an academician. The Academy ignores the public as long as it thinks it can – though really it could ignore it forever if it liked – but it begins to be anxious, and finally sends an ambassador to ask young Mr So-and-so if he is elected a full Academician, without having to be an associate first, will he accept? And he says: 'Oh yes, I don't mind.' But he has to be a genius first for that.

His friends – particularly his women friends – are glad to hear that he is getting sense. 'You know he is getting on' they say 'and it wouldn't do for him to feel out of it'. Out of what? They don't know, and neither does anyone else. But the search for that mysterious something that you mustn't be out of is the chief preoccupation of Academies and Societies for the promotion of this that and the other. In the hunt for it they all do their damnedest to sidetrack each other, and in the heat of the struggle forget that ostensible reason for their existence – namely to promote, or encourage or whatever it is.

It is not possible in the time to go very deeply into their philosophy of tomfoolery, but some of the results of it are that an Academy is a place where tea on exhibition opening-day is more important than cash receipts on closing day. It is also a place where you can spend two hours of a working day debating whether the part-time charwoman ought to have a stamped insurance card or not – and similar important questions. It is in fact the kind of institution which might either redouble its activities or 'cease upon the midnight with no pain' – and nobody would be a penny the worse.

Academies stand in the same relation to art as bazaars do to charity. Promoters of bazaars go to endless trouble. They meet, discuss, arrange, give interviews, get photographed and paragraphed. An ocean of money is subscribed, demanded – and spent like water, on catering, advertising, paying rent, fees, car-fares and the thousand and one unnecessary elaborations. Everybody eats, drinks, spends and talks too much. And when it is all over and the accounts are made up, the charity concerned is presented with about sixpence to every pound that has been spent. If, instead of all this, everybody who wanted to help would give 5 or 10 shillings and be done with it, what a lot of time and trouble would be saved.

But the promoters of the bazaars would probably be indignant at such a suggestion, because spending time and trouble elaborately and uselessly is what they're good at. So it is I think with a lot of the institutions of the world – committees, boards and not least, our illustrious academies of Art.

Glory – but [there is] nothing to give in exchange for it. So they take on the troublesome job of enlightenment – well rewarded if they see their name in the papers or get a handshake from the Great, or those whom they consider to be the Great, or those who happen to be great at the moment. But people, who thirst for limelight without having done anything to deserve it, are not usually of high intelligence, and so the things they undertake to do don't get done. In this world if you want something done you have to pay for it. What you get for nothing is either what you don't want or can't refuse. You can't tell the 'Honorary Secretary' that he is a D---d fool. That is why societies, associations and committees don't cut much ice. The members have to be so civil to each other in public, that it makes them hate each other in private. They form little cliques and talk about art. All try to grab the limelight and there isn't enough to go around.

Snobbery in Art

by John Keating, RHA. [Broadcast 2 June 1931]

Before saying anything about snobbery in art, I should like to be able to define 'snobbery' and 'art'.

All the books written on Art go to show that nobody knows what it is – least of all the artist, and though several artists have written books, their books are never about Art. So I won't pursue the useless quest. Now for snobbery. My own view of snobbery is that it is a valuable human quality ruined by misuse. To admire something, to imitate it, to strive to get it: Is there anything contemptible in such conduct? The answer depends on whether you really admire it, or whether you only pretend to do so because you think you ought – because somebody you respect or envy does so, or because you have heard that it is the thing to admire. That is as near as I can get to it.

Now we have decided, at least I have decided, that I don't know what Art is, and that I can't define snobbery, so now I can, with perfect confidence and authority, proceed to tell you something about snobbery in art. That, I assure you, is the correct method in dealing with the matter of Art. You can always get away with it, because nobody knows any more about it than you do yourself. I am told that in the region of positive science it is different, that there exist persons who know what they are talking about and can communicate their knowledge to others, but I am not a scientist – though I am positive enough.

Returning to our subject. Take for instance the two most famous pictures in the world –famous in the sense that everybody has heard about them: Leonardo's *Last Supper* and *La Gioconda*.[273] When I stand in front of *La Gioconda* what do I see? – a woman of middle age, sensual and sly. The reds in the painting have all faded and left the greys and blacks and blues. The woman looks liverish, and there is the suspicion of a squint. She has the shy blindish look of a kitten or a drunken man. If anybody who has looked at the picture and has seen the beauty and the wonder disagrees, I would ask him had he heard or read anything about *La Gioconda* before he saw it. Had he in fact had his opinions formed by what he read, and not by what he saw? If, on the other hand, anybody has seen in the picture just what I have seen – take courage, friend, there are, at least, two of us.

Now about the 'Last Supper'. Leonardo painted the picture in fresco on a new damp wall in a convent loggia open to the weather. The work was never finished. Now it is a ruin of grey plaster scored with cracks, blotched with damp. But people stand and gape. Copies are sold in thousands. Why? Because even if you do not admire it you must pretend to do so or write yourself down a savage. The only reason for having to choose between these alternatives is the existence of Cant. I have mentioned two pictures the

---

[273] *The Last Supper* (1495-1498) and La *Gioconda* (1479-1528) also known as *The Mona Lisa*.

names of which are associated in the average man's mind with real greatness. But take the name of Raphael. To most people Raphael means Art in *excelsis*. They are not certain that they would recognize a picture of his without a name. But they have never heard of Andrea del Sarto who was a better painter and draughtsman. Both were contemporaries. Both painted the same subjects. One is known to experts only – the other to the entire world. Again – why? I think it is because of the blind chance which made the publicists light on the name of Raphael, and because of the superstitious awe which attaches to the printed word, which is a kind of Cant. Write any kind of nonsense and get it printed, and there will be people – a great many people – who will swallow it as Gospel. We get second-hand general ideas injected into us from books or when we are children at school. We accept them then just as we wear the clothes and eat the food our parents give us. We grow up with them, and only some – comparatively few – of us ever ask ourselves do we like them, or do they suit us – are they what we wanted.

[page missing from original manuscript]

The indifference of the snob – the artistic snob – to things like Mickey Mouse and 'Gentlemen prefer Blondes' gives us a hint as to the nature of a snob, and we might (on evidence offered by himself) define him as one who won't let himself enjoy anything until he has a printed permit signed by authority – what authority he doesn't know and doesn't care. In fact he doesn't want to feel or care or like or hate. He wants to be told. And nevertheless he has a place in the order of things. He supplies with an audience those elaborators who – not being able to see or think for themselves – like to get the sensation of seeing and thinking by telling others about it. 'Blind Mouths' as Milton calls them. We are all familiar with the 'simple lifer'. He eats nuts instead of beefsteak, because although he likes beefsteak in his stomach, he hates it in his mind, forgetting – or not wishing to remember – that he could live happily, or at least comfortably without a mind, but not without a stomach. But then his educators have put into his head that digestion is a base function and intellection a noble one – a Cant distinction – so he refuses beefsteak on principle.

This is a genuine snob. He suffers for his beliefs. He it was whom I had in mind when I said a few minutes ago that his is a valuable human quality ruined by misuse. His standpoint is what is good enough for humanity is not good enough for him. He is an up lifter. So are the saints and prophets and inventors and martyrs – only with this difference which is all the difference – that his opinions and beliefs are not his own and theirs are. But there is another and a commoner kind of Cant merchant, less valuable and more of a nuisance. He is the seeker after cheap limelight. Everybody must have wondered, at some time or another, at the spectacle of people who spend time, money, energy in the administration of affairs which really don't concern them, and for which they get no thanks – but often blame. And one asks oneself why do they do it? The answer is for limelight. The world is full of people who have a raging thirst for the limelight.

Lecture on Art and Cant

by John Keating, RHA. [Broadcast 9 March 1933]

Before beginning to talk about ART and CANT, I should like to be able to define ART and also CANT.

All the books written about Art go to show that nobody knows what it is, least of all the artists, and though several artists have written books, their books are never about Art. So I won't pursue the useless quest.

Now for Cant. I think that it is an off-shoot of snobbery, and that snobbery is a valuable human quality ruined by misuse. To admire something, to imitate it, to strive to get it – is there anything contemptible in such conduct? The answer depends on whether you really admire it, or only pretend to because you think you ought – because somebody you respect or envy does so, or because you have heard that it is 'the thing' to admire. This is as near as I can get to it.

Now we have decided – or at least I have decided – that I don't know what Art is, and that I can't define Cant, so now I can, with perfect confidence and authority proceed to tell you something about Art and Cant. That I assure you is the correct method in dealing with matters of Art. You can always get away with it because nobody knows any more about it than you do yourself.

I am told that in the region of positive science it is different, that there do exist persons who know what they are talking about, and can communicate their knowledge to others, but I am not a scientist – though I am positive enough. But to return: – take for instance the two most famous pictures in the world – famous in the sense that everybody has heard about them – *The Last Supper* and *Mona Lisa* by Leonardo da Vinci. When I stand in front of Mona Lisa what do I see? A woman of middle age, sensual and sly. The reds in the painting have all faded and left the greys and blacks and blues. The woman looks liverish and there is a suspicion of a squint. She has the shy blindish look of a kitten or a drunken man. [Continues from here in the manner of 'Snobbery in Art' 2 June 1931.]

Talk on the Future of Irish Art

by John Keating, RHA. [Broadcast 9 June 1931][274]

I was going to call this talk: ART IN IRELAND, but I decided that there is not enough Art in Ireland to justify me in talking about it. Why is it that we have no Art in Ireland? I think it is because the encouragement of Art is a hobby of the Rich, and in Ireland we have no rich people, or if we have, their attitude towards the good things of life is different from that which distinguishes the Rich of other countries. Perhaps it is that our rich people have a different opinion about what constitutes the good things in life – and that they do not include Art amongst them. But if that were so they would not feel obliged to make excuses for their lack of interest in Art – as they usually do. When anyone points out certain drabness in Irish life – a want of beauty and comfort, a lack of variety in food and amusement – the answer always is that our history has been so miserable, we're so oppressed that the wonder is we are alive at all. But is this a genuine excuse? If it were – if peace and plenty were essential to the existence of Art and Culture, there would be no such thing in the world. Take Italy of the Renaissance.

Not merely did the Italians fight the French, the Austrians, the Turks, they also fought each other. Every big town was the enemy or the ally of every other town. They lived at war, and only made peace to go to war again. But Art certainly flourished.

Take France from 1500 when she became a Nation until 1870 and the 3rd Republic – never at peace for 50 years together. Take the Netherlands or the group of states that is now Germany. They had the 100-years war, the 30-years war and continuous religious wars, but they have all produced a steady stream of noble architecture, painting, sculpture, music, drama, characteristic costumes, good cooking, good drinking festivals, pageantry, and learning – all that makes life good and desirable. Why does a Swedish peasant live in a lovely timber house carved and painted, instead of in a grey stone cabin? His country is poorer than ours. His climate is worse. Why is there a good picture or two in every municipal office all over rural France?

Why do the houses of poor workmen in Germany have carved wood presses full of lovely embroidered linen? What have we to compare with the Passion Play at Oberammergau – played and produced by small farmers and wood-workers?[275] And if we haven't, why haven't we? Because we don't want it, obviously.

If the argument that we were oppressed and ill treated could be sustained as a reason for having no national art – then Europe would have none either. After all, whether you are killed and your house burned by men from across the sea or by men from across the

---

[274] Published in Irish with variations as 'I'd say that it would be better not to hang any pictures than to hang a bad one', in *The Irish Digest*, September 1940.

[275] First dramatized in 1634 by the people of a small village called Oberammergau in Southern Bavaria after it had been ravaged by plague. Repeated every ten years ever since.

road, makes no difference to the result. As far as Ireland is concerned, ethnologically or socially, Sarsfield was as much a hireling as any Black-and-Tan.[276] We owe no more to the Ormondes and the Fitzgeralds than to Henry VII. Art can – and does – flourish in two ways: as a plaything for the rich, and as part of the daily life of the ordinary citizens of a country – a country that has not been industrialized.

The transition from skilful workman to great artist is imperceptible. One might say that a great artist is a skilful workman who has something very individual, original or personal to say, and who says it in a way that can be understood by the normal man.

Now the industrial system does not produce skilled workmen except in a limited way, nor does it tend to produce individual human beings, but rather multitudinous repetitions of the same pattern, so that the probabilities for the existence of great artists or an audience for them is not good. However, the future does not concern us because by the time the future has arrived, we will be the past.

People always excuse themselves for having a dull time – without beauty, comfort, order, health, in the present, by saying that they are working or thinking for the future.

As some American economist said the other day: 'Everybody knows – or should know – that by working very hard, and resisting the temptation to have a bit of fun now and then for twenty years of your life, you can save enough to take advantage of a financial opportunity when it occurs – and lose the whole lot in one lump.'

We Irish have never arrived at the stage when, without being rich, we begin to have nice things in our houses, when country people begin to invent picturesque and beautiful costumes. We have national and religious festivals, but we do not dress up, we have processions with bands and flags, decorated statues, national songs sung by everybody present, but we are not merry in public; we do not eat and drink in public with our wives and families.

Are we the high-spirited, imaginative, warm-hearted, impulsive, quick-witted people that we would like to believe? Of course not. We are dull, sad, and respectable. We mistrust Art. I am speaking now of art in the sense of decoration and beautification of ordinary things, and not of pictures, sculptures, music and drama only.

When I was painting at Shannon, I noticed that when a job was completed, some workmen would get a German and an Irish flag, some green boughs and a piece of ribbon, and make a trophy which would be fixed on top of the structure.[277] The gang would drink each other's health, sing songs, cheer and have a little ceremony for five minutes. There was something lovely in it to me – something that put a finish on things.

---

[276] Patrick Sarsfield (c.1660-1693), born in Ireland but from a family of Norman origin, created first Earl of Lucan, Irish Jacobite who organized the Irish Rebellion of 1641. He helped to organize the Treaty of Limerick in 1691 before going into service in France along with a group of Irish men that became known as The Wild Geese. The Black and Tans, so named owing to their clothing, were otherwise known as the Royal Irish Constabulary Reserve Force employed in Ireland to suppress the War of Independence.

[277] This is a reference to the 'Shannon Scheme' with which Keating has become synonymous. He worked on the site from c.1926 until c.1928.

The bright flags, the green leaves, the display of taste in arranging the trophy, the merry faces, the manly voices singing, authority unbent for five minutes, and I said to myself sadly: 'Here is something we Irish lack. Why do we never let ourselves go, except at a funeral? Why is the agricultural machinery that comes to us so gaily painted, a mass of rust in two years? Why don't we paint the hay-sheds bright red instead of dull red – in a green country? Why don't we pave the yard? Why don't we clean the windows and clip the hedge and wash the car? Because we don't care about the look of things. And yet no nation on earth has more need of the beauties and amenities of life. We are mostly poor. We cannot visit beautiful countries. Our climate is bad. It rains continually. We have had a miserable past, which we would do well to forget. The only chance we have is to get as much inexpensive pleasure out of our daily lives as we can by living in the midst of good and beautiful things, by having varied and interesting food, by singing, dancing, acting, by having carnivals and frolics – by trying to be alive until we die. As a nation it is time we kicked over the traces and had some fun. We should buy Cathleen Ni Houlihan a new dress, take her to the theatre and give her a dinner instead of a box of chocolates.

Personally I think that we might as well all go on the spree as not. Heretofore we were told and believed that economy and prudence were virtues. Now the Governments of all the nations give an example of mad extravagance to their citizens. The most eminent economists tell us that the remedy for economic depression is to spend freely. If you haven't got the money, buy in credit.

Once people used to think of old age, but now if you want a decent human life, you have to work and think so hard that you won't have any old age. It is a cheerful prospect.

Ireland today is developing along the lines of industrialism. Our objective is Americanism – whether we admit it or not. In the opinion of many people well qualified to judge, industrialism or Americanism (the terms are identical), has been tried and found wanting. They tell us that the system contains within itself the germs of catastrophe – that it is inherently unsound, and that the succession of boom and slump exhibits the periodicity of the disease. Some say that this is the last of all the slumps, some say no, but all agree that the patient cannot be ill and recover indefinitely. There is another aspect of it which weakens the chance for the survival of the industrial system as we know it – that is that it has a powerful and intelligent enemy in Russia.

Whatever one may think of the Soviet Five-Year-Plan, of its practicability, of its rightness or wrongness or anything else about it, no intelligent person can pretend to ignore it.

We have lived through the War, and have seen the moral and physical material and political upheaval that followed it – the effects of which we will continue to feel for years to come. With these results fresh in our minds no reasonable person can pretend to think that the results of five years of concentrated thinking and working in terms of construction and systematization are going to be less momentous than the results of five years of destruction, mass murder, pestilence and moral bankruptcy.

The Great War shattered the fabric of Western civilization. Will the impact of the Five-Year-Plan bring it down? We don't know – but we do know that it isn't going to be safe to try the experiment. We also know that our permission to try it will not be requested.

So that, in planning the course of what remains of our lives, we cannot afford to ignore the situation. What bearing has this on the question of Art in Ireland? Well, up to the present, whenever we thought of Art – if we ever thought of it – we told ourselves that it was something that we couldn't afford. Now, according to the newest theory of economics, you can afford anything you fancy. It is your duty to afford it, in order to hasten the general financial recovery. Spend quickly and get rich quicker. Our governments and big businesses give us the example. If you want a picture, go and buy it (though it would not be truthful to say that the government gives you an example of that), order new clothes, pay the first instalment on a bigger and better car, take plenty of holidays. If you are too far down in the social scale to be able to raise credit, tell the boss what you think of him, instead of telling your wife, and go on the dole.[278] In any case you may win a Sweep – or the Five-Year-Plan may be accomplished in three years.[279] The era of middle-class respectability has come to an end. Authority has gone soft, and begun to explain and apologize, so with a clear conscience we can give carte blanche to the artists.

Legislators during the War discovered that the phrase 'the public wouldn't stand it' has no meaning. The public will stand anything – and pay for anything, moreover. So that it would be a simple matter to legislate for Art.

Soon here in Ireland we shall have to have compulsory third part insurance for motorists. Why not compulsory portraiture for motorists? So that every motorist should have to have his portrait painted, to leave his family a reminder of what he was like before the smash – with the proviso that in the event of his survival, or of an improvement in his looks as a result, that he should be at liberty to destroy the portrait and have a new one painted at a price to be calculated by Income Tax officials, in official Income Tax language, so that he shouldn't be able to understand it, but would rage and pay up – as heretofore. Does that sound too ridiculous? Is it more ridiculous than having to pay taxes to keep people idle – or being forced to pay for helping to keep Germany down, in order to please the French? Public Health legislation has had a long innings. Its opponents said that it was too expensive – too utopian. But the public health acts came and nowadays they are part of our everyday life.

In France they have laws to regulate the design and character of buildings in towns and cities, so that anyone that has the money cannot build as he chooses. Why not laws to regulate the dress of the citizen? So that it would be illegal for a small bow-legged man with red hair to wear a blue tie and plus-fours and a bowler hat – whereas he should

---

278 The dole is another name for unemployment assistance. It was introduced to Ireland in 1933. Keating believed that the dole was encouraging unemployment because working people paid taxes to keep those who were not working 'idle'.

279 Keating refers to 'the Sweep' which was the Irish Hospital Sweepstakes, set up in 1930 and disestablished in 1987. It provided funds raised from betting on horses which were channelled into building hospitals all over Ireland.

according to Section X of the 1974 Regulation of Dress Act (Sub-section 13, paragraph Q), wear dungaree overalls with Wellington boots and a gas mask. What an opportunity for the experts, legal, aesthetic, medical, medico-legal, simple-lifers, dress-reformers, busybodies whose self-appointed task it is to find out what the citizen wants to do and to prevent him from doing it. But what a heaven for the Artists.

Art as a Career

by John Keating, RHA. [Broadcast 4 August 1931]

In Ireland there are a great many young artists. I know this because their mothers write to me from time to time to tell me about them, and having described the symptoms, they ask me if I think that their goose is going to be a swan. I generally say yes, because I know that the ladies in question don't want advice – but only confirmation of what they know. And *even I* sometimes like to tell people what they want to hear. There is Scriptural justification for this (as well as for practically everything else) if one wanted to find it: –' Answer a fool according to his folly' says the Psalmist.

Now I don't mean by this that the mothers who write to me are any more foolish than the rest of us. It is only that our follies are different.

If my children should happen to show any of the symptoms that the letters describe, I shall know that there is nothing to be done about it. For becoming an artist is not just acquiring a profession. It is contracting a disease – as incurable as golf.

If your child is not an artist, there is (fortunately) nothing you can do to make him one. And if he is an artist, there is nothing you can do to stop him. He will be one – not because of you, but in spite of you. Whether you clap your hands or wring them matters not two hoots. So why do either? Here is one of the rare and precious occasions in life when one is fully justified in pursuing a course of masterly inactivity.

But ever-conscientious parents will begin to worry about how to have the child taught and what art school to send him to. That also matters not at all. They might, for peace sake, send him to the nearest school or if inconvenient, not to any school. If the child is an artist he will continue to draw and paint, and will do nothing else. If he is not an artist – but only an amateur, he can wait. It is wonderful how long an amateur can wait. I have seen them and admired their tenacity. Elderly ladies armed with a brand new outfit, the very latest model paint-box, palette and brushes, patent folding easel and stool, with automatic sunshade attached to protect the complexion during out-door 'sketching'. They are generally docile and eager to learn, and I marvel at such belated enthusiasm. Later on they tell me about it. They had always wanted to paint – ever since they were girls. But an invalid aunt left alone in the world had required constant attention and company. So it was only last month, when the old lady died, that they were left free to do what they had always wanted to do. What is one to say to such heroic devotion?

C'est magnifique, mais ce n'est pas l'Art.

The explanation of all this is that everybody is incurably romantic. In the course of having to grow up, the romance gets hunted out of one place after another, but always comes to rest again in some corner of our heart that the business of our life has left undisturbed. Thus one meets seamen who have romantic illusions about life on shore. Just as town-dwellers have about a life on the rolling waves etc. How many respectable and elderly persons see themselves as vamps and sheiks, if only life had placed them in other circumstances, and so on? And because Art is one of the things that seldom touches the life of the average man, it is precisely the region where his starved romantic imagination comes finally to rest. And one of the cruellest spectacles in life is the belated and final disillusionment of the man or woman who has to be told in the latter half of a life of drudgery that, in Art also, you must put in more than you can ever hope to get out. In the case of the young there is still time to change one's mind – provided always, that one has a mind to change.

And so I tell the mothers what they want to hear – because I like making people happy (so long as it does not cost me anything). And telling a loving mama that her child is probably going to be a 'great cubist' generally pleases her very much. It is one of those rare occasions when you can please everybody. The lady is pleased, because every lady knows, at the bottom of her heart, that she is 'very artistic' and that her children take after her. It pleases the husband and father because he thinks that it isn't going to cost much. He finds out about that part later. But paying up is his job anyway. It pleases the young person concerned because it generally means getting out of the bosom of the family (in order to come to Dublin).[280] (They like to come to Dublin – even when they're not from Cork). It has always interested me to notice the strong family affection of our country, and the intense desire of the young to get out of it at the earliest possible moment.

There is another reason for advising parents to send their child to an Art School. A constant supply of young aspirants (artists) is a very necessary factor for the existence of Art, because it enables manufacturers to produce materials at a reasonable price, and provide Schools of Art with a reason for existence. When one remembers the number of big firms engaged in making paints and brushes and canvas – all the extensive and expensive equipment for Art students and schools of Art, and the great number of cultured and distinguished persons engaged in furthering the acquirement of artistic knowledge, one realizes the importance of the question: 'Has my daughter talent?' and 'Do you think that she should take Art as a profession?' In order to realize what it would mean if the reply were: 'No, she hasn't' and 'I don't' one has only to think of what would happen if, for instance, nobody were to break the law ever again. Not that that is likely to happen. Without wishing to institute any unseemly comparisons, I think that there is a certain similarity between the raw material of art (in the sense of Art students) and the raw material which keeps in use the majestic machinery of law and justice. In both cases the young person concerned shows early a strong disinclination for work, and a great capacity for amusement, a vivid imagination, and a contempt for property – (other people's property), a distaste for literal statement, and a preference for the romantic amplification of dull facts, a dislike for going to bed, and a perfect hatred for getting up. That is what is called 'temperament'. In the case of the young law breaker, it is not encouraged. But the glamour of Art, God knows why, outweighs all the obvious disadvantages. The income from Art is precarious, for the painter, unlike certain other

---

[280] Keating wrote 'delete' at this point.

professionals, has no stranglehold on the public. But that fact is discounted. Papa and Mama must look forward to the prospect of having to keep the future artist until very possibly the greater part of his future is behind him. But that does not deter. The morals of artists are not generally believed to be ... – but that does not repel.[281] How is it that all the things that in an artist are romantic would, in the case of any other profession, be judged as evidence of a passion for drink? Of course this is a dangerous subject to pursue, because the variety of human folly is endless and entertaining, and one cannot do much about it – in a quarter of an hour. But certainly it has always seemed to me that parents with artistic offspring to dispose of are capable of a display of vanity, muddled thinking, and indifference to the evidence of the senses, [which is] hard to equal. All schoolmasters will know the kind of exhibition to which I refer.

There are ordinary decent human beings who feel in their hearts that they always loved art (but of course Father wouldn't hear of it) and so they, having become fathers in their turn, are going to give a chance to their children who inherit their genius (this part is sub-conscious). These people are genuine and to be pitied, because suppressed romantic longing will NOT emerge as artistic ability – no matter how suppressed, nor for how long.

The only reliable indication of an inclination towards Art is a point blank refusal to do, or be interested in, anything else – under any compulsion whatever. A good artist – or one who is likely to be so – should have the diabolical cunning of a monomaniac, the devotion of a young lover, the patience of a mother for her child, the ruthless selfishness of egomania. If you feel that that just describes your young artist, bring him right along. The one great advantage he will gain by formally entering the ranks of the profession is that other artists will help him if he is genuine.[282]

Artists don't feel much moral responsibility for others. They have more than enough to do to meet the insatiable demands of the Demon within. But they will help another artist, if he IS an artist – or the makings of one. On the other hand, when it is a question of pseudo-artists, amateurs, limelighters, mountebanks, and the entire crowd who swarm about the fire which they have never helped to keep alight – towards these gentry the artist feels dislike. He would much prefer black beetles.

But if you are prepared to take the consequences of being an artist, that is if you are prepared to be a celluloid cat with tallow legs, pursued through hell of this world by the asbestos dog – whose name is Time – be an artist by all means. If you ARE an artist, you won't have any choice anyway. So you might as well begin now. If you are an amateur, you will know where to stop. To go all out would cost you too much. It would mean indifference to worldly advancement or reward, and very often to family affections as well. It would mean absence of human respect, contempt for suffering, a determination to attain your ends by fair means, or foul – fair of course preferred, because it is much

---

[281] Keating wrote 'aha...ahem...a certain laxity,...ahem' and then crossed it out.
[282] Keating wrote in Irish by hand at this point 'Aitheann ciarog, ciarog eile' which roughly translates to 'like recognises like'.

simpler. It would also mean a total indifference to abstract questions of right and wrong – justice, reason, etc., a preference for instinct and feeling rather than logic or common sense, a great power of attention and concentration on the job in hand regardless of any considerations of the value or necessity of the thing when done. If you feel [that you have] these qualities within you, or if you are a parent and see them in your child, you must only resign yourself to your fate. But in looking back over the qualities just enumerated, I think it unlikely that any mother will decide that such qualities (which are absolutely essential in the artist) are present in her child. Nevertheless, if the child wants to go to a school of art, let him. It will do him no more harm than any other school and he might find it less dull.

It has often occurred to me that it is a great pity that the education of the young should be largely in the hands of gentle, timid, well-intentioned, over-instructed people with no experience of life outside of class-rooms. The copybook virtues are brittle in texture and do not travel well. A School of Art can, at its best, be a happy place, and at its worst, it is only a place or state of punishment where some souls suffer for a time – before they get a job.

Talk on Art and the Cinema

by John Keating, RHA. [Broadcast 28 August 1931]

Everybody goes to the Cinema now and again. Do they get what they want or do they take what they get? If you talk to people – not high-brows or culture mongers, but ordinary people – you get the impression that they go more on the chance of seeing something to interest them, rather than with a reasonable certainty of being amused. Most people laugh at Vamps, Sheiks, Bad Men, Gun-Men, Foreign Legionaries and all the rest of the bag of tricks. Most people dislike vice, crime, violence, bloodshed. But this is the stuff out of which ninety-five per cent of the films are concocted – to which we all go.

Most people – on the other hand – love travel, strange peoples, [and] the sea. Most of us would love to spend a day in a coal-mine, or at a foundry or a ship-yard – or at the building of a sky-scraper, or at a hundred and one human activities about which we know nothing, and shall, in all probability, never know. Most of us have a very deep and real human interest in famous people. We want to know what kind of house they live in, what they eat and drink, whether they sit or stand at work. Thousands of people who adore bodily activity have never had the chance to practice any. All the things in life that we miss – for everybody misses something – could be supplied to us by the Cinema. Open air, foreign travel, [and] the marvels of modern industry, the unbelievable interest and strangeness of practical science. I leave out, for the moment, the exquisite beauty of slow motion pictures, which would have driven the designers of old crazy with admiration and envy. Instead of this food for the mind what do we get?

Well, you can take your choice. You can have silly sentimentality, the beautiful lady who breaks all the commandments, the strong, silent jackass, the gambler homicide with a heart of gold – that unusual organ. Or you can see some noisy, ill-bred bounder getting himself into painful and humiliating situations, hitting people with articles of food, tearing his own and other people's clothes, breaking windows and generally misbehaving himself. For the humour of the Cinema never gets beyond the age of ten. There is of course plenty of silliness in every department of life. But why should all the different kinds be collected into a solid mass to form the material out of which the cinema creates its productions? In ordinary life there is a small proportion of reason and truth. This is the cement which keeps human society together. In the cinema this necessary human element is absent, or mostly so. That is why going to the cinema for refreshment and amusement is like smoking when you are hungry. Your hunger leaves you, but you don't feel fed. The cinema is just dope except of course on rare occasions. I remember particularly one. It was a film showing a few days in the life of an Eskimo family.[283] They hunted, fished, built a house, visited a trading post, cured skins, trained their dogs, cooked food, went to bed and got up – and so on. Nobody was shot or beaten, suspected, robbed, or made ridiculous. It was full of beauty. The little children were exquisite. Snow, the shining black rocks, the wet black seals, the penguins like solemn dwarfs in evening dress, with horn-rimmed spectacles, the gleaming fish and shining ice, made a patterned background of black and white [and] the incredible swiftness strength and skill of the man in the hunting and fishing scenes. The frightful suspense when he harpooned a big seal and was dragged head first into a hole in the ice, and how he hung desperately on to the rope and harpoon and seal, while little dots – his comrades far away on the shore – came racing desperately to help him, jumping across the lanes of black water. How they hauled man and seal, rope and harpoon out of the hole, all in a tangle. How they fell upon the seal, killed it and skinned it, laughing, shouting, stumbling, and doubtless cursing and swearing if one could hear them. They set off in a canoe – dogs, people, pots, pans, nets, sleds, weapons, snow-shoes and everything they had on earth, and having arrived, the woman started unloading the canoe and lifted out now a baby and now a puppy and now a bundle of skins, and now another baby, until one wondered where they had all fitted. How the audience laughed. Not the stifled snigger that creates the double-meaning, but honest laughter. The white trader at the post gave the little Eskimo children biscuits plastered with margarine, which they swallowed like jujubes. Then their little faces began to twist, and they roared with colic, when, producing a bottle of castor oil, he doled out large doses, which they swallowed greedily and begged for more until they emptied the bottle. Then the audience, weak with laughter, cheered and clapped for five minutes. The whole thing was perfect Art. The idea that simple so-called uncivilized people knew nothing of Art is an error. At least they can never be vulgar. The principal actor – the Eskimo and his family – were probably paid with five shillings worth of groceries and a half-pound of tobacco.

I have seen other pictures, where, after quarter of an hour of tedious blatant advertising written in what the producer imagined to be English, the story begins. And what a story! This story, generally adapted from some novel, about people such as have never existed, has been 'improved' by the producer. A producer has been variously described as 'a man who knows what he wants – but can't spell it,' and as 'a man who thinks that an antidote is a funny story'. He has a low opinion of the average intelligence, so he writes down to it. His real subconscious reason is that he couldn't write up. He thinks that his audience wouldn't understand him if he didn't, because he is ignorant, and devoid of imagination, and can imagine nothing better than himself. There is no art in him, but he supplies the want of it with plenty of impudence and bad taste. So he is well qualified to translate bad literature into worse pictures. The process may be

---

[283] Keating refers to *Nanook of the North* which was directed and produced by Robert Flaherty in 1922. Flaherty and his wife moved to the Aran Islands in the early 1930s to produce *Man of Aran*.

described as the making of a silk purse *into* a sow's ear – when the purse isn't silk, but shoddy. Or to put it another way: the average film is a stupid illustrated book – with the book left out. The story is never clear, and the trail of the Censor is over it all. And in that story everybody is doing the most unnatural and astonishing things. Virtuous young women are constantly suspected of misconduct by their nearest relatives on the flimsiest evidence. Loving fathers throw their daughter out of the house for having come home late. Sons of loving fathers forge their loving father's name to cheques for paltry sums. The wicked bank-manager who has designs on the loving, honourable, grey-haired father's daughter, holds a mortgage on the father's property, which he will foreclose unless ... But the wicked bank-manager's ne'er-do-well son loves the daughter, and robs his father's bank – getting shot in the process. The loving daughter nurses him back to health in time for the inevitable tableau, and so on. And they all go around hiding their despair by leaning their heads up against walls, and on roll-top desks, and by throwing away perfectly good cigarettes, which they had just lighted. In the case of ladies and 'gents' – I say advisedly 'ladies and gents' – by the manner in which they are leaning up against each other. And then, to make everything clear the Censor cuts a lump out of the middle of it. But why not cut it all out which brings me to the point I want to make:

I believe that the Cinema is predominantly ignorant and unwholesome, that it gives a false view of life, and that its object is to make money for capitalists. Whether we like it or not the Cinema has come to stay. Otherwise conducted it would be the most powerful instrument of general enlightenment that has emerged. Educationalists are well aware of this, and films of great beauty and interest are made and used in scientific and physical laboratories. But these the public never sees. The unjustified assumption is that the public doesn't want to see them. The public wants to see everything, and, given a choice, will always choose what is good.

Shakespeare and Shaw, Goldsmith and Sheridan, Gilbert and Sullivan are best-sellers. Robinson Crusoe and Don Quixote have never ceased to sell – and never will, while people continue to read books. In the Cinema this is equally true. The Miracle, the Birth of a Nation, Charlie Chaplin will never cease to draw. Because these things are Art, and the much-derided public knows it, without knowing how they know – or wanting to know. So that Art pays – in the long run.

But Art has a better justification than that. Art does not have to rely for its effects on the presence in human nature of base instincts. It appeals to the love of Beauty, Truth, Reason, Order, and just proportion. If you have no Art you must either hold your tongue, or make a vulgar noise. You will be able to get the attention of the brutal and the ignorant, and those who take what they get, instead of what they would like. But why should the intelligent go hungry, so that the ignorant may feed on garbage?

Twenty-five years ago the Cinema was in its infancy, but it was only too evident from the sort of up-bringing it was having at the hands of those who elected themselves to be its parents, what the adult was going to be like – ill-bred, ignorant and vicious. If any future historian writes on education in our times, he will find it hard to explain the utter indifference of the educationalists and humanists to their plain duty to guide and control the destinies of this portentous infant – the Cinema, with its enormous possibilities for good and evil. What the rulers and their advisers did not do then they think to do now by the appointment of censors with limited powers to control the uncontrollable. The adult Cinema of today – rich and established with its offspring-Talkies and Television – is directed by people who care only for money.

All civilized governments practice the right to protect the public from its own ignorance. Medical Councils, Law Societies, Associations of Authors and Artists, and many others have powers over the members of their professions – backed by legal enactments, so that penalties attach to ignorance or misconduct. Public authorities have powers to destroy bad food. To sell bad food or drink, to practice on life or limb without qualification, to supply dangerous substances without precautions, to endanger the public health in any way, is a crime in civilized countries. We are simply not permitted to be dangerous, even through ignorance.

While everybody admits that an injury to the mind is infinitely worse than an injury to the body, nobody seems to think that the production of a universal commodity, such as the Cinema certainly is, ought to be supervised at the source. A Council composed of people of attainment and character in literature and art ought to have the authority in matters of the Cinema that the Medical Councils have in Medicine.[284] But that is not likely to happen, as long as countries spend millions on the upkeep of ornamental personages – armies, navies, diplomacy and all the rest of it, while they leave hospitals, housing and research on charity. As long as private enterprise is allowed to conflict with the general welfare, so long will millionaire producers sell vulgarity, sensationalism and clap-trap – because it is cheap. The Cinema today is simply dope.

---

[284] Keating is indicating the need for some form of arts council. He was aware of Thomas Bodkin's reports in this regard.

Another Talk on Art

by John Keating, RHA. [Broadcast 28 November 1931][285]

Tonight I should like to talk about something else for a change, but, because I make my living out of art, I am not expected to talk about anything else. Or if I do, I must do it in private, and expect in doing so to have interruptions and contradictions. A broadcaster is like a preacher in his pulpit, or a magistrate on the Bench – he is immune for the moment. He can get away with statements that would not pass in conversation.

I have already given talks on Modern Art, Snobbery in Art, Art as a Career etc., etc. This talk will be about Art. Just Art. Probably a legitimate and respectable pursuit in itself, but it has about it an attraction, glamour, a legend that puts it in the same class as Hy Brasil, Perpetual Youth and the Philosopher's Stone – something too good to be true, or something so good that it must be a sin. The public buzzes round like bees round a hollyhock, full of real interest in Art and Artists as known in cinemas, theatres and novels – and full of pretended interest in *real* art and artists. When they find that the real artist does not live up to the film producers' conception of him, either in the speed with which he produces masterpieces, or in the numbers of his creditors and his amours, they are disappointed and annoyed. They almost begin to shout for their money back – until they remember that they haven't given any.

There is another reason for the existence of popular misconceptions about art and artists. It is the amiable habit that most artists have of giving a silly answer to a silly question, the silly answer that turns curiosity into wrath when the enquirer has had time to think it over. And in return for having had his leg pulled, he dismisses the artist saying to himself, 'Ah, he is just a clever fool.' It may be argued that the Artist's conduct in this case is inexcusable. But is it any worse than might be expected from a member of any other trade or profession in similar circumstances? I imagine that an operation performed by a skilful surgeon must be very interesting to watch, but I know that an operating theatre is a Holy of Holies into which no one is admitted except those whose business it is to be there. Imagine the feelings of the surgeon if the patient's mother-in-law were to stand at his elbow discussing his every move with him, in what she imagined to be technical language acquired from the study of A THOUSAND MEDICAL HINTS or HOME SURGERY FOR ALL ... yet this is analogous to what happens to artists every other day. Hence the silly answers to the silly questions – leg-pulling as a means of self-defence. This sort of thing, for instance: some old lady (of either sex) who thinks art is *so* interesting, meets a painter. Being the victim of the delusion that artists eat, drink and breathe nothing else but art, she begins with some banal compliment, and to impress

---

[285] Keating published this article, with slight changes, under the title 'The Voice of One' in *The Leader,* December 17, 1938, pp. 391-393.

him with intelligent interest asks, 'And tell me, do you use varnish?' The painter, knowing perfectly well that she cares nothing for painting (why should she?), instead of saying 'stupid woman, go to the devil', says 'that, as a matter of fact is the whole secret – very clever of you to have noticed it. Yes I do use varnish, but it is rather a special kind'. 'Oh, *how* exciting, tell me.' 'Well, since you're interested, I will, but don't pass it on'. 'Oh, no, indeed I won't'. 'Well then, my varnish is made of Stockholm tar, treacle, rotten eggs, cod liver oil and formalin. The Stockholm tar is to supply the resin. The treacle is to give it body and colour. The rotten eggs are to supply the sulphurated hydrogen, in order to prevent the coal-gas products in the air from attacking the metallic oxides in the paint and turning them black. The cod liver oil is to prevent the mixture drying too quickly. The formalin is to kill off the microbes attracted by the other ingredients and to neutralize the smell of the eggs.' If she laughs, you can then converse with her as a human being. If she swallows the information, it is a thousand to one that she rushes off to tell everybody. Nothing will be lost in the telling. And thus a mere brick is added to the façade of Bunk in Art.

Take another type of enquirer – suppose a 'Photographic Artist' who thinks it would increase business, and distinguish him from the mere photographer, if he could supply his patrons with 'genuine, hand-painted oil portraits'. He goes to the School of Art, interviews the authorities, pays his fees, gets his receipt, time-table, dockets, tickets, schedules, syllabus etc. Everything as simple and straight forward as can be. He wonders why he didn't do it long ago. No fussy preliminaries. No stupid questions, no entrance examination. Everybody is polite, helpful and optimistic. And the fees are very moderate. He thinks: How different from the pretentious formalities to which I should have had to submit if I were entering for the study of law or medicine – or architecture or science, or almost any trade or profession. All kinds of impertinent questions about my ability, my previous studies, my general education, my financial resources, should have had to be answered, and my entry would have cost me more pounds than I have just paid shillings. And he comes to the study of art full of delightful anticipation. His reception at the threshold has been such as to cause him to forget that most excellent maxim: –Blessed is he that expects nothing, for he shall not be disappointed. But once in Life Class, what a disillusionment! There he is with paint brushes, boxes and palette, all the paraphernalia, everything that can be imagined in the way of apparatus. But he can make no progress. He asks questions, such as: 'How do you paint a nose?' and expects to be told the formula – to be given the key. Instead he gets an answer which he can't understand. He flounders, idles, gets bored and gives it up – generally after three months, convinced for evermore that artists are cheats and mountebanks. They have a damned little trick. They promise to show it to you for money. They take your money. They show you the trick. But somehow you can't just get it. Of course, what should have happened is this: the would-be painter should have had it explained to him at the outset that if he feels an irresistible impulse to paint or draw, and if he is prepared to work very hard all day and every day for about three years, he will then be able to judge for himself whether he has any ability or not. He should be told that private income sufficient to keep him in health is absolutely necessary. He should be told that an intense desire for expression is no proof of having anything to express. He should be told that a robust constitution and an endless resistance to mental and physical fatigue are essential. He should be advised to listen with docility, and to be inflexible in holding to his own ideas at the same time. If he were to be told all these things – all simply true, he would have gone away in a fury, convinced that he wasn't wanted, and that it was all trade union humbug.

Thus, for one reason or another we have, on the side of the public, a notion that artists are – well artists. Let us look at the artist's side of it. Not that I want to make any apologies for him, but merely to suggest some of the causes which might be responsible for his idiosyncrasies, real or imagined. To begin with, there is his experience in a School of Art – that Mecca towards which he has been struggling since the first manifestations of his disease. This part of his existence is comparable to being skinned alive – a necessary operation because the art is presumed to be inside, under all the skins. It sometimes happens that when all the skins are removed, there is no inside and consequent to the process, no outside either. But it is a very fruitful process nevertheless, because in the course of it the searcher comes to be acquainted with many of the innumerable varieties of human folly and ineptitude as exhibited in himself and his fellow sufferers.

He spends the impressionable years of adolescence, so full of vague dreams of ambition, of beauty and of luxury in working very hard, and being (as a rule) very poor, [which is] not the best way to sweeten the temper. To spend the best part of one's life like the blind man in the dark room looking for the black hat which may or may not be in that room is a good way to cultivate bleakness of outlook. One learns to know that frustration is the price of enthusiasm and one learns to dispense with the comforts of sentimentality.

Later he realizes that he has to have money in order to get some money. Now the way to get money is to have painted the Rich, and the way to get to paint the Rich is to have a reputation. It is not so much a vicious circle as a barbed wire entanglement in the no man's land of the financial system. But having confined himself as part of his discipline to an exclusive diet of 'the unleavened bread of sincerity and truth', he finds that confectionary makes him ill, so that he is not good company at the tables of the Rich. He has only too much reason to suspect that his culture – so dearly bought – is a second-rate affair.

His instructors are 'akademickers' as the Germans say, elaborators, examination wallahs and the like, so that he tends to look over the fence of reputation and authority, and find nothing behind it but a lot of empty tin cans rusted with vile gut glue sticking to their labels. Having studied to be inexorable in the pursuit of truth – even against his natural sympathies, he becomes inevitably an iconoclast. And iconoclasts are not popular.

If the public would look upon artists as being also God's creatures and not merely the embodiment of a talent, to be hung up behind the door until required for use, and if artists would refrain from drawing overdrafts on people's tolerance and credulity, both parties would learn much about each other that it would be well for them to know. But that an artist can tell the public anything about art I very much doubt. Art is an experience not be described. Trying to describe it is like trying to describe the taste of an egg. What the taste of an egg means to you and what it means to me, could only be described to either of us by a third person who knew what it meant to each of us separately, as well as what it meant to him. Thus he would have a basis of comparison. But the taste of an egg is simply the taste of an egg and we need to know more. We can always produce the sensation with an egg.

The forgoing, which is self-evident nonsense, is the exact equivalent – minus the pretentious terminology – of discussions and writings and lectures about art. If you like eggs, eat eggs. And if you like art, look at pictures, sculpture and architecture. You will never know more about it than can come through your eyes to awaken what is in your heart. And if you don't feel anything when you look, go your way, and bless God that you have no heart to feel anything about anything very much, or very long, having had it all frittered away in the process of growing up and getting on.

[Keating added by hand:]

He spends the years of adolescence, half in a world of romantic dreams of beauty and ambition, and half like the India rubber cat with tallow legs, being chased through the hell of this world by the asbestos dogs of Time and Death. The years when he might have grown straight and strong in a kindlier environment are spent like a blind man in a dark room looking for a black hat which may be in that room – a good way to cultivate bleakness of outlook. One becomes acquainted with frustration and learns to dispense with the comforts of sentimentality. One is very poor, works very hard and has no fun because fun is expensive. Later he discovers that the region of his mind most valuable to an artist is out of his power to exploit, because it consists of a large empty space of the extent and shape of that amount of humanism and culture which his progenitors did not absorb and assimilate during a period of about three hundred years, so that in order to have a future he must provide himself with a past. He must learn how to flourish in barren ground without the customary aid of roots. And thus he becomes a sinister caricature of what he might have been under humane conditions in fertile ground, watered by tenderness, fed on beauty, sheltered by love. Instead of which he lives in Heytesbury Street on a Scholarship of £60.00 per annum, payable for ten months of the year. If you don't believe it, ask the Department of Education.

He begins to have reason to suspect that his culture – so dearly bought – is a second rate affair – an 'Ersatzkultur', an attempt to gatecrash the Parnassus by claiming to have an acquaintance with the Immortal Gods based on a study of cheap plaster casts.

Having confined himself as part of his discipline to an exclusive diet of 'the unleavened bread of sincerity and truth', he finds that confectionary makes him ill, so that he is bad company at the table. He regrets that he should have rationalized his poverty by pretending that he was practising austerity when he was enduring want and so robbed of the only lesson that was in it – that poverty is a sin.

Later still he realizes that he has to have money in order to get some money. Comfortable people don't like the poor. They fear that they are going to be asked for a loan or get fleas and they are quite right. It is no use saying 'I am hungry' or ' I am bored' or 'I lack cultivated feminist society', one must pay for these things, or seem to be able to do so. Now the way for an artist to get money is to paint the rich and to get to paint the rich one has to have money and reputation.

Art in Ireland

by John Keating, RHA. [Broadcast 23 April 1932]

If a Frenchman were told that he would become the owner of six French paintings provided he was able to name them, he would have no hesitation in trotting out the names of six French artists –his favourite work of each, its whereabouts and (most likely) the catalogue price. Could an Irishman name six Irish pictures – not to mention Irish artists? I do not think so – unless he was a highbrow or a dealer. A Frenchman walking about Paris can take in the story of his country through his eyes. If he were deaf and dumb and illiterate he could still understand what is meant by '*La France*'. Would Dublin or Cork tell an Irishman as much? I doubt it.

The fact is that in France and other continental countries interest in Art is almost as common as interest in food – too normal to be boasted about or apologized for. In Ireland, on the contrary, it has no place in the lives of ordinary people. In the words of the song: Nobody knows, nobody cares – except the people who are officially interested in Art. And yet I believe that the Irish have artistic sensibilities, and are capable of artistic expression and appreciation. I hold this belief on the evidence of Irish music, Irish dancing, colourful speech and rich vocabulary and also in the Irish incapacity for real vulgarity. With regard to pictures I have learned to value very highly the criticism of persons who are still unselfconscious in their attitude towards Art. But most Irish people if asked what they think of a certain picture or piece of sculpture will put on an expression of wariness, or embarrassment, or just boredom. They will begin by saying: 'Of course I know nothing whatever about Art' as if it were something remote or inhuman. I think that such an attitude is not natural in Ireland – any more than it would be in France or Spain. It is borrowed English convention – that is to be well-informed is 'ungentlemanly'.

Hitherto in this country as part of the British system, the encouragement of Art has always been *de haut de bas*. The patron was well repaid in prestige. One could be a Maecenas for an expenditure of twenty-five pounds a year.[286] One could be a connoisseur on fair words.

The Church (in Ireland) ignored the Arts and bought what was required at a wholesale shop. The system of Art Education was that inaugurated by Prince Albert – when the Department of Science and Art came into existence. This system – severely damaged by time – still operates.[287] It cannot be said to work. It consumes a great quantity of money, time and energy without much result – unless the manufacture of teachers for when there are no jobs can be called a result. A glance at the account of such

---

[286] Maecenas was a Roman statesman and patron of literature c. 70-80 BC. Keating uses the name to allude to generous patronage.

[287] It was the same system that was in place when Keating wrote his report on the DMSA in 1925. The system did not change until 1937.

an institution reveals the relative importance in which the student stands to the machine. Of course it has no connection with Art or Science – and never had. But it was part of the Victorian smoke-screen of Democracy and Humanitarian Liberalism behind which went on the real business of Empire – mad industrialism and privilege.

All this is thoroughly realized by most Irish people of today. It is, I think, the principle reason why we have no characteristically national 'school'. Another reason is that most of our best artists had to go to other countries where they got a better chance of making a living by their work. Whatever the reason, the fact remains that no Irishman has done for the Irish what Courbet, Monet or Manet did for the French, what Goya did for the Spaniards or Zuloaga for the Basques, what Rapin did for the Russians, Zern for the Swedes or Segantind for the Italians. I leave out of consideration those painters who – no matter when they lived – or where – turned away from life about them to paint pseudo-classicism or historical anecdote. It is generally forgotten that the 'Old Masters' were [the] modern of the 'Moderns' when they were alive.

Now I personally admire the English School of Painting. English painters are generally excellent craftsmen. They are full of love of their country. They see her beauty and they extol it. But they have a strong fixation in the past, and they love a picture which 'tells a story'. They have little regard for logic – and prefer not to have. The Englishman, at bottom, is a youthful sentimentalist, the Irishman a realist and an adult. We are their temperamental opposites. In this connection, as in most other human relationships, respect and esteem are sounder than the flattery of imitation. We can never build an Irish 'school' of art out of the debris of the Ascendancy.

We have in Dublin two good galleries. The National Gallery is, for its size and revenue, one of the best all-round collections that I know of. Such pictures as Rothwell's 'Callisto', Goya's 'Lady in Black Shawl', Franz Hal's 'Fisherboy', Walter Osborne's 'Lustre Jug' and Ribera's 'San Procopius' would – any one of them, I think – justify its existence. But the scarcity of works by Irishmen of the fist rank is very obvious. The Municipal Gallery of Modern Art has Brangyn's 'Mars and Venus', John's 'Head of a Lady', Glyn Philpet's 'Mocking of Christ', Le Sidanier's 'Twilight in a Village', Corot's 'Rome from the Pinsio' and others that one can never see too much of. But here too the flavour is distinctly British – and of the past. The Gallery – except for a few additions – ceased to grow at the death of Sir Hugh Lane, to whose generosity it owes the best that is in it. In England, Municipalities – even of quite small towns – levy a rate for the purchase of pictures. This, as well as numerous gifts from individual donors, ensures constant additions to the Municipal Galleries, and provides a market for works of merit by younger artists, whose prices are still moderate.

In Dublin, although the Municipal Gallery is supported by rates, there is no allocation for the purchase of pictures, and people in Ireland apparently do not contribute to any extent. A fine new Municipal Gallery constructed on the most modern lines has been provided in Charlemont House. It is to be hoped that a fund will be forthcoming to purchase pictures for it. As it is there is no evidence in either gallery of the existence of an 'Irish' school. If the labels were removed I defy anyone – no matter how expert – to distinguish the Irish painters from the British by any internal evidence of a common tradition or a national culture. Yet we have in Ireland at the moment a number of young Irishmen of talent and individual character – actually painting Irish things in Ireland. Here is all the material for an Irish School, if the individuals were sufficiently self-conscious and cohesive to be aware of it, and if they were given the necessary encouragement. This must be in the form of a provision for continuous work on public buildings, offices, Churches, theatres and the recording studio. I think I have an idea about how these facilities if granted could be used to the best advantage so as to produce a native Irish School of Painting.

Talk on Art

by John Keating, RHA. [Broadcast October 30 1932]

I want to talk tonight about an Irish School of Art. I don't mean any existing institution, but one that could and should exist. At this moment I imagine that a number of my auditors will reach for the knob – but hold on – I am said to have a 'swell line of drip'.

Now this School of Art, what is it? Is it an imposing building with a large staff, apparatus etc., and a grant of money, or is it a living organism with a tradition, a conscious aim, a creed, a national consciousness? Is it a design for a temple to false gods made by a deluded amateur architect eighty years ago, or is it a home for certain living creatures of the Irish nation – present and future [and] to whom God has given the job of providing a culture for their county?

I ask, because on the answer depends the answer to the question whether we are already well provided with a School of Art or not. (I use the word 'School' here as meaning more than the walls and the roof). Let us go back a little. In 1859 or so, Prince Albert, the husband of Queen Victoria, (*le mari de sa femme*) conceived the idea of the DEPARTMENT OF SCIENCE and ART. He was an intelligent and able man, but he had delusions common to his time. He thought that you could marry SCIENCE AND ART TO INDUSTRY AND COMMERCE, and that a civil servant was the noblest work of God – next to the aristocracy. He also thought that the British Empire was the supreme manifestation of the Divine Will. But he was sincere, exact and serious according to his lights, so he didn't last very long. (Incidentally his memorial in London is a supreme example of the kind of bad design of which he was the patron).

Up to Albert's time the artists and the scientists (two names for the same thing) had worked out their ideas for the love of it, as indeed they have always done and always will. But it was Albert who made the match between SCIENCE AND ART and INDUSTRY AND COMMERCE whose misbegotten progeny are with us still. It was a time of bunkum in excelsis. There was no God but Business and Free Trade was his prophet. Art and Science – two brilliant lads to be sure, but not to be trusted – were to be safely married off (no love of course, but plenty of money) and good uncle civil service would look after the double *ménage in saecula saeculorum*. That was eighty years ago and now the family estate is in the hands of the bailiffs, and neither the people behind the scenes in the British Empire nor in any other Empire know where to look for the next move. Fortunately that need not concern us, if we use the brains we have, and develop a system as we can do, that will be suitable to our national psychology.

Admitting for the sake of argument that a School of Art is not merely one of a number of similar machines, intended to produce designers and teachers of design, and official artists whose job it is to advertise the ideals of Empire and Privilege and Rank and Big Business and all the rest of it – but a cradle for the development of a national culture, and supposing that we want such a thing, have we got it? I don't think so.

The system initiated by Albert, our system up to the present day, is, when you come to analyse it, an attempt to manufacture Art, and the manufactured product bears the same relation to art that margarine does to butter – the synthetic as compared to the natural. The vitamins are lacking, and we cannot feed on it.

At this point I imagine laughter at the grotesque analogy, but let me add that a hen knows more about the making of eggs than all the chemists that ever concocted egg-powder, but she knows it in a different way, and she couldn't tell you how she does it, and there is no reason why she should, but when you want eggs you go to a hen. All she wants is a nest and enough to eat.

It is the same with art. Get one or more artists, put them in their natural surroundings, give them food and shelter and as the Cork man said: 'Let Nature take her course'. Then you will get pictures and statues and books and music. The artists will bring forth fruit in season. That fruit will come straight out of the earth. It will be made of the land from which we spring. Its flavour will be of the soil of Ireland, and we can feed it spiritually and keep our physical health – for not by bread alone doth Man live.

Or we can do the other thing. We can raise chickens in ever-heated incubators, and feed them on foreign food, and keep them from the wind and the sun and the rain – the devil an egg will ever be laid or, if it is, it will have a foreign flavour.

The worst element of our present system is that is exalts the system at the expense of the aim. As long as the machine is revolving, as long as the students are passing examinations which lead nowhere (except to poorly paid jobs as teachers), so long is the end considered to be attained. Early in its career the system became a mere copy factory. You haven't anything to say? Well, copy the renaissance and improve your taste – or copy the Gothic, or the Moorish or the Chinese. Nowadays it is the Egyptian, West African, South Sea Islands or the Eskimo, – never thinking that all these styles were evolved by people, often quite simple and primitive, who were intensely national and individual, because they had never heard or dreamt of being anything else. We could start now and in twenty years have something as utterly Irish as the Chinese is Chinese. Where would we start? In the Gaelteacht – with white-wash and thatch, and red and white flannel, and black shawls, and rush bottomed chairs and baskets.

Out of the rocks and sky and the native language, and the noble forms and proportions of the people's faces all the rest will come. Heretofore when such a proposition was advanced it used to be said: 'What! Turn ourselves away from European culture? Turn our backs on the wonderful achievement of the machine age? Nonsense.'

Well, it seems to me that we have no choice. European culture and the machine age have given us the Great War, the Treaty of Versailles, thirteen years of neurasthenia, war debts and influenza – and now the Great Slump. And in the realm of Art where, at least, one might have hoped to find a refuge for the humanities, with what a flood of nonsense, chaos, ugliness, have we been bedevilled? What charlatans, mountebanks and imposters have got away with it during the last thirteen years? The Gadarene Swine are in full cry, and it is time for us in Ireland to call a halt.[288]

We are adding to our manpower at the rate of fifteen thousand a year. We are piling up a flood of energy that must find an outlet. Heretofore the flower of our people, the man of energy and ambition, the man who wished to live fully, who wanted to rid himself of his inferiority complex – all cleared out at the first opportunity. And the opportunity was never lacking for very long, because he who wants a chance badly enough makes it for himself, so that we have had hitherto an undue proportion of the timid and non-adventurous in our population – the sort of people who take the line of least resistance. So that life was for the greater number dull and sad. That is going to stop. It is a long lane that has no turning, and we have reached the turn. There is no reason why we should not have a renaissance – not a literary cultus merely, but a quickening of the national consciousness over the whole field of existence. Always in Ireland Art has been patronized *de haut en bas*. As long as you didn't 'get fresh' as the Americans say, you could always get a cup of ascendancy tea, and sometimes an ascendancy sandwich, or a stale ascendancy cigarette – or you could be sure of a remark or two in the best Oxford Irish. If you were an aboriginal, and could not find anywhere in your ancestry a Cromwellian or a turn-coat, if you were the sort of person whose progenitors had had to choose between Hell and Connacht, if you didn't like being patted on the head, you had to get out of Ireland – and you generally did. If you were innocent enough to think that you might live in Ireland as an artist, you found that the price in loss of self-respect was too heavy to pay. One could not flourish in that atmosphere of back-drawing room treason, Oxford Irish and intellectual fox-hunting imperialism. But now that snobocracy is up against the ropes and one punch will finish it.

I repeat that we are not going to build a national culture out of the debris of the ascendancy. The Ireland that is emerging will not be fully satisfied with fox-trotting to the Hamitic rhythms of the saxophone – nor will it sit puzzling in the moral blackness of the picture-house, over the blanks left by the Censor in stuff that ought to have been condemned *en bloc* – for mere imbecility.

It will not be satisfied to read the wretched dope that comes to us from the heart of Empire – not because it is British, but because it is blither. It will not be satisfied to go to highbrow theatres run by cliques who think that they are improving the drama when they are only depressing the audience.

Where will Young Ireland turn for the food of the mind? Let us first learn to speak Irish – that will put the tin hat on the language of Carmelite Street, the medium through which the Empire expresses its want of a creed. Not ENGLISH, the tongue of

---

[288] Keating refers to the 'Gadarene Swine Fallacy'. It is the fallacy of supposing that because a group is in the correct formation that it is therefore on the right course. Moreover it is the fallacy of presuming that that if an individual is not in formation with the group, that he or she is off course.

Shakespeare, Pope and Addison, but the BRITISH language – the language of advertisements addressed to anxious couples in search of furniture on easy-payment, and beauty ready-made in a box, with full directions for sixpence-halfpenny – so that every factory girl can marry a millionaire, the language of the motor-car blurb, the patent lie about patent medicines for baldness, fatness, plainness and old age – written by office boys FOR office boys.

I have a picture in my mind of an Ireland, self-supporting, self-confident and self-respecting – an Ireland rid of idlers and wage-slaves, an Ireland with an economic equilibrium that could be trusted to stay put – where the Ivar Kreugars and the war-monger kings of the millionaire press would have no power to rob, kill and corrupt the citizens.[289] I imagine a time when Bulls and Bears will have joined the lion and the unicorn in the limbo of forgotten things, a time when the awful doctrine of every man for himself and devil take the hindmost – that damnable first article of the creed of all imperialists and money-grubbers – will stand revealed as an insult to man's intelligence. That doctrine does not work, as we see today. The hereditary fools at the top, the hypocrites in the middle and the slaves at the bottom may very shortly be striving together for a piece of bread. And when that day of wrath is come, where shall we stand in Ireland unless we begin now to make Ireland a land fit for Irishmen to live in.

The only kind of man for whom I care anything is he who produces with his hands or out of his brain, something that wasn't there before that other human beings can use or enjoy. So far reason has been exalted over instinct. Where have abstract philosophy and speculative reasoning led us, but up to our eyes in the Slough of Despond. For that reason I look forward to a sort of life dominated by artists and engineers. Of the two sorts I think the artist the more valuable to the nation. Don't laugh until you hear why I think so. Up to the present the engineer has done more to enrich the millionaire, and to make war more destructive, than to release humanity from the slavery of monotonous work. The capitalist has always bought him and put him and fruits of his genius in his pocket. The capitalist has never troubled himself about the artist. He isn't a proposition as the Americans say, until he is dead. And so the artist can look the Empire finance conspiracy in the face, and see it for what it is and tell the truth about it. And if you want an anti-toxin for hum-bug you will get it from the artist. If it is worthwhile to keep dogs at the Pasteur Institute to supply a serum for the cure of rabies which kills individuals – and that rarely – why not have a pack of artists to provide a serum against economic and financial rabies, which destroys whole nations by recurrent epidemics of war and starvation.

---

[289] Ivan Kreugar was a Swedish businessman known as The Match King. He was director of Kreugar and Toll, a multi-million dollar match (for lighting cigarettes) conglomerate. The stocks for the company were popular in America but after the financial crash in 1929 it was revealed that Kreugar had been operating a pyramid selling scheme. The company went bankrupt in 1932 and investors lost millions of dollars. Kreugar was found dead in March of that year.

I have a plan for the foundation of such an institute in Ireland. It would cost a twelfth of what we spend on Art with poor results as at present, and I shall be very happy to describe it to anybody who wants to hear how it could be done.

Art Does Not Get a Chance in Ireland!

by Sean Keating, RHA. [Response to the question 'Is there any rage in you against our cultural shortcomings? – Published in *The Irish People*, (Muinntear na h-Eireann), 29 February 1936, p. 4]

Much has been written and argued about the necessity for a national culture; ways have been pointed out by which culture could be promoted speedily and cheaply and with existing personnel and equipment.

Having seen the promise of better things dawn and fade more than once under the new regime, I conclude that these arguments and proposals have not succeeded because they were premature. The word CULTURE with all that it implies is still in Ireland one of the Cant terms that go to make up the democratic intellectual vocabulary – that liturgy or humbug which has to be recited at public functions, like prayers at the opening of legislative assemblies, or speeches at Private Views or Public Dinners.

As a step towards bringing about a state of things in which art would flourish – as part of the life of the common people – we would have to begin by eliminating this cultural liturgy and talk of pictures and books and buildings frankly and sincerely as we do of bread and boots. Hitherto the discussion of cultural questions has implied an attitude *de haut en bas*. This attitude is a mixture of Liberalism, Nonconformist Conscience with its insistence on social betterment, and Trade Unionism with its inevitable underdog complex. Individuals of those groups are often sincere and high-minded, but they have a tail of legal reformers, anti-vivisectionists, culture hounds, up-lifters, elaborators, nosy parkers and Protestants with a small P – and that tail often wags the dog.

It is in the modern democratic tradition that ministers of governments should always pretend to consult and be advised by such bodies of opinion, and in so far as this does not interfere with the real business of getting into power and remaining there, they do consult and take advice and even act upon that advice, provided it does not cost too much or otherwise interfere with 'practical' matters. Art is, I suppose, the outcome of man's desire to impose his concept of order on the beauty of the world, to bring it into line with his idea of logic and reason, and thus to make the sensation of pleasure recur at will. This may not be a good definition – all definitions are necessary evils – evils because they limit and perhaps distort, but necessary in so far as they make analysis possible.

First in any intelligent operation comes the question of precedence in order of importance. What has to be done first and why? Assuming that a reaction to beauty is in part a reaction from ugliness, that a notion of order arises from a notion of disorder, it would seem to follow that in Ireland we are not taking the first step first, because there is no evidence to show that we do hate disorder, but very much to the contrary. We condone and accept ugliness in many forms and that even in personal matters easily in our power to alter. If this is admitted it follows that we in Ireland have a lot to do to clean the windows and sweep the floor and kill off the parasites and arrange for the ventilation and free circulation of ideas, and do whatever is necessary to make the place habitable before we start on the decorations. As long as we permit little boys of ten to push loaded bicycles through traffic or dress them in silly uniforms and stand them at swing doors we have no right to think of art. As long as we condemn young women (future mothers of the race) to stand behind counters all day to sell tawdry fal-lals to tasteless old women from ugly suburbs, we have no right to think of art. As long as we permit lying advertisements worded in revolting terms to cheat sick and frightened people out of money for nostrums, we have no right to think of art.

As long as we permit anyone who thinks himself a builder to run up an ugly structure in any place that suits him for any purpose – however unnecessary – we have no right to think of art. As long as private interest can postpone or defeat schemes for improvement or draw rents from slums, we have no right to think of art. As long as we build hospitals in noisy and depressing slums and let private jealousies defeat necessary and obvious amalgamations and constantly protect privilege and authority against reason and common sense, we have no right to think of it. As long as the whole mental background of the people is formed on the concept of a remorseless struggle for existence presided over by an angry god or (for those who dislike the god hypothesis) by a soulless machine – the State, there is no room for beauty or culture. You might as well hope to grow flowers on the floor of a slaughterhouse.

How can we expect people who have grown up stunted and warped by fear of authority and fear of want, pushed headlong into the first job that offers, intimidated and frustrated all their days, to have any faculty or desire to exercise the right to choose?

If a man lacks the desire to choose a wife or a house or clothes or a job that would suit HIM, is he likely to choose pictures or books or the good use of his free time? And if he cannot or does not want to do so, what then becomes of art or culture?

The assumption that freedom in any real sense exists in the modern democratic state is false. Try it, and you will find out. There is the freedom of the prison yard – the freedom to choose between a black eye and a kick in the pants if you break the rules. Who wants to live in such a world? Certainly not artists. Not that that would make any difference to the propagation of art and culture as presently understood. All the artists could be hanged or otherwise eliminated tomorrow, and art and culture would flourish as before – official art run by official democratic machinery could and would operate in a vacuum. There are too many interests involved for it to be allowed to stop. There are ministries of art, chairs of art, schools of art, art galleries with staff and equipment all complete, books on art, art periodicals, writers, critics, dealers, social climbers and all the rest.

And that mysterious entity – the People – for whose benefit all this expensive and imposing façade is supposed to be maintained, would still pass by in a hurry about their business, and neither know nor want to know anything at all about it.

If I were Director of Broadcasting

by John Keating, RHA. [Broadcast November 14 1936]

If I were Director of Broadcasting – I wouldn't be Director unless I could be Dictator as well, in view of the reforms which I would ordain. The job would be like that of a strong-minded nursery governess who takes over the management of the unruly children of a nouveau riche family. We can reconstruct the scene, say little Tommy's birthday party. The floor is littered with expensive mechanical toys, into the making of which has gone much thought and a high degree of intelligence and imagination. The children, bored and excited at the same time, are eating over-rich and varied food that they don't want. They have lost the taste for simple things, because ignorant and excessive variety has been their normal regime. There are vulgar comic papers, story books with elaborate, sophisticated illustrations, a gramophone, a mechanical piano-player, wireless etc., provided under the delusion that the more gadgets the greater the enjoyment. There are crackers, bonbons, light, noise, indigestion and ill-temper. That is the picture I have in my mind of the worlds of listeners. Anybody who has lived in a large family knows the difficulties of making arrangements for anything – whether it is what to have for breakfast, or where to go for an outing, or any other question which may have to be decided. In practice this difficulty can be solved in either of two ways. Either the most selfish person goes for what he wants and the others acquiesce, or everybody gives in to everybody else, with the result that nobody is pleased.

Something like this happens in broadcasting, when the rival claims of everybody to have what he wants are put against the rival claims of everything for a share of attention and award. Then one cancels the other out and nobody is pleased. I would eliminate all that by being exactly what I wished myself, and incidentally I might please a few other people.

Now it seems to me that you only get real fun out of something which is hard to get, and which you have wanted for a long time – something in which you are sufficiently interested to bring to its enjoyment some degree of attention when you do get it. It is like smoking. If you smoke only when the wish to do so becomes insistent, you then enjoy it. If you smoke because everybody else is smoking, or because you are bored, or from mere habit, or because you are not a separate human individual – conscious of what you want and why, or for any reason other than the fact that you feel a pressing need to smoke; then a potential source of legitimate pleasure becomes a joyless mechanical habit. It is the same with wireless. To put an endless opportunity for choice before people who have no desire to choose, and no preference to guide them if they had, is to make a choice impossible. It simply leads to knob twiddling and dissatisfaction. I believe that if the variety were restricted, and the supply curtailed, that people would be obliged to choose as a result of preference decided upon under pressure and in advance with a great heightening of attention and enjoyment as a result – a gain to all concerned.

The energy devoted to the seeking of endless variety on the part of the Director could be censored and put to better use in searching for quality. If one orders a good dinner, and gives a certain amount of thought to choosing the different courses, he shouldn't spoil it by tea and snacks beforehand.

Broadcasting, as I see it, is a reflection of the times. The Public is assumed to have certain wants which it is the Director's job to satisfy. The Public – that mysterious entity – with whom nobody has ever come to grips, only manifests itself by symbols, such as; 'they say', 'it is believed', 'people think', 'it wouldn't do at all', etc., a kind of mirage which dissolves at close quarters.

That is why, if I were director, I should have to be Dictator too. Dictators have no illusions about what the public wants. They waste no time in pretending to consult the people. They satisfy the need to be ordered about and told what to think which arises from not wanting or not being able to think for oneself. And it is a question whether good comes into the lives of the people through the activities of energetic and domineering men who know what they want, or through the activities of those who approach their aims by means of appeals to reason, commonsense, justice, liberty and other abstractions – ideas of which there is no evidence to show that the public has any grasp at all. Dictators don't have any doubts, don't have to argue, are never contradicted, are the idols of the people, get photographed every day, have large lumps of property given to them, and have great fun in every way. All that their country has to offer of beauty, luxury and grandeur is theirs for the taking – with a little beating and killing thrown in if they should feel bored. Radio Dictatorship would get rid of that ridiculous, antiquated, reactionary figment – the Public and how to please it. It is so simple, so obvious, [and] so reasonable that it hasn't the slightest chance of being instituted. Nevertheless it would save people from the mental anguish of having to make up their minds, and would relieve them of the intolerable burden of having to think and act for themselves. In return the Dictator would claim license to contradict himself and be illogical as often and as completely as he liked (after all, what is Truth? And hence, what is logic?).

Assuming myself in the position of Dictator, it would be part of my procedure to close down completely every now and then, at times known to myself, and with such modifications as I thought fit, in order to recall to the public that wireless programmes are an amenity and in a sense a privilege, and not a natural phenomenon like the sun's light. It is amusing to think of the fury caused by the withdrawal of something which is not necessary at all, which the one who habitually enjoys has done nothing to deserve, and which a little time previously was quite undreamt of. This notion is an offspring of the idea that anything can be bought if you have the money to pay for it – irrespective of any moral, physical, social or other values attaching to it or to the purchaser.

Since I think this notion quite wrong, I would, as Radio Dictator, try to find out what intelligent people wanted, and give them half of it at rare intervals to make it more valuable. I should institute a 'Bureau of Grievances' where people could let off steam – but only if they were such as rage makes eloquent. I should claim for their utterances parliamentary immunity. It would be more amusing than the Dáil, because the speaker's time would be limited, his indignant eloquence would be genuine as compared to professional, and, if necessary, we could always arrange for a 'technical hitch'. The people with a grievance would not be paid, but would gladly pay for a chance to let go, before an audience consisting of the whole nation – as they imagine. Because it is a delusion cherished by people with broadcasting that everyone listens in, whereas thousands and thousands do not. And thousands and thousands more turn on the wireless and do not listen either.

I should like to have some sort of attachment on every set whereby listeners would be prevented from changing in the middle of an item, or cutting somebody off because they didn't like his voice, or his views – until they had put a penny in the slot. The money thus collected could be expended on the publication of a paper – giving the interrupted details in full, and the names of the interrupters – collected from the sets along with the money. These names could be published with their owner's views, as a kind of counter-fan mail. Or the listeners could indulge their bad manners, and want of respect for the performers, and evade publication, by pressing a button and inserting a further penny in the machine. Because, after all, if you distribute synthetic amusement by machinery to people who aren't interested, why not turn their boredom and internal vacuity to account – as is done at railway stations – and provide automatic machinery which will separate them from their petty cash by means of little knobs.

I would institute a change of venue for listening in too – for instance, a lunatic asylum on a moonlight night, a country dispensary, a pawnshop, a public house at closing time on Friday night, lunch hour on a building site, the direction of a film in the making – dealing with a temperamental star, a newspaper office during a general election, or the cross-examination of a lying witness (if there is such a thing) in a case of assault and battery, a tramcar to Inchicore on a rainy Saturday in Winter, a guard on point duty at O'Connell Bridge rebuking a driver from the country. Or we could have a big steamer getting away from the docks on a rough day – donkey, engine, crew, captain, pilot on bridge, harbour-master, tug-boat, quay-side loungers etc. Assuming that the essential quality of drama is its power to evoke feelings of pity and terror, and further assuming that drama is a high form of entertainment, I would exploit it to the full in my programme of broadcasting.

I think it a waste of time, however, to go on the lines that broadcasting drama consists of – effects contrived in the studio – steam-whistles, horses galloping, the howling of the gale, the pouring out of a drink etc. I should prefer to broadcast the drama of daily life in its lesser known aspects, or perhaps I should say, its common aspects seen from an unusual angle. With sound effects, characterization, drama, horror, suspense, fear, anxiety – all complete and genuine – a hundred per cent verity instead of verisimilitude. There would be a magnificent crop of nervous break-downs and hysterics as a result, but nobody could complain that the program was dull. In addition to running commentaries on football matches, motor races, boxing contests etc., I should stage for instance, a broadcast of a critical surgical operation. The commentator should of course be an able man. One can imagine something of the thrill we should get from the introductory remarks –the brief, dramatic description of the scene, the rustling of the starched overalls, the clattering of instruments, the staccato remarks, [and] the atmosphere of nervous strain. Like this: 'The surgeon is now making the incision – something is wrong – no, no, it is all right – now he is pushing back the subcutaneous what-you-callum – clip, tie, clip – another clip. The patient is being kept under with great difficulty – his breathing isn't good (close up of breathing, [and] possibly heart action as heard by the stethoscope). The surgeon is working against time – now the anaesthetist is looking very anxious – hurry up – I can't give him much more – hold on, I haven't got it yet – well, I can't risk it – you've got to risk it – ha, here it is – swab, scissors – hurry up, a nurse has just toppled over' and so on.

Then there is something completely rotten in a state of things which permits nothing provocative, contentious, heterodox or disrespectful to authority to be said. Criticism is a tonic, a purgative, a febrifuge and an antiseptic. It is fatal to fools and cowards – but good for healthy organisms. To forbid it on the grounds that it can be abused is to drive it underground, lower the quality of it, give a monopoly of it to rascals and do generally what prohibition did to alcohol in America, with terrible results. The results of license are awful – but not so awful as the results of complacency, and immunity from the necessity to defend a point of view. For this reason I would promote discussions and controversies on everything under the sun [and] the more acrimonious the better. One never knows how much illumination can come out of a royal row, until one has tried it. What endless complications would be unravelled and misunderstandings cleared up; what suspicions dispelled or justified, what wrongs righted, if only people told the Boss what they tell their wives they told him. This is very obvious and banal, of course, but it is the Director's job to tell the people what they already know if they would give themselves the trouble to think.

These radio rows would afford an opportunity to gladden the ears of the English-speaking world, with our magnificent vocabulary of abuse – [a] gracious offspring of the marriage of Elizabethan sonority with the rich imagination of the Gael. It might even be found possible to collect the choicer efforts and print them in a little book for the use of the fillers up of Income Tax Forms, or the Post Office might print them on forms for the use of families, as they do in America – where you can send a telegram ranging from 'love and best wishes' for 25 cents to the 'song of Solomon' for one dollar fifty, for the use of those whose command of eloquence is not equal to the intensity of their feelings – or whose social betterment is impeded by the want of knowing the proper thing to say.

In my programmes I would cut down music to a minimum. There is a kind of general impression in people's minds that music and entertainment are synonymous, and with this I don't agree. I think that music is an unsatisfactory substitute for fooling and thinking and that – as a means of killing time – it is a little inferior to novel reading. I wonder how many people agree with me – or would agree with me if they were not intimidated by fearing to appear uncultivated, or wanting in sensibility if they were to say quite frankly want it means – or fails to mean – to them. From this rule I would exempt the music of Handel, Back, Scarlatti, some of Gluck, some of Beethoven and Boccherini. And I'd boycott music in proportion to its distance from the formal pattern music of the 18th century. Wagner I consider as an example of what unrestrained romanticism can do on a great intellect. Debussy is just a wet Sunday evening among the Elgin Marbles.

I make these remarks well knowing the howls of rage that will result, but it must be one of the most delightful privileges of a Dictator to be able to put out the greater part of his tongue at the populace, instead of having to keep it between his teeth out of respect for the feelings and opinions of others.

So instead of music I would promote discussions such, for instance, as would arise if a musician were to reply to my remarks. (Of course, as a Dictator, I wouldn't dream of letting him do any such thing). The public – who probably weep secret tears of boredom at recitals would come to life and begin to enjoy themselves as they heard the argument proceed from deadly politeness at the beginning, to the crash that tells the audience that the microphone has been knocked over.

I forgot to mention that in the event of my being appointed Director of Broadcasting; I should require to be given – not only the powers of Dictator, but also a steamer ticket to an unknown destination, a supply of get-away money and an armed escort to the nearest port of embarkation.

Talk to Children

by John Keating, RHA. [Broadcast October 28 1937]

I am going to talk to you about Art. I know that generally when grown-ups talk to children, the children find them hard to understand, because the big people use long words and talk about dull things, and, most of all, they hate to be asked questions.

Now I think that children must ask questions because there is such a lot that they want to know, and they have no way to find out but to ask. Of course you'll think that it is easy for me to say that now, because I am talking through a microphone and you can't talk back to me. But what I would like is if we could all go for a walk on a fine day, and talk as we went along the road. But that can't be either. Because there would be too many of you and only one of me – and we only have ten minutes anyhow, so I must hurry.

Well, I remember when I was young, I liked pictures and drawings better than anything else – except playing in the open air. I was very bad at school, except at reading and composition and learning poetry. In those days things weren't nice at school. I haven't been in a school now for a long time, but my children tell me a lot about their school, and things seem different and much better. Their class rooms are nice and bright and warm, and they don't have to eat their lunch out of a school bag, but have tables and chairs to sit at, and there is a stove where somebody makes them hot drinks at lunch-time in winter. Their classes are not all on arithmetic and geography and things like that. Some lessons are about animals and flowers and they make things out of wood and coloured paper, and they paint them and model things in plasticine, and they have little gardens of their own, where they sow whatever seeds they like – and so on. All this, I think, is very good, because everybody, young or old, has a right to be happy; unless his or her way of being happy interferes with the happiness of other people or animals. But the one thing that I think is more important than almost anything else in life, is that people should be honest and sincere. When they are asked what they like they shouldn't begin to think of what they OUGHT to like, or what answer is expected of them, and they should never say yes when they mean no. You may think that all that has nothing to do with Art, but I'm coming to that.

When I was at school, children and big people too seemed to have got the idea from somewhere that if you didn't like things like pictures and music and poetry, you were ignorant and stupid. They thought too that a man that worked in an office or a shop was a nicer kind of man than one who worked in the fields or in a factory or workshop. They also thought in those days that it was better to pretend to be a little richer and grander that you really were, and people used to try to talk like the English which was very silly. Then everybody pretended that they were interested in paintings and books and music – whether they were or not. Now I want to tell you that you should never pretend to know or like anything if you don't really, and that there is no reason to be ashamed if you would rather be making hay than reading books, or – if you are a girl – that you would rather be knitting yourself a jumper than listening to music. One sort of work is just as good as another, if it is useful. One sort of accent is just as good as another, if you don't make mistakes in grammar. A mechanic or a carpenter or a farmer is just as good a man as a civil servant or a clerk or a shop-keeper. A solicitor is no better than a civic guard – nor worse than a judge; that is if he is a good man and knows his job.

Most of us, big and little, have to do everyday things we don't like – tiresome, dull things, but everybody ought to try to find out while he is young what he does like, so that when he grows up he won't have to spend his life doing something he doesn't like in order to make a living. Making money is not much good if you hate the work you make it at. Because most of your life will be spent at the job, and only a little bit of it in enjoying the money you earn. But if you love your work, you are happy and the time flies. You know how it is when you are playing, and it is bed-time before you have played enough. Well when you are at work you like, it is just like that. You only stop because you are tired or hungry or because night has come. There are thousands and thousands of jobs to be done in the world when you grow up, and a big choice – if only people didn't think that it is bad to have to dirty your hands or take off your coat or put on an apron to do it. There is also an idea that it is a finer thing to work with your brain than with your hands – but that is not true. There are some people I know who seem to have all their brains in their hands, and very useful people they are too. Anyway, the world needs both the people who think things out and the people who do things. I am always painting and drawing because I like it, and I took it for my trade because I liked it better than anything else. But my sons don't want to be painters. One wants to be a mechanic, because he loves machinery and understands it, the other doesn't know yet what he wants. He is interested in a lot of things – in the meaning of strange words and in people and in reasoning about things. He might grow up into the kind of man who thinks things out and tells other people what to do when they want advice. Anyway they are both going to work at whatever they like best.

Now there is a thing called Art that I started to tell you about. People spell it with a capital A when they want it to mean only paintings and statues and music, but I think there is artistry in anything that is done with great skill, and that carpenters and blacksmiths as well as dancers and actors and story-tellers can be artists if they are experts. All real art is produced by people who like doing it – firstly because they like doing it and secondly, to give pleasure to people's' minds. You know when you eat sweets, or come in to a warm fire on a cold day that it gives pleasure to your body. Well, people find as they grow up that their minds like pleasure too, and that is where Art comes in. A few feel that they want to produce art themselves – to play the music or paint the pictures or write the books. But the greater number – no matter what their job in life is – enjoy the result of the artist's work. And every one of you listening to me will probably begin to enjoy some form of art. With some it will be listening to music; with some it will be looking at paintings or handsome buildings or plays or expert dancing. And if you discover what form of art appeals to you personally, and if you see or hear as much as you can of it, until you begin to appreciate the best in that particular form of art

– then you can look forward to a lot of pleasure in your life that you would otherwise have missed. But you won't get any fun out of it unless you really like it. It is no good to have to pretend you do; that only bores you and makes you hate it. When I was young there was an idea that all really 'nice' children had to learn to play the piano or to be able to sing a little song for visitors – whether they had any real taste for music or not. And the child who could play his or her little piano piece on the piano was considered far superior to the one who was only an expert with a skipping rope or at a high-jump. Yet I think that to watch an athletic boy sailing over a high-jump like a bird, or a graceful girl skipping like a ballet-dancer gives more aesthetic pleasure – that is pleasure to the mind of the audience – than the second-rate playing or singing of a child who has not much ear for music.

But to come back to my own job, which is pictures. If you have never taken much notice of the pictures you see around you in your homes or at school, I want you to look at them. You may not like them, but they are not the only pictures in the world, so don't decide straight away that pictures are dull things and an unnecessary waste of wall space. There is a Society in Dublin that sends prints of good pictures to schools throughout the country. They know the kind of pictures that children – and grown-ups too –generally like. There are also books that can be bought in parts that come once a month and cost about a shilling. They have good pictures in colour that have been painted by good artists and picked out for these books by people who know what is good.

To know and like good pictures used to be a thing only for the rich. But now, because good prints and books on Art are cheap, and because there are picture galleries in Dublin, Cork and Limerick (and other towns will soon have them) children living in the country can see good pictures. But remember not to let anyone shame you into pretending that you like them if they mean nothing to you. There is more pretence (I think) about Art than about any other activity in the world, and there is no reason that I can see for that pretence. There is almost sure to be some form of skill or expert work that will interest each of you. Stick to that – and don't despise others who happen to have different tastes.

'The Voice of One'

by John Keating, RHA. [Published in *The Leader,* December 17, 1938, pp. 391-393. Broadcast, with minor changes, as 'Another Talk on Art', November 28 1931]

Art is probably a legitimate and respectable pursuit in itself, but it has about it an attraction, a glamour, a legend that puts it in the same class as Hy Brasil, Perpetual youth and the Philosopher's stone – something too good to be true, or something so good that it must be a sin. The public buzzes round like bees round a hollyhock, full of real interest in Art and Artists as known in cinemas, theatres and novels – and full of pretended interest in *real* art and artists. When they find that the real artist does not live up to the film producers' conception of him, either in the speed with which he produces masterpieces, or in the numbers of his creditors and amours, they are disappointed and annoyed. They almost begin to shout for their money back – until they remember that they haven't given any.

There is another reason for the existence of popular misconceptions about art and artists. It is the amiable habit that most artists have of giving a silly answer to a silly question, the silly answer that turns curiosity into wrath when the inquirer has had time to think it over. And in return for having had his leg pulled, he dismisses the artist, saying to himself, 'ah, he is just a clever fool'. It may be argued that the Artist's own conduct in this case is inexcusable. But is it any worse than might be expected from a member of any other trade or profession in similar circumstances? The difference is that the people in other jobs are protected against such circumstances. I imagine that an operation performed by a skilful surgeon must be very interesting to watch, but I know that an operating theatre is a Holy of Holies into which no one is admitted except those whose business is to be there. Imagine the feelings of the surgeon if the patient's mother-in-law were to stand at his elbow discussing his every move with him, in what she imagined to be technical language acquired from the study of *A Thousand Medical Hints*, or *Home Surgery for All*. Yet this is analogous to what happens to artists every other day. Hence the silly answers to the silly questions – leg-pulling as a means of self-defence. This sort of thing, for instance: Some old lady (of either sex) who thinks art is *so* interesting meets a painter. Being a victim of the delusion that artists eat, drink and breathe nothing else but art, she begins with some banal compliment, and to impress him with her intelligent interest ask: 'And tell me, do you use varnish?' The painter who knows perfectly well that she cares nothing for painting (why should she?) instead of saying, 'Stupid woman, go to the devil,' says, 'That as a matter of fact is the whole secret – very clever of you to have noticed it. Yes I do use varnish, but it is a rather special kind.' 'Oh, how exciting, tell me.' 'Well since you're interested, I will, but don't pass it on.' 'Oh no, indeed I won't' 'Well, then, my varnish is made of Stockholm tar, treacle, rotten eggs, cod liver oil and formalin. The Stockholm tar is to supply the resin. The treacle is to give it body and colour. The rotten eggs (are) to supply the sulphurated hydrogen, in order to prevent the coal-gas products in the air from attacking the metallic oxides in the paints and turning them black. The cod liver oil is to prevent the mixture drying too quickly. The formalin is to kill off the microbes attracted by the other ingredients and to neutralize the smell of the eggs.'

If she laughs, you can then converse with her as a human being. If she swallows the information, it is a thousand to one that she rushes off to tell everybody. Nothing will be lost in the telling; and thus one more brick is added to the façade of Bunk in Art.

Take another type of inquirer – suppose a 'Photographic Artist' who thinks it would increase business, and distinguish him from mere photographers if he could supply his patrons with 'genuine hand-painted portraits'. He goes to the School of Art, interviews the authorities, pays his fees, gets his receipt, time-table, dockets, tickets, schedules, syllabus, etc. Everything is simple and straightforward as can be. He wonders why he didn't do it long ago. No fussy preliminaries. No stupid questions. No entrance examination. Everybody [is] polite, helpful and optimistic. And the fees are moderate. He thinks: how different from the pretentious formalities to which I should have to submit if I were entering for the study of law or medicine – or architecture or science, or almost any trade or profession. All kinds of impertinent questions about my ability, my previous studies, my general education, my financial resources should have had to be answered, and my entry would have cost me more pounds that I have just paid shillings. And he comes to the study of Art full of delightful anticipation. His reception at the threshold has been such as to cause him to forget that most excellent maxim 'blessed is he that expects nothing, for he shall not be disappointed'. But once in the Life Class, what a disillusionment! There is he with paints, brushes, boxes and palette, all the paraphernalia, everything that can be imagined in the way of apparatus. But he can make no progress. He asks questions such as, 'How do you paint a nose?' and expects to be told the formula, to be given the key.

Instead, he gets an answer which he can't understand. He flounders, idles, gets bored and gives it up – generally after three months, convinced for ever more that artists are cheats and mountebanks. They have a damned little trick. They promise to show it to you for money. They take your money. They show you the trick. But somehow you can't just get it. Of course what should have happened is this? The would-be painter should have had it explained to him at the outset that if he feels an irresistible impulse to paint or draw, and if he is prepared to work very hard all day and every day for about three years, he will then be able to judge for himself whether he has any ability or not. He should be told that private income sufficient to keep him in health is absolutely necessary. He should be told that an intense desire for expression is no proof of having anything to express. He should be told that a robust constitution and an endless resistance to mental and physical fatigue are essential. He should be advised to listen with docility and to be inflexible in holding to his own ideas at the same time. If he were to be told these things – all simply true, he would have gone away in a fury, convinced that he wasn't wanted, and that it was all trades union humbug.

Thus for one reason or another we have, on the side of the public, a notion that artists are – well, artists. Let us look at the artist's side of it. Not that I want to make any apologies for him, but merely to suggest some of the causes which might be responsible for his idiosyncrasies, real or imagined.

To begin with, there is his experience in a School of Art – that Mecca towards which he has been struggling since the first manifestations of his disease. This part of his existence is comparable to being skinned alive – a necessary operation because the art is presumed to be inside, under all the skins. It sometimes happens that when all the skins are removed there is no inside, and consequent on the process, no outside either. But it is a very fruitful process nevertheless, because in the course of it the searcher comes to be acquainted with many of the innumerable varieties of human folly and ineptitude as exhibited in himself and his fellow sufferers. He leaves behind him his hide, his hopes and his illusions, but acquires an indifference to human respect, a clear sense of personal values and a good-humoured cynical persistency. But a School of Art is not – like other training colleges and universities –a place where one's mania is investigated – chiefly by oneself. His instructors are 'akademikers' as the Germans say, elaborators, examination wallahs and the like, so that he tends to look over the fence of reputation and authority, and find nothing behind it but a lot of empty tin cans 'rusted with a vile repose' but still sticking to their labels. He spends the years of adolescence, half in a world of romantic dreams of beauty and ambition, and half like the India rubber cat with tallow legs, being chased through the hell of this world by the asbestos dogs of Time and Death. The years when he might have grown straight and strong in a kindlier environment are spent like a blind man in a dark room looking for a black cat which may be in that room – a good way to cultivate bleakness of outlook. One becomes acquainted with frustration and learns to dispense with the comforts of sentimentality. One is very poor, works very hard, and has no fun because fun is expensive. Later he discovers that the region of his mind most valuable to an artist is out of his power to exploit, because it consists of a large empty space of the extent and shape of that amount of humanism and culture which his progenitors did not absorb and assimilate during a period of about three hundred years. So that in order to have a future, he must provide himself with a past he must learn how to flourish in barren ground without the customary aid of roots. And thus he becomes a sinister caricature of what he might have been under humane conditions in fertile ground watered by tenderness, fed of beauty, sheltered by love, instead of which he lives in Heytesbury Street on a scholarship of £60 per annum, payable for ten months of the year. If you don't believe it, ask the Department of Education.

He begins to have reason to suspect that his culture – so dearly bought – is a second rate affair, an Ersatzkultur, an attempt to gatecrash Parnassus by claiming to have an acquaintance with the immortal gods based on a study of cheap plaster casts. He fears that he may unknowingly arrive at the state of that man who, when asked how he came and what he was, answered, 'I done it through striving for to self educate myself.' Having confined himself as part of his discipline to an exclusive diet of 'the unleavened bread of sincerity and truth', he finds that confectionery makes him ill, so that he is bad company at table. He regrets that he should have rationalized his poverty by pretending that he was practising austerity when he was enduring want and so robbed the situation of the only lesson that was in it – that poverty is a sin.

Later still he realizes that he has to have money in order to get some money. Comfortable people don't like the poor. They fear that they are going to be asked for a loan or get fleas, and they are quite right. It is no use saying 'I am hungry' or 'I am bored' or 'I lack cultivated feminine society': one must pay for these things, or seem to be able to do so.

Now the way for an artist to get money is to paint the Rich, and to get to paint the rich one has to have money and reputation. It is not so much a vicious circle as a barbed wire entanglement in the No-man's land of the financial system.

Having studied to be inexorable in the pursuit of truth – even against his natural sympathies – he becomes inevitably an iconoclast. And iconoclasts are not popular.

If the public would look upon artists as being also God's creatures and not merely the embodiment of a talent, to be hung up behind the door until required for use, and if artists would refrain from drawing overdrafts on people's tolerance and credulity, both parties would learn much about each other and it would be well for them to know. But that an artist can tell the public anything about Art I very much doubt. Art is an experience and not to be described. Trying to describe it is like trying to describe the taste of an egg. What the taste of an egg means to you and what it means to me could only be described to either of us by a third person who knew what it meant to each of us separately , as well as what it meant to him. Thus he would have a basis of comparison. But the taste of an egg is simply the taste of an egg, and we need to know no more. We can always produce the sensation with an egg.

The foregoing, which is self-evident nonsense, is the exact equivalent –minus the pretentious terminology – of discussions and writings and lectures about art. If you like eggs, eat eggs. And if you like art, look at pictures, sculpture, architecture. You will never know more about it than can come through your eyes to awaken what is in your heart. And if you don't feel anything when you look, go your way, and bless God that you have no heart to feel anything about anything very much or very long, having had it all frittered away in the process of growing up and 'getting on'.

A Spanking for 'Intellectuals'

by John Keating, RHA [Condensed from *The Leader* and published in *The Irish Digest*, March 1940, pp. 18-21.]

A famous artist puts certain unenviable people across his knees.

If I believed in argument – which I do not – I would support the view that people should be free to voice their likes and dislikes about everything, to give reasons for their preferences and to argue about them forever if they so pleased. But to voluntarily take on oneself the task of teaching or expounding to others is, I think, a mark of little intelligence.

The more people know the less convinced they are of the rightness or wrongness of anything. Ignorance, on the other hand, is confident. People who reason don't usually think that they do, because they think that mental discomfort is a mark of intelligence. The effort of most self-determined Intellectuals to understand things without the use of study and practice or natural ability involves them in a perpetual quarrel with their environment.

Their incapacity to do things well, to come to terms with their surroundings, to take a job and stick to it, to learn by experience, marks them, in their own eyes, as 'different' and better because in their own case they cannot distinguish between different and better. Looked at from this angle it is possible to explain why a great many critical, self-conscious people – highbrows, teachers and preachers etc. – are incapable of understanding their relation not only to Art but to life itself, sufficiently well to make a job of their personal existence –an incapacity which, if they were capable of judging impersonally, would prevent them from talking or writing.

One of the results of that sort of instruction out of books which is miscalled 'education' is to give people the illusion that they understand things because they are familiar with the names loosely applied to more obvious aspects or attributes of things.

Most people are familiar with that psychological dodge by which we evade the doing of unpleasant but inescapable things, by doing other less necessary things instead. I believe that this is the fundamental fact about the critic. His desire to improve and instruct is a measure of his unwillingness to tackle the job of finding out something about himself.

How many dogmatists, legalists, formalists, fanatics are there whose whole system is based on a subconscious, determined refusal to look into themselves and their relation to their environment, and thus find out why they are unhappy? They know – whether they admit it or not – that one's first job should be to improve oneself, to acquire skill, to practise patience and to bring forth fruit in season.

This discrepancy between the high sentiments and aspirations, and the absurd inefficiency and lack of continuity exhibited in the lives of so-called Intellectuals, is not due – as they think –to the difficulties created by the stupidity of the herd, but to their own incapacity to relate ideas to facts, to distinguish between things and the names of things, to realize the absurdity of trying to force living things into dead logical systems. Their mental distress arises from having to face again and again the necessity for overcoming obstacles from which they have recoiled before, and about which they refuse to think, which stand eternally in the way – inevitable yet insurmountable.

This is probably the explanation of that shocking display of envy, malice and all uncharitableness which shows itself in the conversation of Intellectuals. They have a large vocabulary, no knowledge of the technique of any single human activity, a perfunctory acquaintance with philosophical terms, a tendency to loose thinking, low power of attention, no insight nor continuity. One comes to the conclusion that the self-conscious Intellectual is a mental vacuum which Nature in her abhorrence has filled with all the sawdust, chips and shavings that result from the activities of the doers and makers of the world.

The fault of the Intellectuals lies not in the fact that they have unlimited access to the debris, but in that they consider that they have therefore a right to interfere in the direction of the machine without practical knowledge or skill or creative imagination. True, the more harmless Intellectuals choose to interest themselves exclusively in the Past. There everything may be treated as debris – subject to any system or classification that may be imposed upon it, however futile. Pre-digested food for weak minds.

Most people nowadays have not the slightest understanding of the system by which they exist. They would perish in a week if it broke down. But the first to perish would be the Intellectuals who (though they can discuss Economics) can see no further into the mysteries of bread and wine than the baker's van and the glass bottle. These people have the illusion of being competent and intelligent inversely as the complexity and artificiality of city life makes it difficult to apprehend in terms of reality.

Or to put it another way – in proportion as the necessity for understanding and being able to do simple things ceases to arise, so is the illusion created of understanding everything in minds not called upon at any time to exercise skill, knowledge, dexterity or practical imagination.

Everything comes out of a slot or out of a book or out of some apparatus, and if the machine sticks or the light goes out or the gadget won't work, then send for the technician whilst we discuss the Universe – whose laws, it is to be presumed, are at least as difficult to understand as the workings of a wireless-set. It is possibly a disaster for the human race that ability to read and recite inspires so much reverence as to entitle fools who are literate to be listened to with respect.

Whenever something superlatively silly is said in dignified language it is almost always by one pedant about another. For example: 'He took all knowledge for his province.' Imagine one technician saying of another: 'He took all dynamics – or all chemistry – for his province.'

It is to be noted that a state of ignorance and inefficiency unthinkable among ordinary workaday people has come to be the distinctive mark of pedantry and pedagogy – for example – the comic professor, the 'literary' man. What would be thought of the surgeon who left his instruments in the train, or the lawyer 'who penned a stanza when he should engross'?

It is possible that the universal respect attached to literacy is a hangover from the time when 'literate' and 'clerical' were synonymous – a reasonable view in a world which held as an article of religious belief that the then existing state of things was eternally and immutably right.

Later, in the 17th and 18th century, literacy was a part of the education of the upper classes to enable them to get more pleasure and interest out of their privileged position and guaranteed financial security. Literacy thus gained an additional reverence from the common man as the external mark of the enviable superior being. What literacy had lost on the religious swing it [then] gained on the aristocratic roundabout.

When – on the coming of the Machine Age or the so-called Industrial Revolution (wherein, by the way, nothing revolved but the machinery) – education of a cheap utilitarian sort began to be broadcast among the common people, it was only for the purpose of making them more efficient slaves, and not to enlarge their minds or teach them to think. And henceforward literacy began to lose both on the swings and the roundabouts. The common man began to find himself in the position of the South Sea Islander who said that he didn't like the missionary because he told him what a grand place Heaven was – 'ever so much better than the South Sea Islands –' and how nearly impossible it was to get there.

Alexander III emancipated the serfs and sent their sons to Universities, but did not foresee the necessity to provide a future for the need which his action had created. He was blown to pieces by a bomb, and his descendants perished at the hands of a mob tortured and maddened by visions of a life that they could imagine but not realise.

Nowadays kings and princes are gradually fading out or are being preserved only as museum pieces. It is unlikely that any more bombs will be wasted on them. Presidents must soon become vice-presidents to dictators – military or financial – or else submit to bureaucracies composed of gentlemen who have been educated out of books and not by contact with men and things – a world within a world, separated by training and temperament from the common man.

Meanwhile the Intellectuals go on talking about Art, Religion, Politics, Economy – everything. Nobody listens to them, and they don't listen to each other. And the common man – like the maddened beast in a forest fire – stands bewildered amid the glare and crash of falling bombs and shattered hopes, with nobody to lead him into the light.

This is where the Intellectual would like to intervene. But it is to be noted that, though the Intellectual is convinced that he understands the common man and is forever trying to improve and educate and uplift him; although he believes that the welfare of the 'masses' is pre-eminently his affair, the common man does not return this interest. He ignores the Intellectual; he resents him, despises and distrusts him because by his realistic factual standards the Intellectual is a renegade, a condescender, a parasite or a mountebank.

The workers will have to use their heads as well as their hands – and the Intellectuals their hands as well as their heads if the human race is to survive. Think or die. Work or rot.

I'd say that it would be better not to hang any picture than [to hang] a bad one: **The Art of Pictures from Eire**

by Seán Céitínn [Published in Irish in *The Irish Digest,* September 1940, pp. 89-91. Broadcast, with some minor changes, as 'Talk on the Future of Irish Art' June 9 1931]

As far as Art in Ireland was concerned, it had no foundation as a guide for literary archaeologists. No other country was as desolate as Ireland in regard to an artistic foundation or relics. Maybe you would try to contradict me by reminding me of the great Gospel of Colmcille. But the great Gospel of Colmcille is not really an Irish book. It belongs to the Age of the Monasteries. There were monks in other countries too who decorated their books with the ornamentation that we call Celtic ornamentation. And let's suppose that we, and we only, had that craft of ornamentation, would it be right for us to say that the visible beauty of the world should be reduced and diminished until it were something bloodless, lifeless, soulless, like a serpent and dry geometry – a Christian version of Moses' authoritative order: 'Do not carve images.'

I admit that we had, as had a lot of other countries, the Stone Age, the Bronze Age, the Age of the Monasteries and then – as far as Ireland was concerned – Nothing. When someone reminds us of the gloominess in the Irish way of life – the lack of beauty and luxury, the lack of variety regarding food and pastimes – the most usual reply is how miserable our history was; it's amazing the race survived at all considering how much the violence and the lawlessness hurt us. But is that a worthy excuse? If it were, and if it were a case that art and refinement depended on peace and great wealth, they wouldn't exist at all. Not only were the Italians attacking the French, the Austrians, the Turks but they were attacking each other. Every town was on the side of, or against, every other town. They never ceased fighting and even when peace was made; it was only to give them breathing space. But there's no doubt but that Art grew and flourished. There was no 50-year period in which France was at peace from the time she was declared a nation down until 1870 and the Age of the Third Republic.

Have a look at the Netherlands and the group of states that is called Germany today. They had to suffer the 100 Years War, the 30 Years War and small wars about religious issues. Despite that, there is not a country nor state among them that didn't do its best for great craftsmanship, painting, carving, music, plays, education, beautiful clothing, festivals, good cooking, not to mention good, strong, tasty drink – everything needed to make life happy and cheerful. Why aren't the country people of Sweden living in dark, sad, cold houses instead of being happy and comfortable in a lovely little carved and colourful house? Their country is poorer than ours and the climate in which they have to live is much worse.

Why are there at least one or two pictures in every City Office in the countryside in France, pictures that are worth seeing? Why are there carved wooden presses full of beautiful embroidered linens in the houses of poor workers in Germany? Have we anything that could compare to the passion play in Oberammergau? A play in which only farmers and poor carpenters take part? And if not, why not? Because it's clearly evident that we don't think it's worth it. If the tyranny and ill usage forced on us were an acceptable excuse for not having National Art, every country in Europe could have the same excuse.

It doesn't matter at all to someone in the end of the day whether it was foreigners or their next door neighbours who burned their house. As far as Ireland is concerned, the Black and Tans were no worse than Sarsfield. We are no less under a compliment to the Thomondites and the Fitzgeralds than we are to Henry VII.

The church was patron and guardian to the Fine Arts in other Christian countries – the ark in which everything we treasure and we like is kept. As for the storm of the dark age of ignorance – it didn't matter to the Church whether it was there or not, as far as this country was concerned. If you are doubtful about this, all you need to do is to look inside any church or chapel or cast an eye at the window of any Catholic depository. If it's said that, in these cases, certain parishes cannot afford to assist good art, the answer is that it's not the amount of the money but the lack of choice which is their biggest difficulty. I admit there are chapels, and beautiful chapels, where this is not the case and we have every hope that the numbers of chapels like those will increase.

When a copy of Michelangelo's *Virgin and Child* can be bought for 10 pounds, there is no excuse at all for buying a miserable, obscene, coloured trinket for 15 pounds, made by some student of the school of Ice Cream and Fish and Potatoes (if we have to have schools). I know that even 10 pounds is an amount beyond measure to some poor parishes but as Dickens said in Bleak House: 'It's better to hang the wrong person than not to hang anyone!' I'd say myself that it would be better not to hang any picture than [to hang] a bad picture.

Another reason why the situation is so bad is the lack of interest that the governments before now had in the story. I know that the government we have now has great interest in the efforts being made to rebuild on the old foundation of refinement, but up to now they did not do a thing to help painting and carving. It's not up to me to say what place Art has on the programme of things to be done, but I think I could say it's not nearest the top. As I am on the subject, I can say that the Hospitals' Trust is the only group that are enabling workers and craftsmen of Ireland to survive and get a bite of food in this country.

The reasons I have mentioned brought about another reason for the poor state of painting affairs. Any painter who was born in Ireland and was not wealthy had to head off and settle in another country – that or stay at home without even getting alms.[290]

What other protection, apart from that, has he got against the obscenity of the Englishman? When we make an attempt to copy Blackpool or the Daily Mail I know it's a

---

[290] As the article pre-dates the foundation of The Arts Council, Keating may have meant social welfare or unemployment assistance, otherwise known as 'the dole', which was introduced in Ireland in 1933.

miserable effort. The artistic wealth of an Irish person will nurture the music, poetry and dance of this island because the Irish person is a person who has a soul.

The country now has a good few intelligent Irishmen who are putting certain aspects of the life of the nation on canvas. Here is the material for a native school if the pupils could get the encouragement and the facilities that they badly need. I think I know how those facilities, if they were made available, could be used to found a native painting school. And though my respect for a school, built on the carcasses of painters who are dead for years, would be small, I'd have great trust in a school of pupils of young men with truth and energy.

As for this school of Art, what is it? A big showy building, a big staff and lots of material etc, and of course, where would you leave a good grant of money? Or is it a vigorous live thing which knows its aims and its opinions, a school which has an Irish basis? Is it a house which will only be a refuge for false gods, the work of a declining architect, 80 years of age, whose life went astray on him? Or will it be a refuge for our own people – now and in the future – who God has chosen to promote the learning of their race.

The question is for you and it's for you to answer, because it's from that answer we'll understand if the school that's already there is sufficient or not.

Happiness to you.

'Déarfainn féin gurbh fhearr gan aon phictiúr a chrochadh ná droch-cheann': Ealaín na bPictiúrí As Eire

Sean Céitinn, RHA a scríobh. [Published in *The Irish Digest,* September 1940, pp. 89-91]

Chomh fada agus a bhain an scéal le hEalaín in Éirinn, ní raibh aon bhonn ann mar threoir do shean-dálaithe liteartha. Ní raibh an tír sin ann a bhí chomh feidheartha le hÉirinn maidir le bonn nó iarsmaí ealaíne. B'fhéidir go bhféachfadh sibh le mé a bhréagnú ach Soiscéal mór Cholmcille a mheabhrú dom. Ach ní leabhar Gaelach dairíre Soiscéal mór Cholmcille. Is le Ré na Mainistreacha a bhaineann sé. Bhí manaigh i dtíortha eile, freisin, a mhaisigh a leabhair leis an ornáid a dtugann sinne an gréasadh Ceilteach sir. Agus cuirim i gcás gur againne agus againne amháin, a bhí an cheird ornáideach sin, arbh in-mholta dúinn a rá gur chuí agus gur chóir áilleacht so-fheicthe an domhain seo a laghdú agus a chúngú ionas nach mbeadh de scód ná de thalamh aici ach rud éigin gan fuil gan feoil gan anam, ar nós nathrach nimhe agus céimseata tur tur – leagan Críostúil ar ordú údarásach Mhaoise: 'Ná snoígí íomhánna.'

Admhaím go bhfuil againn mar a bhí ag a lán tíortha eile Ré na Cloiche, an Chré-Umha, na Mainistreacha, agus ansin chomh fada agus a bhain an cúrsa le hÉirinn – Neamhní. Nuair is mian le duine duairceas éigin sa saol Gaelach – easpa áilleachta agus sócúlachta, easpa éagsúlachta maidir le bia agus caitheamh aimsire – a mheabhrú do dhuine is é an réiteach is iondúile a chloisfidh tú ar an scéal a shuaraí agus a bhí an scéal againne ó thaobh na staire; a mhéid is a ghoill éigean is aindlí orainn, gur mór an t-ionadh gur mhair an cine ar chor ar bith. Ach an leithscéal é a bhfuil aon bhunús rathúil leis? Dá mb'ea, agus dá mba rud é go mbeadh Ealaín agus míneadas ag brath ar shíocháin agus ar ollmhaoin, ní bheadh siad ann ar chor ar bith. Ní hé amháin go raibh na hIodálaigh i gcochall na bhFrancach, na nAstrianach, na dTurcach, bhíodar féin i gcochall a chéile. Bhí 'chuile bhaile mór ar thaobh nó in aghaidh gach baile eile. Ní bhíodh iabh orthu ach ag comhrac agus nuair a dhéantaí síocháin ba le anáil a thabhairt dóibh féin é. Ach níl amhras ar bith nár bhorr agus nár fhás an Ealaín. Ní raibh síocháin sa Fhrainc leathchéad bliain as a chéile ón uair ar gairmeadh náisiún di anuas go dtí 1870 and ré an tríú Poblachta.

Féachaigí ar an Ísiltír agus an comhluadar stát ar a ngairmtear an Ghearmáin de inniu. Bhí orthu An Cogadh Céad Bliain, An Cogadh Tríocha Bliain agus mion-chogaí faoi chúrsaí creidimh a fhulaingt. Mar sin féin, níl tír ná stát acu sin nach ndearna a cion féin ar mhaithe le hardsaoirse, péintéireacht, snoíodóireacht, ceol, drámaí, oideachas, cultacha ornáideacha, féilte, dea-chócaireacht gan trácht ar ól maith bríomhar blasta – le gach ní is gá leis an saol a dhéanamh soilbhir suairc. Cén fáth nach i dtithe fuara dorcha duairce atá cónaí ar thuathánaigh na Sualainne seachas a bheith sásta sóch i dteachín gleoite, snoite, daite? Is boichte a dtír ná an tír seo agus is measa go mór fada an síonrith ina bhfuil orthu maireachtáil.

Cén fáth a bhfuil pictiúr nó dhó ar a laghad i ngach Oifig Chathartha amuigh faoin dtír sa Fhrainc, pictiúir is fiú a fheiceáil? Cén fáth a bhfuil cófraí adhmaid greanta agus iad lán le línéadach álainn bróidinéireachta i dtithe oibrithe bochta sa Ghearmáin? An bhfuil tada againne a bheadh inchurtha le Dráma na Páise in Oberammergau? Dráma gur feirmeoirí agus siúinéirí bochta amháin a bhíonn páirteach ann? Agus mura bhfuil, cén fáth? Mar gur rífhollasach nach fiú linn é. Dá mba leithscéal ionghabhtha *[inghlactha?]* dúinn gan Ealaín Náisiúnta a bheith againn an t-ansmacht agus an ainíde a imríodh orainn, d'fhéadfadh an leithscéal céanna a bheith ag gach tír san Eoraip.

Is cuma sa tubaiste do dhuine i ndeireadh báire an daoine as tír isteach nó a chomharsa béil dorais a dhóigh a theach. Chomh fada agus a bhaineann na cúrsaí le hÉirinn, níor mhó de mhogha aon Dubh-chrónach ná an Sáirséalach. Ní lú atá muid faoi chomaoin ag na hUrmhuimhnigh agus ag na Gearaltaigh ná táimid ag Annraoi V11.

An eaglais a bhí mar phátrún agus mar chaomhnóir ag na Mín-dana i dtíortha Críostúla eile – an airc in ar chuir gach ní is geal agus is luachmhar linn. Síon ré dorcha an aineolais de – ba chuma léi ann nó as í, chomh fada is a bhain sí leis an tír seo. Má tá sibh faoi amhras i dtaobh an scéil, is leor daoibh féachaint ar aon teampall nó séipéal taobh istigh, nó súil a chaitheamh ar fhuinneog aon taisceadáin Chaitlicigh. Má deirtear sa chás seo nach bhfuil paróistí áirithe in acmhainn cuidiú le hEalaín mhaith, is é an freagra atá ar an scéal nach é méid an airgid ach laghad an rogha a bhíonn acu an deacracht is mó. Admhaím go bhfuil séipéil ann, agus séipéil áille, nach mar seo atá an scéal agus tá 'chuile shúil againn gur chun líonmhaireachta a rachaidh séipéil dá shórt.

An lá ar féidir cóip den 'Ógh agus an Naí' le Michelangelo a cheannach ar £10, níl aon leithscéal ar chor ar bith samhlacháinín suarach gráisciúil daite a cheannach ar £15 ó lámh dhalta éigin de scoil Éisc is Fataí (más éigin dúinn scoileanna a bheith ann). Is eol dom gur luach as miosúr £10 féin ag paróistí bochta, ach mar a dúirt Dickens i *Bleak House*: 'Is fearr an duine mí-cheart a chrochadh ná gan éinne a chrochadh!' Déarfainn féin gurbh fhearr gan aon phictiúr a chrochadh ná droch-cheann.

Tá cúis eile faoi go bhfuil an scéal chomh dealbh maidir le cúrsaí ealaíne – an neamhshuim a bhí ag na rialtais sa bhí ann roimhe seo sa scéal. Tá a fhios agam go gcuireann an Rialtas atá anois againn suim mhór san iarracht atáthar ag déanamh le hath-thógáil a dhéanamh ar an seanbhonn míneadais, ach go dtí seo dheamhan faic a rinne said ar mhaithe le péintéireacht agus snoíodóireacht. Ní agam-sa atá a ra cén t-ionad atá ag Ealaín ar chlár na rudaí atá le déanamh, ach measaim go bhféadfainn a rá nach don bharr is gaire é. Os ag caint air sin é, tig liom a rá gurbh é Iontaobhas na nOspidéal an t-aon dream amháin atá ag cur ar dheis oibrithe agus ceardaithe na hÉireann maireachtáil agus greim béil a fháil sa tír seo.

Tháinig de na cúiseanna atá luaite agam cúis eile faoin drochbhail atá ar chúrsaí péintéireachta. Aon phéintéir a rugadh in Éirinn, agus nach raibh gustal aige, bhí air greadadh leis agus cur faoi i dtír éigin eile – sin nó fanacht sa mbaile agus gan an déirce féin le fáil aige.

Cén chosaint eile ach é atá aige in aghaidh gráisdiúlacht *[gráisciúlacht ?]* an tSasanaigh? Nuair a dhéanann muid iarracht ar aithris a dhéanamh ar Blackpool agus ar an 'Daily Mail' tá a fhios ag mo chroí gur suarach í mar iarracht. Is í an acmhainn Ealaíne atá ag an nGael a chothaíonn ceol, filíocht agus rince an oileáin seo, mar is duine é an Gael a bhfuil anam ann.

Tá sa tír seo, ar ala na huaire, roinnt mhaith Éireannach éirimiúil agus iad ag cur gné áirithe éigin de shaol an náisiúin ar chanbhás. Seo againn an t-ábhar i gcomhair scoile dúchasaí dá bhfaigheadh na daltaí an t-ugach agus na saoráidí a bhfuil said go géar ina gcall. Sílim go bhfuil a fhios agam an chaoi a bhféadfaí na saoráidí sin, dá gcuirtí ar fáil iad, a úsáid le scoil dhúchasach phéintéireachta a bhunú. Agus cé gur beag mo mheas ar scoil a tógfaí ar chonablach péintéirí atá sna Flaithis leis na cianta, is mór an mhuinín a bheadh agam as scoil ar dhaltaí de fhir óga le fír is fuinneamh.

Maidir leis an scoil Ealaíne seo, ceard í? Foirgneamh mór feiceálach, foireann mhór agus leor-fhearas, etc., agus, ar ndóigh, cá bhfágfá deontas maith airgid? Nó an rud beo bríomhar í ar eol di a cuspóir agus a tuairimí, scoil a bhfuil bunús Gaelach léi? An teach í nach mbeidh inti ach tearmann do dhéithe bréige, saothar ailtire meata, ceithre scór bliain d'aois, a ndeachaigh a shaol amú air? Nó an tearmann í dár muintir féin – anois agus amach anseo – daoine a bhfuil sé ag Dia faoina gcomhair saíocht a gcine a chur ar aghaidh?

Is oraibhse an cheist agus is libhse freagairt, mar is ón bhfreagra sin a thuigfear an leor dúinn an scoil atá ann cheana féin, nó nach leor.

Sonas oraibh.

J'Accuse! 'We are a dishonest lot, or we have been deceived …'

Seán Céitinn, RHA. [*Comhar,* May/June 1942, pp.5-6. Published in Irish]

It happened in the City Gallery, Parnell Square – a wet afternoon in the middle of spring. An exhibition of the works of Andrew O'Connor was being formally and officially opened. [Andrew O'Connor was] the sculptor who died recently, having left those works, with great generosity and munificence, as an heirloom to the people of Ireland.

By this time, a speaker was praising the dead person in the words commonly used on occasions such as these, his great deeds, the eternal renown he earned for his country, the fame he won in countries abroad, the greatness of his good example, the victory of intellectual elements over worldly elements, and so on.

The boring words [were] falling on the skulls of the non-plentiful audience just as the rain was falling on the pavements of the street outside – and maybe both had only the same result!

The strong, truly beautiful, truly eternal pieces of marble and bronze under the grey light of that spring afternoon were telling a different story: that is, that O'Connor has not died and that he will not die – but the people themselves, ah! A docile, easily swayed, tired, crowd – they had little liveliness.

Disgraceful neglect

The main point in the speech of everyone who spoke was that O'Connor was a genuine Irishman– we deserve no thanks for that chance of fate, alas. We would deserve some of the gratitude if it was our luck to keep O'Connor in Ireland! He returned to his native country early in the 30s of this century, with a wide international fame, great wealth and great ability to match. He didn't ask us for a thing – we had nothing to give him that it would be worth his while to accept from us except one small thing, public respect and esteem: the sun shines in the dark but the darkness doesn't appreciate it – he returned to London of the Galls and if he did, it was to die.

What right or what entitlement have our office crowd and our public officials to be sunning themselves finely, airily, cheerfully and self-indulgently in the light of the glory he attained for himself and for his art?

All that we gave him in the end of the journey [was] six feet of clay.

He wasn't granted any *honoris causa* degree. He wasn't given any Order. No local or city authority gave him a distinction of the town or city. The people of Ireland were not told – or if they were told, they didn't care whether they heard it or not – that Andrew O'Connor had returned to the native sod.

Our national eternal fault

The reputation abroad of the people of Ireland is strange – the inferiority complex – which is always held, the eternal memory they have of old complaints and ancient enmities, and their cursed reluctance to boast of the great intelligent men of their own race or to give them recognition, until they are corpses in the graves and have no interest in or attention to their praise or criticism.

It's our national fault that we don't have the insight to estimate the harmful damage the eternal slavery has done to our intellect. If we knew, we'd have a cure and in the first instance, what we'd do, and [we'd do it] in a hurry, we would drive out the broad group of false intellectuals, a small, stupid, haughty crowd who have not got any standard of judgement in their skulls which could be compared with a standard of judgement as would be understood in any country in the world....

Cultural panel – and Horse Doctors

And to say the glory of Ireland is based on the works of the spirit! We have a 'cultural panel' in the Seanad and most of them are horse doctors! Either way, we are a dishonest lot or we have been deceived by the size of our own ignorance.

When someone said in the Dáil recently that there wasn't a person to be found in Ireland who was suitable to be a Director of the 'National' College of Art, there wasn't a Christian to be found who would deny him. Alas! As the people who applied for that job are still alive it's probable that official recognition can't be given to themselves or to their artistic ability.

The damage the Saxons did to us, it wasn't the possession of the country and the evils that followed it that were the greatest part but the laziness of heart and the weakness of mind and the sleeveenishness they left begot in us, kneaded into us and imposed on us in the name of Democracy – God help us.

True Art and Dishonesty!

The life of the artistic man has always the penetrating searching of heart and mind, the eternal trials, the hard work, the patience and devotion. And it's the same for the good nation. But on the other side of the story, those good characteristics do not match well with promises and treachery, with 'praise-my-hand', with 'I'll go with them', with laziness of heart and mind, with sentimentality and false honesty, with swashbuckling, and with pretence – the visible signs of the crowd who are in charge of intellectual matters these days.

And as for supporting, nourishing and promoting the arts, it's not right that that would only be a coldly asserted cause from national false goodness, to be put in front of the public in boastful speeches at funerals and at remembrance assemblies!

J'Accuse! 'Is dream mí-mhacánta sinn, nó táimid meallta …'

Seán Céitinn, RHA. [*Comhar,* Meitheamh 1942]

In Éalaíonlann na Cathrach, Cearnóg Pharnell, a thit sé amach – tráthnóna fliuch i lár an Earraigh. Bhíothas ag oscailt go foirmeach agus go hoifigiúil taispeántas d'oibreacha Andrew O'Connor, an snoíodóir a fuair bás le déanaí tár éis dó na hoibreacha úd a fhágáil le barr féile agus flaithiúlachta mar oidhreacht ag náisiún na hÉireann …

Faoin taca seo, bhí cainteoir ag moladh an duine mhairbh sna focail is gnách le haghaidh ócáidí den tsaghas seo, a chuid gníomhartha uaisle, an ghlóire bhuan a ghnóthaigh sé dá thír, an clú a bhain sé amach i dtíortha thar lear, maitheas a dhea-shampla, an bua atá ag nithe na haigne os cionn nithe saolta, agus mar sin de.

Na focail leadránacha ag titim ar bhlaoscanna an lucht éisteachta neamh-líonmhair faoi mar a bhí an fhearthainn ag titim ar lic na sráide amuigh – agus b'fhéidir gan ach an oiread céanna toraidh leo araon!

Bhí a mhalairt de scéal á insint ag na píosaí beoga fíor-áille fíor-bhuana marmair agus cré-umha faoi ghlas-sholas an tráthnóna earraigh sin: mar atá, nach bhfuil O'Connor tar éis bháis agus nach bhfaighidh sé bás ach an oiread – ach na daoine féin, áfach, dream so-lobhtha *[so-lúbtha (?)]*, tuirseach, ba bheag den bheocht sin a bhain leo siúd.

Faillí Náireach.

Ba é an pointe ba mhó i gcaint gach duine a labhair ná gurbh Éireannach ar a bhoinn é O'Connor – seans ón gcinniúint nach bhfuil náid dá bhuíochas ag dul dúinne, fairíor. Bheadh cuid den bhuíochas ag dul dúinn, ámh, dá mbeadh sé de chrann orainn O'Connor a choiméad in Éirinn! D'fhill sé ar a thír dhúchais go luath i dtríochaidí an chéid seo, faoi chlú mór leathan idirnáisiúnta, saibhreas mór aige agus cumas dá réir. Níor iarr sé faic na ngrást orainn – ní raibh pioc againn le tabhairt dó go mb'fhiú leis a ghlacadh uainn ach aon rud beag amháin, gradam agus urraim phoiblí: Taitníonn an solas sa dorchadas ach ní thuigeann an dorchadas dó – d'fhill sé ar Londain na nGall agus má d'fhill, ba chun báis a fháil é.

Cad é an ceart nó cad é an teideal atá ag ár lucht oifige, agus ár bhfeidhmeannaigh phoiblí chun bheith á ngrianadh féin go breá aerach saighiléartha (?) i solas na glóire a bhain sé amach dó féin agus dá cheird?

Ba é ar bhronnamar air i ndeireadh na scríbe thiar – sé throigh cré.

Níor bronnadh aon chéim *honoris causa* air. Níor tugadh aon orduithe dó. Níor thug rialtas baile ná cathrach gradam baile ná cathrach dó. Níor insíodh do phobal na hÉireann – nó má insíodh ba chuma leo é a chloisteáil – go raibh Andrew O'Connor fillte ar an bhfód dúchais.

Ár mbuan-locht náisiúnta.

Is aisteach an teist atá amuigh ar mhuintir na hÉireann, an 'coimpléasc íochtaránachta' atá á sealbhú riamh, an buan-chuimhne atá acu ar shean-ghearáin agus ar fhaltanais ársa, agus an leisce mhallaithe atá orthu mórtas a dhéanamh as na fir mhóra éirimiúla dá gcine féin ná aithne a thabhairt dóibh – go dtí go mbeidh siad ina gcoirp san uaigh agus gan aird ná suim acú i gcáineadh ná i moladh.

Is é ár locht náisiúnta nach bhfuil sé de léargas ionainn a mheas cad é an díobháil urchóideach atá déanta ag an sclábhaíocht bhuan dár n-intleacht. Dá mbeadh a fhios againn bheadh leigheas againn agus, ar an gcead ásc, 'séard a dhéanfaimis, agus sin le dithneas – an ruaig a chur ar dhream leathan na n-intleachtóirí bréige, dream bocht amaideach uaibhreach nach bhfuil caighdeán breithiúnais dá laghad ina mblaosc gur féidir a shamhlú le caighdeán breithiúnais faoi mar a thuigtear i dtír ar domhan é ...

Painéal Cultúrtha, – agus Dochtúirí Capall.

Agus a rá go bhfuil glóire na hÉireann bunaithe ar oibreacha an spioraid! Siúd 'painéal cultúrtha' sa tSeanad againn agus gan ann ach dochtúirí capall a mbunáite! Ceachtar acu, is dream mí-mhacánta sinn, nó táimid meallta ag méid ár n-aineolais féin.

Nuair a dúirt duine éigin sa Dáil le déanaí nach raibh duine le fáil in Éirinn a oirfeadh chun bheith ina Stiúrthóir ar Choláiste 'Náisiúnta' na hEalaíne, ní raibh Críostaí an Luain le fáil ann a bhréagnódh é. Mó léan géar! Toisc go bhfuil na daoine a chuir isteach ar an bpost sin ina mbeatha go fóill, is dócha nach féidir aitheantas oifigiúil a thabhairt dóibh féin ná dá n-acmhainn ealaíne!

An díobháil a rinne na Sasanaighh dúinn, níorbh é sealbhú na tíre agus na hoilc a lean é an chuid ba mhó di ach an leisce chroí agus an mheirtne aigne agus am tslíbhíneacht a d'fhág siad ginte fuinte istigh ionainn agus a cuireadh siar ionainn in ainm an Daonlathais – go bhfóire Dia orainn!

An Fíor-Ealaín agus Mí-mhacántacht!

Is í an ghéar-scrúdú croí agus aigne agus na trialacha buana, an dian-saothar, an foighne agus an caoindúthracht , beatha an fhir ealaíne riamh. Agus ní taise don náisiún mhaith é. Ach, ar an taobh eile den scéal, ní ró-mhaith a réitíonn na tréithe fónta sin le gealltanas agus feallaireacht, le molaim-mo-lámhadas, le 'gluaisim leo.', le leisciúlacht croí agus aigne, le maoithneachas agus neamh-ionracas, le buailim sciath agus le cur i gcéill – comharthaí so-fheicthe an dreama atá i gceannas i gcúrsaí intleachtúla inniu.

Agsu maidir leis na healaíona a bheathú, a chothú agus a chur chun cinn, ní ceart nach mbeadh ansin ach cúis fuar-mhaíte as bréag-mhaitheas náisiúnta le cur faoi bhráid an phobail i gcainteanna bladhmannacha ar shochraidí agus ar thóstail chuimhnimh!

Reflections

by Seán Keating, RHA. [Published in *The Irish Art Handbook,* 1943, p.29-30].

Art, in the sense of artists and their productions, will always appear in every country and community, quite irrespective of a sympathetic Government or a receptive public. It is an odd fact that art flourishes in time of war, perhaps because of a heightened consciousness or as a reaction to the horrors of the outside world. And since all art is to a certain extent 'emotion recollected in tranquillity', it is not unlikely that present conditions will produce the tension that is the essence of creative work.

The only honest contribution that we in Ireland can make on behalf of art and civilization is to make the best possible use of the comparative peace we *have* got, to allow freedom and facilities to creative workers, and to leave art to look after itself. The question for artists, as for all men is: What do you want? How much do you want it? What are you willing to contribute in return for it?

There is always the danger that art institutions starting as incubators –to which, at first, the entrance fee consists of a normal physique, including human faculties in good working order, good character and an authentic vocation – tend to degenerate into refrigerators to which the entrance fee is paid by cheque and no questions asked. This is the history of most institutions. But life – of which art is a part – is dynamic and changing continually. That which is not changing is dying, and that which cannot change is already dead.

Then there are the critics. They are not dead, but most of them are sterile. Criticism can be valuable if it is done by people with unbiased, objective and constructive minds who know what they are talking about. And for art critics it is not enough to have read a few histories and compilations and lives of artists, and to have been escorted round the Tate, Louvre and Prado. They should be soaked in their subject, preferably in some practical aspect of it. The criticisms of aesthetes and busybodies are quite useless, and generally arise from a snobbish inclination to display information which is out of the reach of the fellow they are talking to. It is no good trying to build up a system of criticism on intellectualized jargon. The highbrow stuff intrudes itself between the artist and the public and means nothing to either. Much of what passes for criticism is the output of minds which lack the initial creative impulse, but which, when attached to a spiritual self-starter, can operate forever, without, however, producing anything but noise and friction. Our newspaper reviews, with few exceptions, consist of meaningless laudatory phrases, especially in the case of an artist who is already established; while sometimes a little mild reproof is administered in the case of non-established artists, and a not-so-mild reproof to somebody at whom the critic, for reasons of his own, wants to have a crack. An odd magazine here and there provides blurbs for friends. But the art of criticism in Ireland is not flourishing.

Painting in Ireland Today

by Seán Keating, PRHA. [Published in *The Bell,* December 1950, pp. 17-18]

From which point of view? [That] of painting or [that] of Ireland? Or of which Ireland – the small farm or the Tea, wine and spirit merchants, Fitzwilliam Square or Crumlin, the Gaelic League or the Palace Bar? Or might it be from the point of view of the artist who is not usually very concerned about the other points of view? He generally conforms in his life to the famous Italian dictum: 'Me dead – all dead.' Recognition and its rewards are very fine things, and nobody knows this better than the artist, and nobody knows better how little they matter. He knows that whether laurel-crowned or not, the passage of time presents in him as in everybody else the inevitable and dreary spectacle of a transition from the state of bones and hopes to fat and regrets.

The first necessity for the artist of bourgeois or more frequently proletarian origins is to organize himself so as to be able to grow without the customary aid of roots – material and spiritual. He has to avoid the psychological and physical dangers which attend those who persuade themselves that they are practising austerity when they are really enduring want. He is often a sinister caricature of what he might have been had he been grown on kindly soil – sheltered by respect and tended by affection. Why should he expect such favours? He does not – though he would be fully justified if he did on the grounds of what he had read in 'Appreciations' and 'Tributes' and heard in 'Opening Day' speeches on that Inestimable Thing – that fine flower of civilization, which is Art.

From the public's point of view the answer to the question about the position of art in Ireland today depends on the answer to another question – namely: Is there and will there be an increasing or decreasing number of people who think that spiritual food in the form of art is a necessity? What do they think of the expenditure on sports grounds, race-tracks, cinemas and other organized and commercialized amusements compared to the sums spent on concert halls, experimental theatres, picture galleries and exhibition rooms for cultural non-earning amenities?

In the old days a certain degree of pseudo-cultural activity administered by Civil Servants was regarded as part of the business of Empire, and it provided a means of cheap reward for 'other ranks' who had outlived their term of active service. A cane chair in a museum and a sufficient sum to enable a pensioner to live on tea and central heating was one form of art patronage.

The coming of national ballyhoo as a permanent activity of the State, plus the emergence of a new class of leisured people not rich enough to be idle, nor poor enough to have work, has opened up a new field of activity hinging on Art. The younger generation of this class is now passing from part-time to full-time dilettantism and, with a fair degree of literacy and a lot of fluency, its members will provide the personnel of the new Arts Councils and Cultural Bodies. Their transformation into civil servants will only require a stroke of a pen, and lip service will graduate into Civil Service, with the customary rewards. There is always more than enough aesthetic material in existence to provide subject matter for comment and assessment in *saecula saeculorum*. The function of the commentators will be to inform the public on the history of art up to and including yesterday. If this job were to be tackled comprehensively and with realism, the creative artist might become superfluous. He might nevertheless be difficult to eliminate. His failure to reach a working agreement with his public without the intervention of middle-men, would not necessarily disprove his genius, but would be due to the fact that he lacks 'what it takes' and this is true of all men in all situations.

The question for the public is: Does it value Art enough to give all the artists all the chances they ask for? Some will be worth it; many will not. When armies are recruited either for spiritual or temporal defence, the recruits are not asked to give a certificate of heroism. The incidence of heroism is not high and everybody knows it. But defence is a real issue, or so people think. By this criterion Art is not.

The artificial antithesis between Art and Modern Art is largely a by-product of phoney journalism. It equates with Loch Ness Monsters, Yellow Perils and Flying Saucers. Art was always modern in the sense that sincere artists were always experimenting, and insincere ones were always imitating them in the hope of attaining the end without understanding the means. In Art, as in other things, movements are inspired by saints and missionaries, and stifled by theologians and functionaries.

Post Mortem

by John Keating, RHA. [Date of broadcast or talk unknown but c.1940s]

One morning recently I got an invitation to go to hear some people discussing or lecturing on the question 'What is wrong with Art in Ireland?' I knew one of the answers – that there is too much hypocritical talk about it – so I did not go. Not because I thought that the people who were going to talk at that meeting were necessarily hypocrites, but that the uneasy feeling that suggested the question for debate was based on a false approach to the whole subject.

Most people in Ireland think that Art is a very nice hobby – a suitable pursuit for semi-invalids and women of independent means, but ridiculous as a profession and subversive as a creed. If the artist succeeds in becoming solvent his unorthodoxy is forgiven, because that end justified any means. Consequently it is more important to arrive than to accomplish anything *en route* – better to annex many things than to make anything. Hence a general contempt, perhaps unconscious, for technical knowledge, craft or skill, and in that atmosphere parasites are more conspicuous than practitioners.

If Irish artists succeed in reviving their Medieval Guild, the crest on their armorial bearings should be an Amateur Rampant. We find him everywhere, the eternal amateur, always disgusted at his non-success, but not sufficiently to learn a technique or give it up. In a simpler age and not so long ago, a man was a workman while at work and a human being the rest of the time. Now, our artistic amateurs are never at work but are all the time, ad nauseam, artists 'without expression'. To express themselves in house painting, tailoring or carpentry would require an apprenticeship and the attainment of some standard of proficiency, so they choose 'Art' which is comfortably vague and in which they need fear no qualifying test.

As a result of the ha'penny of literacy which passes for education in our day, we know the names and technical terms of every activity and the nature, study and practice of none. Hundreds of inconsequent lads who have been expensively schooled are rambling through the years of early manhood like puppies out for a walk, smelling at everything and forgetting everything between one lamp-post and the next. Their rudimentary noses go into everything – literature, art, the cinema, the stage, the radio and their intellectual pubs, bottle-parties and week-ends in the mountains where the old bones are dug up for another chew. 'Impressionism', 'Expressionism', 'Plastic Volume', 'Rhythmic Unity' and so on from the 1st January to the 31st December. That was alright in England where a futile generation was 'blowing in' the accumulation of fifty years of money-grubbing imperialism and four years of Great War profiteering. But in Ireland, where there is no accumulation of moral or physical resources to be wasted, such a state of things amounts to national suicide.

A predisposition to suicide may be the subconscious fundamental fact of the Irish psyche. There is certainly sufficient evidence of death worship. I remember when a lad going with my father to a wake in a poor cabin in the mountains, where, in company with twenty or thirty other people, I was given a teacup full of whiskey (which I thoroughly enjoyed) from a large jug which was kept circulating and refilled continually. I said to my father afterwards 'But are these people not very poor?' He said, 'Yes, but you must know that even the poorest and most miserly become princely for a funeral.' I did not know then, but I do now, and it has explained many a morbid phenomenon to me since.

When a people, for one reason or another, can only receive mental stimulation from a mixture of alcohol and some primitive emotion, it is probable that their reaction to Art will be lip service only, because Art in any form seldom comes home to them as a personal thing. It is simply a name – respectable or otherwise – and an artist requires to die before people can really let themselves go about him. Anyway they think that, being an artist, he must have been a round peg and a round peg is probably less comfortable in a long box than in a square hole. Also he was one of those fellows who manage to get paid for doing what they like – writing things down in books and painting pictures while they themselves had to work.

Even if there is no conscious envy of the living man, it seems to me that there is always a note of subdued relief in the panegyric – that behind the official tributes to a dead genius one can detect gratitude for being finally rid of him. The panegyrist is a lucky fellow. For ten minutes or longer he stands in the reflected glory of something bigger than himself, something which he, [and] possibly he alone, has never really understood. He satisfies both his conscience and his audience by delivering a high-minded and generous critique without the danger of being contradicted in public by the subject of his criticism. True, he may often have felt like paying a few compliments to the fellow himself, while he was alive, but then there was the awful possibility of being asked for a loan or about wangling a sale. One had to be careful, but one can and does send a beautiful wreath to be laid on the coffin. *'De mortuis nil nisi bonum.'*

Indulgence in post-mortem flattery is not confined to the Irish. Many satires have been written about what happens when so-and-so comes back from the dead and calls his panegyrist's bluff, but they have not stemmed the tide of Appreciations, Tributes, and Analytical Surveys etc., – the wife, mistress, sister, cousin and aunt versions, safe at least from contradiction – 'my Laurence', 'Tomkins as I knew him', 'the hidden Hodge.' Here at least is a subject on which foreigners can teach us nothing. The Irish native is a past master of the liturgy of ceremonial humbug and this talent is traceable through our whole social system.

In countries such as ours, where political upheavals have accelerated the process of the ascent from class to class which is the underlying motive of all bourgeois society, people whose abilities are sufficient to enable them to conduct a farm or a shop or a routine activity with tolerable success, find themselves in charge of affairs, the social import of which they have no conception of. At the same time they are, by reason of their sudden advancement, tempted to think that their personal abilities are the source and the only source of their success. It is to their credit, under the circumstances, that swelled head is the exception rather than the rule. Some, indeed, are sincerely well-meaning and are willing to ask advice and who can give advice except 'practical' people? Now, if one wants to understand the extent of the gap between the mind of the man who wishes to 'become' – by, with and from within, and the mind of the man who wishes to 'arrive' – at possessions, power and freedom from work, one has to talk to so-called 'practical' people and examine their reactions to what they call 'intellectualism'.

Their attitude is partly the contempt of the countryman for the townsman, whom he regards as the helpless ignoramus about things of practical importance. It is partly due to the feeling that the town draws its subsistence from the country and that it is populated by deserters, who prefer a soft job. The townsman, who is himself a countryman once removed, and who is often engaged in a perfunctory, ornamental or redundant activity where inadequacy does not spell disaster, regards the countryman as a fellow who literally has not the sense to 'come in out of the rain'.

In Ireland these extremes are accentuated by historical events and [by] the fact that enterprise and personal qualities have been drained away in a steady stream, leaving an impoverished residuum to carry on an increasingly difficult and complex economic structure, which is made more unstable by a fantastic bureaucracy. Under such a set of conditions, there is little hope that Art will be officially recognized as of vital importance in the development of our race.

The cultural future of a nation depends on whether it chooses a positive or a negative philosophy. Puritanism is negative. Its arch-enemy is not the devil, but the artist. Joy and Beauty are suspect. Life itself is suspect. Hence, death worship in Ireland is a dangerous symptom. Other symptoms of the disease of Puritanism are the substitution of bigotry for faith, drunkenness for gaiety, hypocrisy for virtue, sentimentality for art and prohibition for temperance. It is not an accident that 'Temperance' is a child of sectarian religion divorced from humanism and culture. The difference between art and sentimentality is the difference between Wine and 'minerals', and that is why 'Art' in puritanical mammonistic communities is mostly wind – a perpetual morning after without a night before.

A Modern School of Painting
by John Keating, RHA. [Undated][291]

I don't believe in Schools of Painting as commonly understood. I know that great painters have lived and worked. They also probably drank, married and got into debt, had theories and were jealous when other painters got the jobs they thought they ought to have been given. But all that is, I think, of no importance. When I want to know anything about a painter – ancient or modern – I look at a picture he has painted. That is enough for me. I don't want to know how he mixed his colours, nor how he compares or contrasts with so-and-so, nor how he was influenced by somebody else, nor what 'school' he [may have] belonged to. In fact I don't believe that any Schools of Painting existed in so far as the painters were concerned. The painters were presumably, like all genuine artists, intensely individualistic, egotistical, self-willed and self-centred, not knowing or caring two straws whether they were advancing or retarding the cause of art in Florence or Siena or Umbria or wherever it was. More probably they were, like all artists, doing exactly what they liked and as they liked, and endeavouring to get paid for so doing.

It was the literary aesthete who came along later, and who, presumably not having much of his own to say, dug up the remains of the painters and performed a post-mortem for the benefit of later generations. It was they who collected, 'restored', explained, dated and docketed them, 'interpreted' them and pigeon-holed them – all ready with stacks of data for the next crop of their own calibre. It is obvious that if artists thought it of any importance that lives of them should be written, that their language of form and colour should be translated for the amusement of the crowd, they would have done it for themselves, as they had painted and sculpted themselves, and if they cared about it (as they obviously did not), thus prevented the production of an immense mass of pseudo information and pseudo culture, a barren no-man's-land rummaged and ransacked by literary ghouls. These post-mortem interpreters of an artist's work do about as much for art as the Bacon-Shakespeare does for literature. An artist appears, fulfils his destiny and dies. And, lo! Half a hundred ink-slingers, gossip-mongers, hero-worshippers (now safe from contradiction) start to write of conversations which they never heard, of theories and tenets which their victim never held. Never pausing to ask themselves this question: 'How is it that I, who cannot write of what I see about me, who can conceive nothing vividly enough to turn it into the substance of Art, yet think that I am equipped to explain, comment upon, criticize and evaluate, to place in historical and social perspective, to translate into terms which shall be clear to others new and hence-

---

[291] Possibly delivered to students at University College Dublin in November 1948 – Keating had been invited to deliver a talk on Modern Art.

forward, the dreams, the aims and activities, the accomplishments and failures of a different order of being.'

These remarks are intended as an introduction to a theory of mine that a School of Art – Irish or any other kind – does not, and has not and cannot exist as described unless in the minds of literary men. At different times and places individual painters have worked side by side or independently and alone, but that they consciously or unconsciously formed a school, I doubt. In Ireland, so far as art was concerned, the literary antiquarians had nothing to go on. No other country was so devoid of artistic remains. You may attempt to refute me by pointing to the Book of Kells, but the Book of Kells is not specifically Irish. It is Monastic. Monks in other countries too illuminated their books with what we are pleased to call Celtic interlacing. And even if it were exclusively ours, could we admit that it is the function of an artist to reduce the beauty of the visible world to an abstract mess of snakes and geometry – a Christianized version of the mosaic injunction 'Thou shalt not make graven images.' I still submit that we had – in common with most other countries – the Stone Age, the Bronze Age, the Monastic Age and then, as far as Ireland is concerned, a blank. When anyone points out a certain drabness in Irish life, a want of beauty and comfort, a lack of variety in food and amusement, the answer always is that our history has been so miserable, we were so oppressed, that the wonder is [that] we have survived at all. But is this a genuine excuse? If it were, if peace and plenty were essential to the existence of art and culture, there would be no such things anywhere in the world.

The cause of that blank is not so much our history as our psyche. Consider other countries. Not merely did the Italians fight the French, the Austrians [and] the Turks. They also fought each other. Every big town was the enemy or the ally of every other town. They lived at war and only made peace to go to war again. But Art certainly flourished. France from the time when she became a nation until 1870 and the Third Republic was never at peace for 50 years together. Take the Netherlands or the group of states that is now Germany. They had the Hundred Years War, the Thirty Years War and continual Religious Wars. But they all produced a steady stream of noble architecture, painting, sculpture, music, drama, literature, decorative costumes, pageantry, festivals, good cooking and good drinking – all that makes life good and desirable. Why does a Swedish peasant live in a lovely timber house, carved and painted, instead of in a grey stone cabin? His country is poorer for sure. His climate is worse. Why is there a good picture or two in every Municipal Office all over rural France? Who do the homes of poor workmen in Germany have carved wood presses full of lovely embroidered linen? What have we to compare with the passion play at Oberammergau, played and produced by small farmers and weed-workers? And if we haven't anything to compare with it, why haven't we? Because we don't want it, obviously. If the argument that we were oppressed and ill-treated could be sustained as a valid reason for having no national art, then Europe would have none either. After all, whether you are killed and your house burned by men from across the sea, or by men from across the road, makes no difference to the result. As far as Ireland is concerned, Sarsfield was as much a hireling as any Black-and-Tan. We owe more to the Ormondes and the Fitzgeralds than to Henry VII.

The Church – which elsewhere in Christendom was the patron and protectress of the Arts, the Ark in which all that is valuable in civilization weathered the Dark Ages – in Ireland ignored Art. If you doubt this, look at the inside of almost any church or chapel, or look in the windows of any Catholic Repository. If in this connection it is argued that some parishes cannot afford good art, the answer is that the difference between good and bad art is not a matter of price, but of choice. Amongst the chapels there are notable exceptions, for example the Honan Hostel[292] and there is hope in the fact that these exceptions are becoming more frequent. While a copy of Michelangelo's *Virgin and Child* – life-size – can be bought for £10 there is no excuse for buying a vulgar, tawdry, painted puppet for £15 – of the School of ice-cream and fish and chips (if we must have schools). I know that in poor parishes even £10 is a prohibitive sum, but to misquote Dickens who said: 'Better hang the wrong fellow than no fellow', I say 'better hang no picture than a bad picture.'

Another reason why we have no School of Irish Art is that our Governments – even our own Irish Government – have ignored it. I know that our present government is sincerely interested in the establishment of a native culture, but so far they have done nothing for painting and sculpture. I do not know what place art holds in the list of things to be done – but it is evidently nowhere near the top. (I may say here that the only institute which today is doing anything to enable Irish painters and craftsmen to live and work in Ireland is the Hospitals Sweep Trust.)[293]

There is a further reason for the blank in Irish Art. When an artist happened to be born and bred in Ireland, and if he had no private means, he had to go and live in some other county, or stay at home and starve.

I know that the Dublin Corporation has spent £35,000 on building and equipping one of the finest and most up-to-date galleries in Europe. It is the only gallery I was ever in where all the pictures can be properly seen at any hour of the day in any season. This project was carried through in spite of all kinds of ungenerous opposition, by the persistency and devotion of a handful of sincerely interested citizens. It does not claim to be a gallery of Irish Art, but a Gallery of Modern Art. The Luxembourg in Paris is also a Gallery of Modern Art, yet probably 75% of the pictures have been painted in France by French men. The Tate in London is a Gallery of Modern Art, and certainly 80% of the pictures are English. Charlemont House, our Gallery of Modern Art, while being a better building for the purpose than either of them, contains perhaps 7% of pictures painted in Ireland by Irish men. This ought to show us where we stand.

---

[292] The Honan Hostel is on the grounds of University College Cork. Built as a result of the Honan Bequest, the chapel was completed in 1915 and contains work by many of Ireland's best-known artists of the time, including windows by Harry Clarke and a tabernacle by Oswald Reeves.

[293] This line is crossed out in the original typed document.

But if we have the disadvantage of having [had] no tradition we have at least been saved from traditionalism – and that is all to the good. *Is treise greim am fhir mharbh na samsein.* I believe that although we have no art tradition, we have the material for a native art. I believe in the latent artistic capacity of the Irish. Nothing else can explain their resistance as a Nation to the virus of Anglo-Saxon vulgarity. Even when we try to be like Blackpool and the Daily Mail we don't succeed. Nothing but a capacity for art can account for the existence of Gaelic music, poetry and dancing. Behind the faces of the Irish there is a soul.

We have in Ireland at the moment a number of young Irish men of talent and individual character – actually painting Irish things in Ireland. Here is all the material for an Irish School if the individuals were given the necessary facilities and encouragement. Facilities, if granted, could be used so as to produce a native Irish School of Painting. And while I do not believe in the kind of school that is created from the bones of painters dead a hundred years, I do believe in a young, working school of living men.

The era of middle-class respectability has come to an end. Authority has gone soft and begun to explain and apologize, or gone mad and begun to beat and kill, so with a clear conscience we can give *carte blanche* to the artists. Artists believe in life with a big L. They respect life and beauty and joy. They look on such manifestations of the divine will as theirs especially to proclaim to all men. They regard themselves as the fingers of God's hand, the God from whom they receive their patent of nobility direct without the intervention of any priest or king. Having seen the results of the activities of theocrats, autocrats, plutocrats and democrats all about us, perhaps it is time to listen to the artists who in return for preaching the gospel of beauty and understanding have never asked for themselves more than enough to eat and a place in which to work.

Talk continues as per 'Talk on Art', October 30, 1932.

Culture and Cant

by John Keating, RHA. [Undated][294]

The word CULTURE with all that it implies is still in Ireland one of the Cant terms that go to make up the democratic intellectual vocabulary – that liturgy or humbug which has to be recited at public functions, like prayers at the opening of legislative assemblies, or speeches at Private Views or Public Dinners.

As a step towards bringing about a state of things in which art would flourish – as part of the life of the common people – we would have to begin by eliminating this cultural liturgy and talk of pictures and books and buildings as frankly and sincerely as we do of bread and boots.

Hitherto the discussion of cultural questions has implied an attitude *de haut en bas*. This attitude is a mixture of Liberalism, Nonconformist Conscience with its insistence on social betterment, and Trade Unionism with its inevitable underdog complex. Individuals of those groups are often sincere and high-minded, but they have a tail of legal reformers, anti-vivisectionists, culture hounds, up-lifters, elaborators, nosy parkers and protestants with a small P – and that tail often wags the dog.

It is in the modern democratic tradition that ministers of governments should always pretend to consult and be advised by such bodies of opinion, and in so far as this does not interfere with the real business of getting into power and remaining there, they do consult and take advice and even act upon that advice, provided it does not cost too much or otherwise interfere with 'practical' matters. Art is, I suppose, the outcome of man's desire to impose his concept of order on the beauty of the world, to bring it into line with his idea of logic and reason, and thus to make the sensation of pleasure recur at will. This may not be a good definition – all definitions are necessary evils – evils because they limit and perhaps distort, but necessary in so far as they make analysis possible.

First in any intelligent operation comes the question of precedence in order of importance. What has to be done first and why? Assuming that a reaction to beauty is in part a reaction from ugliness, that a notion of order arises from a notion of disorder, it would seem to follow that in Ireland we are not taking the first step first, because there is no evidence to show that we do hate disorder, but very much to the contrary. We condone and accept ugliness in many forms and that even in personal matters [that are] easily in our power to alter. If this is admitted it follows that we in Ireland have a lot to do to clean the windows and sweep the floor and kill off the parasites and arrange for the ventilation and free circulation of ideas, and do whatever is necessary to make the place habitable before we start on the decorations. As long as we permit little boys of ten to

---

[294] Similar in wording to 'Art does not get a chance in Ireland', *Muintearr na hEireann,* 1936.
Date of broadcast or lecture unknown.

push loaded bicycles through traffic or dress them in silly uniforms and stand them at swing doors we have no right to think of art. As long as we condemn young women (future mothers of the race) to stand behind counters all day to sell tawdry fal-lals to tasteless old women from ugly suburbs, we have no right to think of art. As long as we permit lying advertisements worded in revolting terms to cheat sick and frightened people out of money for nostrums, we have no right to think of art. As long as we permit anyone who thinks himself a builder to run up an ugly structure in any place that suits him for any purpose – however unnecessary – we have no right to think of art. As long as private interest can postpone or defeat schemes for improvement or draw rents from slums, we have no right to think of art. As long as we build hospitals in noisy and depressing slums and let private jealousies defeat necessary and obvious amalgamations and constantly protect privilege and authority against reason and common sense, we have no right to think of it. As long as the whole mental background of the people is formed on the concept of a remorseless struggle for existence presided over by an angry god or (for those who dislike the god hypothesis) by a soulless machine – the State – there is no room for beauty or culture. You might as well hope to grow flowers on the floor of a slaughterhouse.

How can we expect people who have grown up stunted and warped by fear of authority and fear of want, pushed headlong into the first job that offers, intimidated and frustrated all their days, to have any faculty or desire to exercise the right to choose?

If a man lacks the desire to choose a wife or a house or clothes or a job that would suite HIM, is he likely to choose pictures or books or the good use of his free time? And if he cannot or does not want to do so, what then becomes of art or culture?

The assumption that freedom in any real sense exists in the modern democratic state is false. Try it, and you will find out. There is the freedom of the prison yard – the freedom to choose between a black eye and a kick in the pants if you break the rules. Who wants to live in such a world? Certainly not artists. Not that that would make any difference to the propagation of art and culture as presently understood. All the artists could be hanged or otherwise eliminated tomorrow, and art and culture would flourish as before – official art run by official democratic machinery could and would operate in a vacuum. There are too many interests involved for it to be allowed to stop. There are ministries of art, chairs of art, schools of art, art galleries with staff and equipment all complete, books on art, art periodicals, writers, critics, dealers, social climbers and all the rest.

And that mysterious entity – the People – for whose benefit all this expensive and imposing façade is supposed to be maintained, would still pass by in a hurry about their business, and neither know nor want to know anything at all about it.

Be not Solicitous

by John Keating. [Date of Broadcast unknown – but c.1930s]

One could argue on the lines of that sceptical Divine, who wrote a book on Napoleon, that Ireland's cultural mythology is a figment of the Ascendency imagination. It may have been that when the physical possession of the land of Ireland was taken from the landlords, their grandsons re-created the land of Heart's Desire – a cultural reservation for the invaders instead of for the aboriginals.

It seems to me that traditional music is the only evidence we have that the 'mere Irish' ever achieved a form of self-expression. A Gaelic school of music we certainly have, and it is something to be proud of.

As I began to write this article, I heard a girl traditional singer singing 'Bean in Fir Ruaidh'. The lovely clear notes rippled over the words like a mountain stream over stones. Then she sang 'Spailpín Arúin' a piece of light hearted malice on the gigolo theme, or a melancholy reflection on unrequited love and folly and old age. It can mean either according to your humour, but it is always genuine and characteristic art – typical of our country. And with that – with traditional songs and music – our art ends.

But another thing called 'The Art of Advertising' is just getting into its stride and sometimes our minds get a bit muddled when the two things – Art and the art of advertising burst on us close together. That is what happened to me. As the last notes of 'Cat céim an Fiad' – surely one of the most passionate and lovely songs in any language – faded away, I took up a newspaper or rather an advertisement paper with some news in it – and I began to wonder what a pity it was – or wasn't it – that the lady in 'Spailpín Arúin' had not taken the advertisers' advice about her appearance. When the Spailpín said to her 'A caille buide crón, nior milis lion do póg', it was obviously because she hadn't heard of the removal of superfluous hair. Neither had she 'banished all undainty odours', nor used the toothbrush that removes film, nor the soap that makes her complexion-conscious all over. And when she refers to her 'cipe' and her 'clóca' and her high-heeled shoes and fashionable buckles, she never says a word about having washed her stockings with Mux or Glux, so that they were free from ladders. What sort of a chance did she think she had?

And the Spailpín. If he had only availed himself of a course of Memory Training, or become an artist in his spare time, or bought a bottle of dope to make himself 'slightly handsome' – because it says on the label that handsome men are slightly sunburnt. If he had done any of these things, he wouldn't have to be 'banishing' the 'fogmar come luat seo'. He could have been a movie star or a gigolo, and smoked coupon cigarettes and solved crossword puzzles, and gone to the cinema every evening. But out of the Spailpín and the cailleach 'cailleach buide crón' we have gained an immortal song. That is culture – that was. And it is a measure of the distance we have come that we should be inclined to smile at the notion that a Spailpín or a crone should have a culture. Just that little something that we others haven't got.

As long as advertising consisted of statements like 'Brown's boots are the best' or 'Smoke Smith's cigarettes' or 'Blogg's ointment will cure your bad leg' there is no harm done because the statement was just an obvious lie, or an ill-bred command, or an unnecessary self-evident proposition as the case might be. But should a young Irishman think it reasonable to be invited by a Cockney shop assistant with a snot-mat to smoke ten thousand cigarettes in order to win a cap or a pair of socks, or even a set of electro-plated fish knives?

Is it reasonable that Irish girls should be told that they can never hope to marry if they don't use so-and-so's face cream? Or to suggest that the whole population is going around stinking like pole-cats (even their best friend won't tell them) because they don't use some specific or other? Or to intimidate a citizen by telling him that 60% of people over forty will die of blood poisoning if they don't use somebody's toothpaste? Or to wring the heart of some woman by suggesting that at any minute her husband may be killed in the street, and that she and her children may be hungry just because he hasn't insured himself with so-and-so for so much – with a picture of two little waifs shivering on a wet door-step?

This is where the artist comes in. Artists as a rule are not self-deceivers. They have a pretty clear idea of what they themselves are doing and thinking of, and why and how. To drive their message right home is simply a part of their technique. From this it arises that they sin with their eyes open, which is the worst kind of sin. What is all this about culture and advertising and artists and sin? Well this ...

If you want to sell tuppence worth of lanoline for one-and-three pence you get some artist to make a picture of a lovely girl's head to advertise your tuppence worth for the one-and-three pence and he comes back with what he considers a lovely head (that is if he doesn't know the ropes, and by the time he knows the ropes he has ceased to be an artist). This head has probably in it some human quality, therefore it won't do. It is not utterly dehumanized and doll-like. No, it won't do. The advertiser says that's not what the public wants and he thinks he ought to know. If he is a nice fellow and wants to spare the artist's feelings, he says that the work is too good for the public. That means that it is not bad enough for him. So the artist goes away, and if he happens to be very hard up he falsifies his work and if he is not, he says he is damned if he will. Then the job is given to somebody who will do what he is told – as far as he can, which sometimes isn't very far, and so public taste is debased.

The advertiser says that he is only giving the public what the public wants, but I am convinced that the public doesn't know what it wants until it is told. Then if it is told to want something that is suitable to its environment and tradition, and if it is told in language that is not entirely foreign in thought and expression to its own language and way of thinking, it is very probable that the public will proceed to want these things. There is where, in my opinion, the advertiser is out of his reckoning – as far as Ireland is concerned. That, which appeals to highly systemized, machine-made pseudo-democracies, has less appeal for us. We are a backward nation and believe in God.

It is not yet too late, however. If we believe the advertisers we ought to do something to make Ireland a land fit for advertisers to live in, [and] forget all that old stuff about eternal human values and so on, and live as they tell us we should. Something like this: springing gaily out of our YZ Sprung Nest of Rest we make straight for our Grandpa Liver Beans – (make you feel fine). Then while turning on the gasless geyser, we begin to shave with our anti-anthrax brush and our bladeless patent razor (a child could use it). We have a look to see if eyestrain is spoiling our good looks, and we have a spray of 'Naturestone'. Why be grey? (Why indeed!). Is our skin clean within? Can we say 'Yes'? The real answer is 'God knows' but the advertiser says *yes* because we use such and such ... To breakfast then, via our solidified paraffin (lubricates while you wait), bright-eyed and eager for the grandest cereal there is. Eat more onions. Drink more tea. Chew more string. Then for cigarettes. 'Coward B'... you can smoke yourself to death if you like but they will never hurt your throat. And think of the coupons you can collect. After that with a long day before you in which to 'prevent that stinking feeling' and 'regain lost energy' you can order lots of things – asking gently but firmly for them. Why be vague? I can't imagine boys, why you don't insist. Mine is always a Jeremiah O'Riordan. Then you can drive home in the correct car, glad to know that the man in the garage won't despise you, when you order a pint of the right oil (a smile in every mile).

The question that arises is this: can the race which produced the song and the singer that I mentioned at the beginning – can the same race accept this doctrine of existence? Do we like it? Can we live on such spiritual food? Let us remember that it is a doctrine that is failing all over the world – this doctrine of competition.

We in a sense are a young nation. From what is left to us of such things as our music, we could develop a culture. We have not disappeared or been absorbed. We have resisted all attempts to standardize us. We are a race of individuals. We have humour and common sense. We are children compared to the standards of today, but like children we can easily be corrupted. Surely one of the greatest misfortunes that can befall a people is to have its natural faculty to distinguish between lies and truth blunted and put out of action.

To endeavour to promote a 'social conscience in the Name of God' and, at the same time, to permit – under the guise of modernism and advancement – the activities of a naked commercialism (which has fallen into disrepute among the very people who created it) is a process of auto-frustration. Unbridled self-interest and reckless exploitation of the moral and physical needs of the human race has brought about the state of things in which collapse is inevitable. The real power behind dictators is the accumulated rage and fury of the common man against the unbearable futility of his existence. So that he seeks a victim for his fury and finds it in some bugbear – the Jews, the Masons, the Reds, or the Whites. The message implicit in commercial propaganda is that human happiness is buyable in a shop. That is not so. All the money and all the leisure in the world are useless without a standard of personal values – and the possessor of personal values has no need for advertisements. Tariffs have been imposed on cultural necessities. I suggest that it might be better for us – even from the financial point of view – to take the tax off Beethoven and put it on Ballyhoo.

The Future of Irish Architecture

by Seán Keating, RHA. [Given to the Architecture Society of Ireland][295]

My presence here tonight is contrary to all my rules. Conversation is one of my vices. But delivering lectures and making public speeches and pronouncements is an activity for which I am not qualified and do not usually practice – except of course, for money. My excuse for being here and presuming to talk to you on a subject which is yours and not mine, is the over-powering personality of your President. It is, in fact, the result of a hold-up.

As I was walking along a road one day last summer, a car dashed up, swerved in to the kerb, jammed on the brakes, and pulled up. A man leapt out and confronted me – and before I could be sure that I was not taking part in a gangster film – the man was back in the car and driving away with a promise from me that I would address the Architectural Society of Ireland. But February seemed a long way off, and I didn't worry about it again until a few days ago.

I have no knowledge about architecture, and if my remarks seem to you disorderly and inconsequent, the disorder and inconsequence are the result produced in my mind by what I see around me.

Assuming that a reaction to Beauty is, in part, a reaction from ugliness – that a notion of order arises from the recognition of disorder, if would seem to follow that in Ireland we are not taking the first steps first. Because there is no evidence to show that we might object to disorder, but very much to the contrary, we condone and accept ugliness in many forms.

In France and other Continental countries, feeling for symmetry and design and consequently an interest in architecture is almost as common as interest in food – too normal to be boasted about or apologized for. In Ireland, on the contrary, it has no place in the lives of ordinary people. As the song says:

'Nobody knows and nobody cares.'

So why blame the architects?

It sometimes seems to me that the architectural profession lacked foresight in not procuring for itself a stranglehold on the public such as that enjoyed by the legal and medical professions. Then they might begin to let themselves go – they might, perhaps, with the machinery of the law behind them, recapture for Dublin its 18th century character – concentrating on streets of handsome Georgian façades and – in the good old Georgian tradition – ignoring everything behind the façade. Thus, conforming externally, the citizens would be allowed to live unmolested in the background, indulging their individuality – or lack of it – as they pleased, within the meaning of the Act. I have

---

[295] Undated: possibly delivered in Trinity College in July 1953 – Keating had been invited to give a talk which was delivered on that date.

heard O'Connell Street described as one of the finest streets in Europe. I think it is a fine open thoroughfare – or could be if the trams, Nelson's Pillar and the statues were cleared away. But I confess that the only occasion on which I got from it any spectacular thrill or any feeling of emotion was when it was burnt down. Then the Georgian, the Gothic, the Classical and the strictly utilitarian were reduced to a kind of conformity of ruin. There was a general colour scheme of black and yellow brown; rust, red and white. All the irrelevance of names, signs and the insistence upon personal character were swept away and the street became a unity for the first time.

Anyhow one was aware of some spiritual content in the scene. That may have been really due to the smell of dead horses and smouldering things, but certainly it was there. Possibly a rare memory – a hangover from the innumerable cycles of the past, when the physical reaction to the smell of blood and burnt offerings – or incense – created the spiritual malaise or exultation which passes as religious experience.

I should say here that it is always astonishing to me to remark how deliberate attempts to create specific emotions by means of architecture nearly always fall flat. To me a Gothic church is usually a wedding cake of the fad period in stone – or else it is a set of ninepins or bottles of claret set up to show what man could do by means of dowels and iron to defy the laws of gravity. Speaking for myself, I have always thought that the laws of Nature are the laws of Beauty, and I have never confused in my mind the sensation of interest and astonishment aroused by, let us say, the Forth Bridge or the Empire State Building on the one hand – and the feeling of eternal rightness and conformity to real human instinct expressed in Cashel, or indeed, in any building which grew by the addition of cells or offices to an original parent structure – half dwelling house, half fort.

In this connection, looking at the new County Council cottages dotted about the countryside, I have marvelled at how their designers managed unconsciously to achieve for them such complete incompatibility with their surroundings. The old Irish cottage with its whitewash and thatch had grown naturally out of the mud cabin of our forefathers and was as much a part of the landscape as the rocks and hills. Surely a good designer does not limit his imagination to the square yards enclosed by his foundations. I think it would have been possible to combine some of that essential fitness of form of the old cottages with the more hygienic conditions of the new and thus save us from those crude box-like structures that look as if they had fallen off the trailer of a travelling circus.

It seems to me that fitness to its natural surroundings is one essential of good design and that it is a mistaken idea that in architecture vastness is necessarily imposing. I see no virtue – no spiritual quality – in mere size alone. The waterfront at New York did not impress me so much as the cliffs of Moher seen from the westward at sea level one fine evening when the sun was setting.

The natural mountain licks the artificial mountain hollow. I have been told that the Alps are not impressive because the sky over them is so enormous. Therefore I conclude that a March sky in Ireland will give as good an impression of the grandeur of immensity as any Alp or Himalaya so that architecture in Ireland should never be tempted in the direction of mere size – not that that is an immediate danger. It may come to pass, however, that it will be necessary in the future to design on an enormous scale in Dublin. Either the problem of parking will have to be solved by some method of putting a number of large objects in the space previously occupied by one – or in the space previously regarded as a necessary condition of physical existence under normal human conditions – or else we shall have to restrict the influx of all the inhabitants of Ireland into Dublin. This latter solution is seemingly not practical because it cuts across one of the principal activities of Democracy – namely going down into the country to tell the provincials how to manage their affairs, so as not to upset the schedules and syllabi constructed for them in Dublin. The average young man and woman in the provinces may imagine that they are going to Dublin in order to get rich and become finer and more intelligent human beings, but this is probably a benevolent deception practised upon them by the Time Spirit – in order to get them into Dublin and into an office where they in their turn can spend their time making regulations for the better management of their country or so that they may help to hasten the arrival of bursting point by increasing the internal pressure in the professions.

This influx will have to be met by the provision of increased accommodation. The design of this accommodation will be conditioned mainly on two factors, one of which has already radically changed architectural design – namely, the use of ferro-concrete. And the other, which is of more pressing and vital importance every day, that they should be bomb proof. In this connection it is necessary to point out that the specified quality of modern design as illustrated by the aeroplane, is the use of streamlined curves and the ruthless elimination of all projections and ornamentation. The shape of future things is forced upon us by the necessity of using only such curves as will deflect missiles. The classical example is the military tin hat. The modern building will be a tin hat made of ferro-concrete – [the] ferro-concrete being inevitable because it offers the maximum resistance to tension and compression strains. The building trades may not like it, but the carpenter and the handyman, the fitter and the innominate guy with the pliers and hacksaw are the key men today. The bricklayer and the plasterer are about to follow the stone mason into the limbo of forgotten things. There is a future still for the draughtsman, for the time is coming when the boy in search of romance will read schedules and blueprints from which he can get a more authentic thrill than any that his father got from the histories of brave Britons versus Dirty Dagoes on which the growing mind of the Irishman was used to feeding.

But in visualizing the future of architecture in Ireland, we cannot ignore the possibility of what would seem at first sight a fantastic alternative.

There are prophets who consider that the Future in terms of ferro-concrete need not really interest us. Ferro-concrete, after all, implies cement and foreigners and iron imports and shipping and the use of imagination and dislike for the good old conservative methods, and all kinds of qualities and materials that we don't like and don't want.

On the other hand, we have, it is true, something which doesn't exist anywhere else in the same quantity and quality, something which would enable us to solve two or even three pressing problems at one and the same operation. Why should we change the traditional style of building which we see in our castles, (all built by Normans by the way) when we have hundreds of square miles of limestone lying on the surface, of perfect rectangular fracture, in every thickness, from prisms of four inches wide to slabs of even thickness, four, five, six feet square – coins, lintels, of beautiful texture and colour; the sides parallel, the angles right angles, simply lying on the ground preventing the inhabitants from pursuing their natural inclination to grow things and be comfortable. These people – all congested and romantic and uneconomic through mere excess of limestone – are a problem that must be solved somehow.

To modernize, to rationalize them and their surroundings would be to cut the roots of national culture. What would become of painting and poetry without the Gaeltacht, and what is the Gaeltacht without limestone and the spiritual qualities consequent on malnutrition rationalized as a philosophy of life?

Foremost amongst the prophets of a better way of life today are the people who preach the abolition or restriction of the machine, who see the only hope for art and culture, for humanity and religion in the return to traditionalism and handicraft; who distrust synthetic materials and mass production. They may be right. When conversing with these people one is always impressed by the lucidity of their arguments and the commonsense and humanity of their ideas, so that their most fantastic proposals take on the appearance of reason, expedience and inevitable necessity, and the confusion and instability of the present appear more madly fantastic and unbelievably silly and impractical than the remedies by which they propose to cure them – so that I am encouraged to propose to you a fantasy of my own – an extravaganza on architectural and economic themes.

Suppose we decide that we should build a greater Dublin, big enough to house all the people of Ireland. We could employ all the people in Connemara with all their horses and ponies and creel carts to lift and transport all that unwanted limestone across Ireland to Dublin and tear up the remaining single line of railway to Galway, which would remove an existing danger that we might become strategically important in time of war.

The great stone caravan would become as important a cultural agent as the caravans of Asia. The compulsion to halt and mingle with the locals; the slow rate of progress leading to contemplation; the necessity for consuming the food and drink of the regions through which the caravan has to pass, would all be factors working together to fuse the Gaeltacht and the metropolis. Since there would be no motive power but horses it would not be necessary to tar the roads, and thus a big item of import would become unnecessary. The returning empty carts and creels would collect manure dropped on the roads and this constant supply would be spread over the fields cleared of stone thus enriching and turning it into arable land, incidentally providing that dream of all transport companies 'pay load both ways.' What a job for an architect of the classical tradition to design in limestone a building to house 'The Gaeltacht Rationalization and Metropolitan Buildings Commission', with an imposing façade, and – as the auctioneer said – 'a commodious rear at the back' to facilitate the get-away of the personnel in time of civil disturbance.

Whatever may be the future of Irish architecture, I am optimistic enough, for I believe – in spite of all the evidence to the contrary – that the Irish have latent artistic sensibilities. I hold this belief on the evidence of Irish music, Irish dancing, a colourful speech and rich vocabulary; also in the Irish incapacity for real vulgarity. Even when we try hard to be like Blackpool and the Daily Mail, we don't succeed.

How this potential reservoir of culture is to be tapped as regards architecture is a matter for you to decide; but in considering yourselves as an academic body, do not forget the dangers which attend upon membership of such bodies. Beware of the conservatism, caution and respect for precedent that lurk in such institutions. The iconoclasts of today who have no property beyond youth and high spirits, who are all bones and hopes instead of all fat and regrets, will, in their turn, wear top hats or red robes or whatever the proprieties demand. They too will write letters after their names and will reject and condemn the innovations of their juniors – not because they are bad, but because they are new. To suggest that an Academic society has no use for youth or courage or novelty or enterprise is to declare it dead. It is awful to contemplate how institutions which came into being as incubators end as refrigerators.

Proposal to Create a Travelling Art Scholarship

by John Keating, RHA. [Undated. c. 1940-1950]

I think this an excellent idea. I suggest that it be awarded to young painters who are already over their student-ship and at a stage when they could benefit by the chance of visiting the galleries and art collections of Europe. There should be an obligation on them to produce proofs of study, by making copies etc. I am against the idea of sending younger students to work in foreign art schools – at least, until the epidemic of so-called 'Modern Art', Impressionism, Surrealism or whatever it may call itself has disappeared. There are already signs of a reaction against this aberration, and of a return to sanity in art in America and parts of Europe, and we must be on our guard against adopting as a new discovery something which other countries have finished with and thrown out. Besides it is a fact that we have here in Dublin as good a school of draughtsmanship (which is the basis of all art) as exists anywhere. But we lack examples of the great art of the past – for which books provide an inadequate substitute. It would be excellent, therefore, if the pick of our advanced students, thoroughly trained here in the technique of painting, could have their training enlightened by travel, and their taste improved by studying Classicism and its source.

Commissions for Historical Portraits and Pictures from Davis's Essays and the Young Ireland Movement;

I suggest that the subjects of these pictures should not be confined to the Davis period, nor to the subjects proposed in his essays. A good many historical portraits already exist, and another batch of them would inevitably consist of *réchauffé*. If the idea of portraits of men of the past be adhered to, the artists should be encouraged to paint idealizations rather than realistic portraits. The Americans have done this in the case of Lincoln with better results than if they had simply copied contemporary drawings and paintings. But it would be better, in my opinion, to commission portraits of living men of the 1916-22 periods where the type has not been fixed in the public mind by existing pictures. The last 25 years are full of subjects for Irish historical pictures; [the] repudiation of the ideals of Empire, decision to fight the tariff war, to grow our own wheat, to build cement factories, to maintain neutrality against any pressure, to meet the coal blockade with turf etc.

I consider that one of the blackest marks against our native administrations is the fact that they neglected to provide any artistic record of the history which they were making. Almost any other civilized country in similar circumstances would by now have in its public buildings and parks, a record in paint and stone that it could be proud to leave to future generations. But, artistically, our children are still fed, largely, on the crumbs that fell from the table of Victoria and Albert. The cause of that state of affairs is that

Irishmen who were not intimidated physically by British guns were intimidated intellectually by pseudo-British culture. When the Ascendency was on the run, it took cover in the last ditch – Culture – rightly assuming that it was a ditch that our people would ignore. If Eamon de Valera, Sean Moylan, and the rest, do not know what they want in matters of Irish Art, the Kildare Street Club is not the best place for them to find out. My opinion is that they do know, and that they should trust their own knowledge and judgement, and – like the Princes and Popes did in the great days of Art – order what they want from the people who can supply it, and not allow themselves to be misled by Committees of 'Aesthetes', intellectual busybodies or professional culture-mongers.

Letter from John Keating, PRHA, to the Cultural Relations Committee
[on behalf of the Council of the RHA, 1950]

The Academy wishes to protest against the manner and matter of the preface to the catalogue of the Art Exhibition to the USA. It is, to say the least of it, in very bad taste. From the start it is an inferior kind of apology made up of the most hackneyed clichés and containing unnecessary references to the Academy which are untrue or are half truths couched in such a way that they can only be interpreted as being deliberately malicious. The preface generally is of such a quality that it is a matter of concern that it should be sent to another country especially under government aegis.

Although from the outset the organization of this exhibition was open to criticism, comment of any kind was withheld by the Academy out of respect for the praiseworthy initiative shown in starting such a project and for its objectives; however, when an official project of this kind is used to give weight of authority to statements which bear a definite show of ill-will and contain statements misrepresenting persons or a society, it is felt that a protest must be made.

The statement that 'an Academy without any tradition at all but which at least made provision for an annual exhibition where commissioned portraits and a quantity of unadventurous landscapes were shown' is deliberately offensive as an opening and is certainly unnecessary. The idea of a group of artists starting without 'any tradition at all' is staggering and difficult to reconcile with the sentence immediately previous of a tradition 'unforgotten through seven centuries.' It can only be assumed that it was unforgotten by everybody except the painters, sculptors and architects of the country, who apparently were also completely unaware of the broad tradition of their respective crafts which passed from continent to continent, country to country and from man to man since man drew on cave walls. Contrary to what one would be expected to infer from the preface, the originators of the Academy were not a huddle of shambling primordials blinking in the light of day, but a body of intelligent men who set out to foster the talents of gifted Irishmen and to promote an exhibition with work of a high standard and to end the indiscriminate showing of works which up to then had been the subject of much adverse criticism. The following is an extract from the catalogue of the first exhibition held by the Academy in 1824:

> Much has been said in melancholy despondence of the distresses of Ireland; much has been said in dishonest spirit of the incapacity of the artists; to those who grieved without exertion and to those who exalted without triumph they say nothing but to look upon the works which now surround them on the walls of the Academy.

and in conclusion

> they consider it their bounden duty to use every exertion which may conduce to the advancement of the Fine Arts and hope that those artists who may hereafter issue from

under their care will in their turn endeavour to transmit the honour of their profession unsullied to posterity.

In the catalogue of the sixth exhibition the preface says that the 'Royal Hibernian Academy can at least claim the merit of fostering the native talent of the country'.

While we make no extraordinary claims for the Academy and admit freely that there have been periods when, for various reasons, [both] internal and external, it has just existed and some of its exhibitions have deserved what criticism they have got, we claim without contradiction, that our objectives have been consistently adhered to. In fact, the Academy, and the Academy alone, has been the real source of encouragement and help in Ireland and the present state of art in this country is due to that encouragement and help.

To say as the preface says 'it is not an Academy in the true sense, but a society of artists with some official recognition' is complete impudence and another example of malicious *suggestio falsi*. In the first place any academy is a 'society' of people, the dictionary definition of it is 'a learned society formed from the advancement of the Fine Arts and Sciences'. The Royal Hibernian Academy is a society formed for the advancement of the Fine Arts in Ireland and it has a charter.

It would be tedious and undesirable here to take the preface statement by statement and analyze it but we feel generally that the writer's mind is on France, not on the French art scene, but on the realms of critical literature which grew around and from the defects of an autocratic French Academy of the last century, finally raging not only around the painters and sculptors, but culminating in a welter of criticism of the theories and literature of the critics themselves by other critics. The writer is apparently 'wishing' an analogous situation here since the fashionable practice of attacking academies gives ample scope to the pens of those who write about art.

In the ordinary course of events the Academy would hardly concern itself with a protest, as uninformed criticism is a recurring familiarity, but it is felt that in the interest of art and society a matter of this kind should not be allowed to pass without a strong protest and a request for some assurance that in other similar projects the persons deputed to provide any literature which may be necessary, shall be of a responsible and discriminating nature, if sponsored by a Department of State. I trust Mr Minister, that you will give the matter your sympathetic consideration.

William Orpen: A Tribute

by Seán Keating. [Published in *Ireland Today,* August 1937, pp. 21-26]

William Orpen was a born painter, and showed signs of his ability so soon that his sensible parents, in whom he was fortunate, encouraged him to follow his vocation from the time he was eleven years old. Few people know what they want to do at that age, and fewer still are encouraged to do it.

Orpen was spared the waste of time that is involved in the conventional attitude towards education. He went straight to what he wanted to do, and did it all his life with all the vigour, decision and originality that are the qualities of greatness. He had the faculty to bring all his power of attention (which was enormous) to bear on any problem, and to go at once to the heart of things. While still young he had, by diligent work, accumulated such a mass of experience, and so much judgment and manual dexterity that he could paint as fast as he thought. What he observed seemed to go in through his eyes, was analysed and arranged by his brain, and written down with inevitable rightness by his unerring hand, as one complicated movement of his will. He painted at an incredible speed without alterations or erasures, and then, if it was not exactly what he wanted, he simply wiped it out and began again – but that was seldom. That is why his work is spontaneous, fresh and clean. That is the secret of his quality. He loved paint itself and would say: 'Wouldn't you like to eat it?' He taught that sufficient paint to create the illusion of light and shade, of tone and colour was enough, and laughed at 'touch', 'impasto', '*heureuse saleté*', and to use his own words, 'all that sort of tosh.' He knew how to draw exquisitely with the point, whether with a brush or a piece of chalk or a lead pencil. And, again, to use his own words: 'Either you can draw or you can't, and that's all there is to it.' This mental clarity and hatred of evasion led, as time went on, to the extraordinary breadth, simplicity and conciseness of his later work; the method sinks entirely into the background, and what the picture says is as forcible and laconic as emphatic and as authoritative as the shot of a pistol.

Orpen's work is the product of a great intellect in conflict with a great task; of the innumerable angles from which he attacked; his faculty to absorb and digest the processes of his predecessors and recreate in his own work something entirely new. And yet [he remained] in contact with the classical tradition of faultless drawing, and truthful and naturalistic tone and colour.

Looking at his later work, no one could say whence he derived. He was completely integrated; he had a personal point of view behind his acute observation. His was an attitude begotten of his experience; not injected in youth, nor founded on complacency, for he was a sceptic – alone in his soul. He could not, and would not, accept claptrap, no matter how dignified by general acceptance. That he was an endless seeker is shown in his work, and anybody who is interested can trace the development of his method through all its stages. He never fumbled, and, even in his experiments, he paints clearly, and with a purpose.

Imagine the resources that lay behind thirty years of continual output of high quality: portraits, subject pictures, decorative compositions, endless exquisite studies in preparation – never repeating himself, never stale, never meretricious, never painting to please anyone but Orpen.

He must have been a strange little boy of twelve. One of the things he told me sticks in my head as a perfect illustration of the uncommon mixture of commonsense, practicality and imaginative resource that was Orpen. He said that when the long day of grinding work in the antique class was over, he used to be so exhausted that he could not walk, so he made a bargain with an old cabman to drive him home every evening. I should like to have been present at that deal. The drawings done from the antique at that time give promise of the future master. The system of teaching was entirely formal and academic. The ideal drawing was to be coldly correct – inflexible and unfeeling in outline. There was no insistence on the movement or gesture, no dramatic lighting – nothing that could not be done better by a camera. But Orpen, being a genius, survived this, and even profited by it. And in some strange way these soulless exercises became, under the hands of the boy, something that smelt of Nature, whom he worshipped all his life.

At twenty he was working in London, at the Slade School. There he painted a picture for some competition: 'The Play Scene in Hamlet'. What a picture from a boy ... something of Hogarth, something of Daumier, something of Velasquez, something of Rembrandt, something of – what? One analyses the picture and the influences evaporate and leave the quality of greatness. Orpen at twenty-one was a self-conscious great man who knew what he wanted to say. But, since he was Irish, and middle-class, he distrusted his native language, or perhaps he did not feel that he had a native language. And so he does not know whether he will speak English or Spanish, Dutch or French. And that is the disadvantage that handicaps artists of our race. We have no background and no tradition. But later Orpen invented an idiom for himself, at once individual and universal, acceptable to the student and to the man in the street. Speaking in this clear and intensely personal language, what a range of subjects did he not display? Take, for example, the Mother and Child. The gentle, lovely mother presses the little tender, gleaming body, rosy from the bath against her heart. One says to oneself: That is what a mother feels. Then turn to the War pictures. The smash and stink. The green slime in the bottom of the trench, the pitiful shattered corpses, dismembered, flattened, swollen, hung in fantastic arabesques, in tattered festoons of burnt rags on splintered trees, and the nightmare tangles of rusty wire. The prisoners driven mad with lice – brooding in cages, scratching their dirty wounds – the bedraggled, weary soldiers, loaded down with pots, pans, packs, picks, shovels, saucepans, rifles, rockets and God knows what, sitting with downcast heads in seas of rotten mud. And all this awfulness [is] shown with a terrifying impersonality, with clean colour, and mathematical exactitude, an austere and pitiless statement, a crushing reply to the pronouncements of the Biological

Necessitarians, the disciples of the late Mr Kipling, the chauvinist, and the apologists for war. This is the seamy, not to say the lousy side. Here are no gallant fellows, charging in formations, no colours flying, no rearing horses and flashing sabres, no moderately wounded in the foreground, raising themselves gracefully on one elbow to salute the flag borne by a white-haired colonel. But no one who has seen these pictures can have any illusions about the glories of war. Orpen saw the war as an affair of 'other ranks', but when it comes to the Generals it is worse – faces of arrogant old men, and men who have never grown up. Having looking at these faces, one needs no official historian to tell him the story of Gallipoli, of Loos, of Ypres and the Somme and why five years of mechanical butchery ended in a stalemate.

Then turn to the innumerable portraits of women, exquisitely sensitive and delicate, painted with tenderness and understanding, ranging from the exotic Lady Sassoon to the vigorous Dame Madge Kendal. Then look at the portraits of men – a panorama of the English world – a Forsythe Saga in paint – and all incomparably designed in arrangement and colour – noble like the people of Van Dyck, human like the people of Frans Hals, sophisticated like the people of Goya, assured and well-bred like the people of Raeburn.

I will try to give an impression of Orpen as I knew him. He was a little man – square shouldered, broad-chested, robust, quick [and] alert. He had a remarkable head, noble, severe, almost ugly; a little bit of the stage-Irishman type, except for the lustrous, piercing eyes and noble, finely finished skull. He dressed in the most conventional way – bowler hat, morning coat, pepper-and-salt trousers. He was very vain of his feet, which were extremely small and beautifully shaped. He always wore the most exquisitely made shoes. He was particular to be perfectly turned out, fashionable, but neither a dandy nor a fop. He looked like a lawyer or a surgeon. His speech was very quick and staccato. He loved to abbreviate until it was difficult to understand him. He was various and inconsistent in his conversation – [he] hated to be contradicted, loved to be courted and admired, whilst despising those who courted him – and there were many. He said once of certain people: 'If I spat on the floor they'd cut out the piece and hang it on the wall, and forget me in a fortnight.' His approach to people was like his attitude to his work – simple and direct. He detested elaborators, complicators and pompous people. To deflate a windbag or a snob with a single deadly remark was his delight. He loathed the activities of the official mind, and preached and practised the superiority of works over words. All sorts of people loved him. He was kind and simple; generous and friendly; unspoilt by success. He could meet people on their own ground, and talk to them about their affairs, sincerely and without condescending. He was extraordinarily charitable, and hundreds of foolish, unhappy and unlucky people had reason to thank God for him. He had hosts of friends and acquaintances, but I imagine that he was a lonely man in his heart. I do not think that he was happy in London. He once said: 'The English are not amusing when sober – still less when drunk.' He loved and practised all kinds of skill and dexterity, and was never content to do anything moderately well. He could not bear to sit still. He would start some game, or go somewhere – or play pranks like a schoolboy. He loved noise and horseplay, and would wrestle and box like a mad man. There was a volcanic element in him which was terrifying at times. He was punctual and orderly in his habits, but recklessly extravagant with money. There was an imp of mischief in him. He never restrained his tongue, and would tell the most ludicrously funny and outrageously malicious stories, so that his listeners, shocked into silence for a moment, would explode in roars of laughter. When I first met him I thought him peremptory and harsh. There was an immense disparity of accomplishment and experience between us. But as I came to know him and learn from him, I grew to respect and love him extremely. And now, thinking of him dispassionately (at least as dispassionately as I am able) at the distance of a number of years, I come to the conclusion that *he was* the best and kindest of men.

Why, it may be asked, did such a man go to the War?

In 1916, when I had to leave London, I said to him before I went: 'Come back with me to Ireland. This war may never end and what we know of civilization is done for. It is the beginning of the end. I am going to Aran. There is endless painting to be done. Leave all this. *You* don't believe in it.' But he said: 'No. Everything I have I owe to England. I am unknown in Ireland. It was the English who gave me appreciation and money. This is their war, and I have enlisted. I won't fight, but I'll do what I can.'

Such was William Orpen as he appeared to me. I doubt very much whether anybody really knew him. Of such people only two or three appear in a generation, and there is no standard by which to judge them. I have been accused of hero worship in regard to Orpen. It is a crime to which I plead guilty. Whom should one worship if not heroes? I realize that there was another side to his character, and if anyone wishes to present that aspect, let him who will be Devil's Advocate.

Seán Keating – a Life [Published in the *RTÉ Guide,* December 10, 1971]

I left Limerick when I was a boy of 19. We were very poor. I left because I hated it. I wanted to get out, get to hell out of the place. Limerick was not a nice place to grow up.

I knew I wanted to be a painter. I got a scholarship to the School of Art in Dublin. That's why I loved the old School of Art; next to being in Aran, I liked to be in the school of Art. When I was a student, 'twas a good school and we had good people. It gave you a chance to work and equipment and apparatus and heat and light and a little weekly pension to keep you alive, a subsidy, a scholarship, and people to teach you if you wanted to take it – Orpen, Greaves, Oliver Sheppard.

Orpen was Professor of painting then. Oh, he didn't bother his head about Dublin, because he was on the way up, he was a great man already, we all admired him passionately, I loved him personally. He took me on as his assistant, but after a while, I went to England. That was in 1915. But I had to come back to Ireland because I would have been conscripted in England in 1917. That's the devil of it, you see – the English were everywhere. I don't love the English. They played the devil's own part in the world's history ... I not only admired Orpen, I loved him personally. He was a grand man and a splendid painter. They laugh at him now of course – 'oh a technician' – as if being a technician was a fault.

That's what kills me about the modern life. How the devil can you deride skill? Even a juggler I admire – anybody who does anything skilful. I'd watch a carpenter or a blacksmith at work for ever, for the sheer pleasure of watching him doing a thing well. My god, to see Orpen at work – it was like hearing a good musician playing music. There was no halt in it; there was no break, there was no hesitation, no fumbling. He'd take his pencil and he'd just begin. The thing would go all down the paper and you'd say no, he's not measuring, he's not doing anything, he's just drawing it, and the picture would come, you'd see it come down to the foot and back up along the other side.

I am now (like that). I wasn't then, but now, if I'm drawing, I can't go wrong. It's practise, you know, practise. Then, people like me, you see, accept other kinds of professionals, surgeons and people, they love it so much that they can't bear to stop it and all the accumulated wisdom is behind it. The hand is really as good as ever – the eyes aren't quite as good, but the hand is still as good as ever ... for instance, always enjoying a new sensation, like this morning, with all that powerful light, I can see things that I couldn't see before ... that's the sorrowful thing about getting old – all that knowledge is gone like smoke ... etc.

When I came to Dublin first, it seemed to me a sordid, run-down, battered old hag of a place. It was like a faded old grandee woman, trailing clouds of glory, but it was long since there was any glory around. I lived in Camden Street, and that kind of thing, 'twas not the most noble of backgrounds. I never painted Dublin. I didn't like to. I didn't like the way they spoke. They didn't like the way I spoke either –ah yous is from the country, yous yous!'.

Then I went to London, and London was more sordid. What's the difference between North Strand Road and Battersea Park? Or Tottenham Court and Foley Street, with the dirty chemist shops and all? It's not particularly English, or American or French – it's the modern, cheap, commonplace, pointless, characterless mess.

But Aran was different. Aran was coherent. There was a natural background of quite a different colour, a different palette, as we say, browns, dull reds, greys, silvers, black, yellow – strong clear colours like the wonderful clear light. And the people! Quite different they were. Grand fellows walking about very freely with their long legs swinging from the hips, wiggling like bundles, confident of themselves! And the women – pyramids, with a black upper half and a red lower half! And the little houses, the character they had, dictated by the nature of the place! The people had a monumental calmness, a dignity, a personal dignity, their movements were slow and dignified, they didn't chatter, everybody said the same thing at the same place, at the same hour every day, 'La brea inniu!' etc. Their mentality didn't interest me at all, except their latent savage paganism. They were pagans you know – all Catholicism and piety – but their reactions to the real situations, like danger and quarrelling and drunkenness, completely pagan. 'Dublin, London, New York, Shanghai, Tokyo are monstrosities ... We can't stop, we've got to go on, we're in a stream ... you can swim with the river, or you can swim against it – swim against the river and you'll drown, swim with it and you may survive. But it isn't you that'll decide where things are going – it's the river. We're in the river ...'

Bibliography

Benedict Anderson, *Imagined Communities, Reflections on the Origins and Spread of Nationalism*, Verso, London and New York, 1991.

Bhreathnach-Lynch, Síghle, *Ireland's Art, Ireland's History, Representing Ireland, 1845 to Present*, Creighton University Press, Omaha, 2007.

Bielenberg, Andy, *The Shannon Scheme and the Electrification of the Irish Free State*, The Lilliput Press, Dublin, 2002.

Bowe, Nicola Gordon, *The Life and Work of Harry Clarke,* Irish Academic Press, Dublin, 1989.

Brown, Terence, *Ireland: A Social and Cultural History 1922-2002*, Harper Perennial, London, 2004.

Doherty, Gabriel and Dermot Keogh, *De Valera's Irelands*, Mercier Press, Dublin, 2003.

Fallon, Brian, *An Age of Innocence, Irish Culture 1930-1960*, Gill and Macmillan, 1999.

Gibbons, Luke, *Transformations in Irish Culture*, Cork University Press in association with Field Day, 1996.

Kennedy, Brian P., *Dreams and Responsibilities, The State and the Arts in Independent Ireland*, The Arts Council of Ireland, 1991.

Kennedy, S.B., *The White Stag Group*, The Irish Museum of Modern Art, Dublin, 2005.

---, *Irish Art and Modernism 1880-1950*, The Institute of Irish Studies, The Queen's University of Belfast, 1991.

Keogh, Dermot, *Twentieth-Century Ireland, Nation and State*, Gill and Macmillan, Dublin, 1994.

Keogh, Dermot, Finbarr O'Shea, Carmel Quinlan, (eds), *Ireland: The Lost Decade in the 1950s*, Mercier Press, Dublin, 2004.

Kiberd, Declan, *Inventing Ireland; The Literature of the Modern Nation*, Jonathan Cape, London, 1995.

Luddy, Maria, *Hanna Sheehy Skeffington*, published for the Historical Association of Ireland by Dundalgon Press, Ltd, Dundalk, 1995.

McBride, Ian, ed., *History and Memory in Modern Ireland*, Cambridge University Press, 2001.

MacCarvill, *The Artist's Vision*, Dundalgan Press, Dundalk, 1958.

McCormack, W.J., *The Blackwell Companion to Modern Irish Culture*, Blackwell Publishers, Oxford and Massachusetts, 2001.

Ó'Drisceoil, Donal, *Censorship in Ireland 1939-1945*, Cork University Press, 1996.

O'Riordan, Michael, *Connolly Column*, New Books, Dublin, 1979.

Turpin, John, *A School of Art in Dublin Since the Eighteenth Century*, Gill and MacMillan, Dublin, 1995.

Index

www.ingramcontent.com/pod-product-compliance
Lightning Source LLC
Chambersburg PA
CBHW071124280326
41935CB00010B/1108